GROWING
TOMORROW'S CITIZENS
IN TODAY'S CLASSROOMS

Assessing 7
Critical Competencies

CASSANDRA
ERKENS

TOM
SCHIMMER

NICOLE DIMICH
VAGLE

Solution Tree | Press
a division of
Solution Tree

the Solution Tree
Assessment Center

555 North Morton Street
Bloomington, IN 47404
800.733.6786 (toll free) / 812.336.7700
FAX: 812.336.7790

email: info@SolutionTree.com
SolutionTree.com

Visit **go.SolutionTree.com/assessment** to download the free reproducibles in this book.

Printed in the United States of America

Library of Congress Cataloging-in-Publication Data

Names: Erkens, Cassandra, author. | Schimmer, Tom, author. | Vagle, Nicole Dimich, author.

Title: Growing tomorrow's citizens in today's classrooms : assessing seven critical competencies / Cassandra Erkens, Tom Schimmer, and Nicole Dimich Vagle.

Description: Bloomington, IN : Solution Tree Press, [2018] | Includes bibliographical references and index.

Identifiers: LCCN 2018029561 | ISBN 9781943874729 (perfect bound)

Subjects: LCSH: Education--Aims and objectives. | Education--Evaluation. | Educational change. | Education and globalization. | Education--Effect of technological innovations on. | Education--Environmental aspects.

Classification: LCC LB14.7 .E595 2018 | DDC 370.11--dc23 LC record available at https://lccn.loc.gov/2018029561

Solution Tree
Jeffrey C. Jones, CEO
Edmund M. Ackerman, President

Solution Tree Press
President and Publisher: Douglas M. Rife
Editorial Director: Sarah Payne-Mills
Art Director: Rian Anderson
Managing Production Editor: Kendra Slayton
Production Editor: Alissa Voss
Senior Editor: Amy Rubenstein
Copy Editor: Evie Madsen
Proofreader: Elisabeth Abrams
Text and Cover Designer: Rian Anderson
Editorial Assistant: Sarah Ludwig

ACKNOWLEDGMENTS

Solution Tree Press would like to thank the following reviewers:

Erin Balfour
English Teacher
McNeil High School
Austin, Texas

Paul Cancellieri
Science Teacher
Rolesville Middle School
Rolesville, North Carolina

Karrie Fansler
K–12 Learning Design Specialist
Evergreen Public Schools
Vancouver, Washington

Amy Janecek
Principal
Irondale High School
New Brighton, Minnesota

Geraldine Lawlor
Principal
Mount Elizabeth Middle/
  Secondary School
Kitimat, British Columbia
Canada

Ryan Reed
Social Studies Teacher
China Middle School
China, Maine

Luke Spielman
Principal
Park View Middle School
Mukwonago, Wisconsin

Lana Steiner
Mathematics Teacher
Springside School
Springside, Saskatchewan
Canada

Amber Teamann
Principal
Whitt Elementary School
Sachse, Texas

Dave Wheeler
Primary Principal
Thompson Public School
Thompson, North Dakota

Visit **go.SolutionTree.com/assessment** to
download the free reproducibles in this book.

TABLE OF CONTENTS

4 *Collaboration* *105*

5 *Creative Thinking* *143*

6 | *Communication*. *179*

7 | *Digital Citizenship* *211*

8 *Social Competence. 237*

ABOUT THE AUTHORS

Cassandra Erkens is a presenter, facilitator, coach, trainer of trainers, keynote speaker, author, and above all, a teacher. She presents nationally and internationally on assessment, instruction, school improvement, and professional learning communities.

Cassandra has served as an adjunct faculty member at Hamline and Cardinal Stritch universities, where she took teachers through graduate education courses. She has authored and coauthored a wide array of published trainings, and she has designed and delivered the training of trainers programs for two major education-based companies.

As an educator and recognized leader, Cassandra has served as a senior high school English teacher, director of staff development at the district level, regional school improvement facilitator, and director of staff and organization development in the private sector.

To learn more about Cassandra's work, visit http://allthingsassessment.info or follow @cerkens on Twitter.

Tom Schimmer is an author and a speaker with expertise in assessment, grading, leadership, and behavioral support. Tom is a former district-level leader, school administrator, and teacher. As a district-level leader, he was a member of the senior management team responsible for overseeing the efforts to support and build the instructional and assessment capacities of teachers and administrators.

Tom is a sought-after speaker who presents internationally for schools and districts. He has worked extensively throughout North America, as well as in Vietnam, Myanmar, China, Thailand, Japan, India, Qatar, Spain, and the United Arab Emirates. He earned a teaching degree from Boise State University and a master's degree in curriculum and instruction from the University of British Columbia.

To learn more about Tom's work, visit http://allthingsassessment.info or follow @TomSchimmer on Twitter.

Nicole Dimich Vagle has a passion for education and lifelong learning, which has led her to extensively explore, facilitate, and implement innovative practices in school transformation. She works with elementary and secondary educators in presentations, trainings, and consultations that address today's most critical issues, all in the spirit of facilitating increased student learning and confidence.

Nicole was a school transformation specialist, where she coached individual teachers and teams of teachers in assessment, literacy, and high expectations for all students. Nicole was also a program evaluator and trainer at the Princeton Center for Leadership Training in New Jersey. A former middle and high school English teacher, she is committed to making schools into places where all students feel invested and successful.

A featured presenter at conferences internationally, Nicole empowers educators to build their capacity for and implement engaging assessment design, formative assessment practices, common assessment design and analysis, response to intervention (RTI) systems, data-driven decisions, student work protocols, and motivational strategies.

Nicole earned a master of arts degree in human development from Saint Mary's University and a bachelor of arts degree in English and psychology from Concordia College.

To learn more about Nicole's work, visit http://allthingsassessment.info or follow @NicoleVagle on Twitter.

To book Cassandra Erkens, Tom Schimmer, or Nicole Dimich Vagle for professional development, contact pd@SolutionTree.com.

INTRODUCTION

Lives are changed when people connect. Life is changed when everything is connected.

—Qualcomm motto

People used to be able to keep up with the rate of change. A new invention or technology would emerge, and members of the public would have five to twenty years to weave it into their everyday life or workflow. However, as the rate of change increases, it is hard to catch a breath before the next new technology is changing the way people think, work, connect, or move in the world. The *age of acceleration* (Friedman, 2016) has arrived, and this has important implications for the way teachers educate and prepare learners in today's classrooms for future success.

The Age of Acceleration

It should come as no surprise the rate of change is increasing. Ray Kurzweil, a futurist and inventor (along with Chris Meyer), described this age of acceleration as early as 2003:

> We're entering an age of acceleration. The models underlying society at every level, which are largely based on a linear model of change, are going to have to be redefined. Because of the explosive power of exponential growth, the 21st century will be equivalent to 20,000 years of progress at today's rate of progress; organizations have to be able to redefine themselves at a faster and faster pace. (Kurzweil & Meyer, 2003, p. 1)

This faster pace can be a powerful tool for collaborating and connecting all over the world, allowing learners to develop some of the most innovative solutions to the most pressing problems both locally and globally. This faster pace can also be overwhelming to educators—both complex to navigate through and respond to—as

1

they prepare learners to communicate, source, synthesize, and consume an overabundance of information intended to help them live, work, and contribute to a world in a constant state of flux. Both the type of technology available to learners and the ways in which they might ethically use it to connect, communicate, contribute, and create have potential to provide both opportunities and challenges. Educators are simultaneously faced with many incredible possibilities and daunting decisions as they design student work, assessment, and instruction in this fast-paced world.

If learners are going to thrive in a new reality where change is perpetual, schools and districts must dig into this phenomenon. What are the dynamics causing this acceleration? Thomas L. Friedman (2016), an economist and author of *Thank You for Being Late: An Optimist's Guide to Thriving in the Age of Accelerations*, describes the interdependence of three elements contributing to acceleration: (1) globalization, (2) Mother Nature, and (3) technology.

The first, *globalization*, is the increased interdependence of people, ideas, environments, and economies all around the world. Countries and people are more connected than ever before. Businesses can easily operate in multiple countries or host parts of their operations in different countries. Organizations positioned in different countries can share resources and develop solutions that mutually benefit their countries and the world. This interdependence has incredible potential to uncover creative solutions to pressing global issues, and, simultaneously, holds significant complexity in finding ways to capitalize on the strengths and navigate the weaknesses of individual countries.

Globalization also makes it imperative for learners to explore, learn, and experience this societal interdependence. When people seek to see and understand the experience of others in places beyond their own worldview, school communities begin to be part of the transition to a more innovative global community. This makes it possible for the world to be a place in which people strive to help all thrive.

The second element influencing this age of acceleration is *Mother Nature*, which includes an increase in severe weather events, a change in climate, and an increase in consumption that leads to increased waste. The changing and unpredictable climate has certainly increased levels of uncertainty and anxiety as severe weather events have increased. There is more need than ever to tap both human and financial resources to respond when the consequences of climate change like fire, hurricanes, earthquakes, tsunamis, flooding, or any other natural disaster adversely affect individuals and groups of people. Emerging issues of consumption and waste influence the need to generate more sustainable practices that better serve the health of humanity and the earth. A loss of biodiversity affects ecosystems and their capacity to flourish, which directly influences the likelihood of a sustainable environment necessary to meet the needs of animals and humans. A 2012 study from nine institutions in the United States, Canada, and Sweden notes:

> Studies over the last two decades have demonstrated that more biologically diverse ecosystems are more productive. As a result, there has been growing concern that the very high rates of modern extinctions—due to habitat loss, overharvesting and other human-caused environmental changes—could reduce nature's ability to provide goods and services like food, clean water and a stable climate. (Erickson, 2012)

There are many promising solutions, and globalization has increased one's ability to connect and communicate with others to engage in collaborative problem solving. However, there is an urgency to these changing conditions, which influences the kinds of things students are learning and the skills they must have to solve these inherited pressing issues successfully.

The third acceleration element is *technology*. People communicate, collaborate, create, and problem solve all over the world in an instant. New solutions to persisting and complex problems emerge from putting different ideas together that may not have been possible before this global network exploded. Globalization has occurred because of the increased speed of technology. Co-founder of Intel Gordon Moore, who developed Moore's law in 1965, posits that the speed of a microchip, or overall processing power for a computer, would double every twenty-four months (Friedman, 2016). While speeds currently double between twenty-two and thirty months, the impact is staggering (Friedman, 2016). Friedman (2016) notes 2007 as a pivotal year for the following technology innovations that disrupted the status quo.

- Amazon released the Kindle, allowing instant purchasing of books online.

- Airbnb was conceived (and launched shortly thereafter), revolutionizing housing options for vacationers and small business endeavors.

- David Ferrucci led a team to develop the first cognitive-thinking computer, Watson, that could question more deeply and make sense of large amounts of information.

- Intel developed a non-silicon chip to further facilitate the speed of the microchip, which was in question until this invention.

- Clean energy capacity drastically increased through solar, wind, and other clean energy forms.

- The biotech industry capitalized on new technology to drastically decrease the cost of genome sequencing.

The innovations of 2007 exponentially changed the face of global communication and collaboration and increased the ability and speed of people and countries all over the world to connect.

These three elements—globalization, Mother Nature, and technology—have great influences on the kinds of skills learners need to deal with the demands of a complex world. *Fresno Bee* reporter Tim Sheehan (2017) interviewed Friedman, who articulates the dynamics and interdependence of these three elements: "The three together are what are shaping more things and more places in more ways in more days." Friedman adds, "More technology drives more globalization, (and) more globalization actually drives more climate issues and more solutions to all these problems at the same time" (Sheehan, 2017). As a result, educators are pressed to reimagine what they expect of learners. The critical competencies they learn will undoubtedly impact their ability to thrive in this changing world.

Understanding this phenomenon helps one consider the kinds of competencies learners need to be productive global citizens. This book provides guidance in defining *critical competencies*, or 21st century skills, and direction in the design and use of assessment evidence for ensuring learners in today's classrooms thrive as citizens in current and future society.

The Critical Competencies

The age of acceleration presses schools to address the differing skills learners need to be successful adults and public citizens in changing contexts and circumstances. Friedman said, "If technology is changing every three to five years, we're required to learn all kinds of new things" (Sheehan, 2017). Additionally, Friedman claims, "People need to retool themselves so much faster" (Sheehan, 2017). Learning to learn and adapt is something intentionally developed as adults and explicitly taught and assessed in students. The notion of lifelong learning is no longer a platitude but a necessity.

In the changing world, it is going to be essential for learners to achieve the following seven critical competencies to thrive in this age of acceleration.

1. **Self-regulation:** Individuals and collaborative teams must understand what they know and what they don't know, and how to navigate and learn when they don't know. *Self-regulation* is the ability to recognize the conditions and situations that either motivate or shut down

people—whether as individuals, teams, or systems. Self-regulation is the ability to independently monitor progress and deal with defeat, yet still persist—by learning from previous experiences.

2. **Critical thinking:** Individuals and teams must think critically to analyze, evaluate, and synthesize ideas and information to understand issues, concepts, and other phenomena. Critical thinking helps make sense of the world and sheds light on the steps to create progress. Individuals, teams, and systems must critically evaluate sources of information and determine credibility. Given the plethora of information at one's fingertips in the modern world, the ability to identify surface-level insight, fluffy ideas, meaningful insights, valid information, or plausible ideas is essential.

3. **Collaboration:** Individuals, teams, and systems must work together to communicate and apply information, and creatively solve problems and develop innovative solutions to the world's most pressing challenges. Individuals, teams, and systems must bring together diverse perspectives, work through conflict productively, generate solutions, and create new ideas or products.

4. **Creative thinking:** Individuals, teams, and systems must put unique, competing, and unrelated ideas together to generate new and more innovative solutions. This is imperative to deal with changing demands, changing climate, changing technology, and changing social conditions. Each of these contexts provides rich opportunities for creativity to thrive.

5. **Communication:** Verbal, written, and digital communication is essential to effectively collaborating, problem solving, and creatively engaging with diverse individuals and groups. Learners must use different mediums to clearly articulate and share ideas, as well as debate and provide counter-ideas and counterarguments. Innovation depends on sharing ideas clearly, building on ideas fluidly, critiquing ideas productively, and defending ideas thoughtfully.

6. **Digital citizenship:** Learners must become digital citizens who understand how to ethically, productively, and proactively conduct themselves online. Digital citizens are globally competent and understand the etiquette of communicating with diverse individuals and groups in a variety of online venues. Digital citizens seek to understand diverse points of view and perspectives.

7. **Social competence:** Learners in this new context must be socially aware and learn how to use all the critical competencies to contribute solutions to the larger issues plaguing local and global communities. Socially

competent individuals see how the health and education of both the individual and groups contribute to the whole. Socially competent humans use the critical-thinking competencies to make their own circles, as well as the larger community's, more inviting and inclusive places for all. Individuals and groups that serve the larger community feel connected and part of creating the world in which they would like to live.

These critical competencies should be the foundation of meaningful and relevant learning experiences, including assessment tasks, activities, and the instructional environment. However, current educational practice often focuses on a more short-term goal. School technology experts and authors Scott McLeod and Dean Shareski (2018), in *Different Schools for a Different World*, explain, "As nations perceive their students are falling behind international peers and make specious links to national economic well-being, they focus on narrow academic achievement gaps rather than empowering students broadly for life success" (p. 2). However, Harvard Project Zero founding member David N. Perkins's (2014) notion of the relevance gap illustrates an important distinction: "The achievement gap asks, 'Are students achieving X?' whereas the relevance gap asks, 'Is X going to matter to the lives learners are likely to live?'" (p. 10). Embracing the notion of critical competencies being the *end* and not only the *means* will ensure learners are ready to be productive citizens and to contribute to society in meaningful ways.

The excitement and challenge of these competencies are integrally connected to content. There is only so much time, and thus educators must create a new under-standing of how to connect content with competencies in ways that alleviate the burden of *coverage*. With this new emphasis on critical competencies, subject-specific content becomes not just something to be memorized but instead a rich part of developing and studying relevant and engaging issues and concepts.

The Interdependence of Content and Critical Competencies

Being able to recall scientific concepts, identify historical events, or memorize mathematics facts and algorithms, while acutely impressive, is no longer sufficient to prepare students for the challenging world they will face. Identifying characters, theme, and symbolism used to be the focus of education, and it was enough. In the past, learners would occasionally have opportunities to collaborate, communicate, critically think, and creatively problem solve, but that was the *means*, not the *end*. After engaging in dialogue, problem solving, or analysis, learners would typically take a multiple-choice test, or an essay prompt would ask them to recall details or themes discussed in class. As critical competencies shift to be the *end* rather than the *means*, recalling facts is not nearly as important as being able to find the content, critically evaluate its value and credibility, apply it appropriately in different contexts, or put new ideas together to generate something interesting and original. Content is not obsolete; rather, the memorization (and recall) of it is. More than ever it is essential for educators to provide more meaningful tasks so learners tap into rich content while demonstrating the critical competencies through application.

Exploring what it means to move from isolated content to context-dependent tasks takes intentional planning and thoughtful processes co-constructed with colleagues and learners, and dedicated time for learning and development. The following list provides examples of what it might mean to move from isolated content to context-dependent tasks.

- From memorizing the steps in the water cycle to analyzing how the water cycle is affected in a scenario, such as a drought

- From solving and graphing linear equations to representing patterns in global warming or increased texting and driving using equations and graphic representations

- From identifying verbs and adverbs to applying their use in communicating with an authentic audience in a public setting about an important issue for them to consider (for example, developing an unforgettable infographic that reminds children to wash their hands, or parents and families how to be supportive fans of youth sports)

- From identifying similes and metaphors to using similes and metaphors to help others understand and make sense of events throughout the world

- From knowing the five themes of geography to critically evaluating the impact of location on population growth, deforestation, or thriving economies

These examples, which articulate the necessary connection between content and competencies, only touch the surface of what might be possible with thoughtful assessment design.

Assessment Design Through Collaborative Teams

When critical competencies are the *end*, assessment will be dramatically different from what most people experienced as students. Educators will benefit greatly from collaboratively developing new, interesting, relevant, and feasible ways to assess (and instruct) because doing it alone can feel daunting. Professional learning professor and international consultant Louise Stoll and colleagues (2006), in *Setting Professional Learning Communities in an International Context*, offer the following perspective on thriving in this new reality:

> To succeed in a changing and increasingly complex world, whole school communities need to grow, develop, deal with and take charge of change so they can create a future of their own choosing and prepare students to play their own role as effective agents of change. (p. 2)

It is through working with colleagues and other stakeholders in the community that teachers develop more innovative ways to deal with this increasingly complex set of competencies learners must achieve to be prepared, successful, and productive.

Collaborating with diverse colleagues leads to more enhanced ideas as the team debates issues, experiences conflict, evaluates various options, and moves through the process of collaboration to put forth a potential new way of assessing and developing the critical competencies. These tasks will be even richer as collaborative teams consider partners in organizations and businesses outside the school—those who use these competencies in context. External partners, or collaborators, can offer insight into the criteria for successfully developing the seven competencies and the situations that might provide instruction and assessment ideas. In the words of Stoll et al. (2006):

> It's vital to find the best possible ways to enhance young people's learning—through the actions of professionals—by enquiring into practice, learning new strategies, developing deeper understanding, sharing good practice and creating new knowledge about effective learning and teaching. (p. 2) .

Collaboration is essential in developing the most innovative ways to assess and grow critical competencies that prepare learners to be successful and contributing members of this global society.

When whole schools, teacher teams, community members, and business partners work together in a collaborative culture, striving to achieve the seven critical competencies in learners, they should take the following action steps.

1. Develop a deep understanding of what each competency means and looks like.

2. Identify the nuances of the competency for the grade level or subject-specific content area.

3. Design engaging, authentic assessments; the accompanying criteria; and the attending tools (rubrics, checklists, and student tracking forms) to measure student proficiency.

4. Plan instruction that supports the competencies, including ways to provide feedback, foster self-assessment, and nurture self-regulation to ensure learning.

5. Monitor and track progress on the competencies across units, courses, and grade levels to determine if the tools are leading to learners achieving these competencies.

With the unique perspectives of each team member and a commitment to transforming the culture of assessment and learning, students can develop and achieve these competencies. When students leave with mastery of these competencies, they will be better prepared to thrive in this ever-changing world. These students are the best hope of solving some of our most complicated global issues.

The Assessment Tenets

Educators must be grounded in assessment fundamentals. *Essential Assessment: Six Tenets for Bringing Hope, Efficacy, and Achievement to the Classroom* (Erkens, Schimmer, & Vagle, 2017) outlines a framework through which educators can develop their assessment literacy so that the assessment of any aspect of learning, including critical competencies, is seamless.

Assessment is much more than a clinical exercise in number crunching; it can shape the disposition of our learners and influence their responsiveness going forward. As such, at its core, sound assessment practices foster *hope, efficacy*, and *achievement*. Sound assessment practices will result in an increase in achievement, and will leave students feeling more optimistic and efficacious about their potential success. This can be critical as learners are expected to immerse themselves in critical and creative thinking about increasingly complex and authentic problems, situations, or circumstances. The critical competencies presented in this book guide educators in helping learners achieve these skills in this age of acceleration.

Surrounding this focus on hope, efficacy, and achievement are the six essential assessment tenets that will undoubtedly enhance—or transform—the experience for every learner. Table I.1 (pages 10–11) briefly articulates each of the six essential assessment tenets and outlines its connection to the assessment of critical competencies. While the assessment of critical competencies is relatively new for many teachers, assessment fundamentals themselves are not, which means teachers can lean on their assessment fundamentals to delve into uncharted territory of assessing deeper and more authentic thinking. Assessment practices must build hope, efficacy, and achievement in learners and teachers. In this learning environment, the following six tenets ground all assessment policies and practices (see figure I.1) and connect to the critical competencies in important ways.

Table I.1: Six Assessment Tenets and Critical Competencies

Tenet	Description	Connection to Critical Competencies
Student Investment	**Student investment** occurs when assessment and self-regulation have a symbiotic relationship.	Students must learn to *think* for themselves, which means they need to eventually come to invest in and self-regulate their own *thinking* through assessment.
Assessment Architecture	**Assessment architecture** is most effective when it is planned, purposeful, and intentionally sequenced in advance of instruction by all of those responsible for the delivery.	Assessments must be designed with precision to ensure learners are being assessed at the appropriate level of complexity, especially when what is being assessed is a deeper, more authentic demonstration of learning.
Instructional Agility	**Instructional agility** occurs when emerging evidence informs real-time modifications within the context of the expected learning.	Complex and authentic demonstrations of *thinking* can be challenging to teach and assess, so teachers' clarity of how to make any necessary instructional maneuvers is an even greater priority.
Assessment Purpose	Assessment **purposes** (formative and summative) must be interdependent to maximize learning and verify achievement.	Complex and authentic demonstrations will need time, scaffolding, and practice. This will require an effective use of formative, finite practice to master certain granular skills. As these skills increase to complexity, teachers will verify (summative assessment) that learning has occurred.

Accurate Interpretation	The **interpretation** of assessment results must be accurate, accessible, and reliable.	More sophisticated criteria will require that teachers calibrate along the identified criteria. The criteria for *thinking* is complex and robust, which means the reliability with which teachers identify competence is a priority.
Communication of Results	The **communication** of assessment results must generate productive responses from learners and all the stakeholders who support them.	The communication of assessment results will require a level of finesse and attention since the critical competencies can produce (for example, creative thinking) a level of vulnerability within learners; the residual effect of any assessment (whether formative or summative) should be learners who have the same, if not increased, levels of willingness to keep *thinking*. The communication of results should also not do the thinking for students.

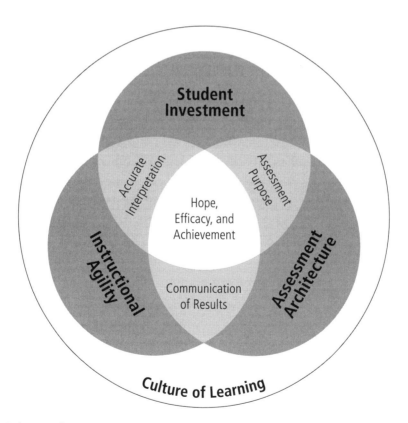

Source: Erkens et al., 2017.

Figure I.1: *The six assessment tenets framework.*

A learning-rich culture provides opportunities for risk taking, productive failure, and celebrating successes. All of this creates a culture of learning, which, in the case of critical competencies, implies a culture where learning to *think* is sustained. Assessment is *essential* to the development of the critical competencies, which means it is both efficient and effective for teachers to be grounded in the six tenets and the ways they can positively impact the assessment experiences for all learners.

In This Book

What it takes to transform the culture of assessment may be a bit counterintuitive; though it may seem a paradox, perhaps, *slowing down* and *reflecting* may be the only ways to effectively deal with accelerated change. Friedman (2016) emphasizes that pausing to reflect in this rapidly changing environment is essential. Friedman (2016) also writes it was the moment the person he was meeting for coffee was late that he realized how to articulate the connection between and among globalization, Mother Nature, and Moore's law (thus, the title of his book *Thank You for Being Late*). It was in that unintended but precious fifteen minutes Friedman found the space to pause and think. Intentionally planning and exploring what new plans might look like with engaging feedback and ideas from learners, and continually trying new ways and ideas, is the way of the future. This book provides a way to begin to *pause* and *design* for the new experiences necessary for education to keep up with the rate of change and prepare learners to thrive.

Chapter 1 provides a broad introduction to the critical competencies by discussing how teachers can cultivate habits of mind and develop more sophisticated ways of thinking in learners. It discusses how teachers must become habitual about eliciting evidence of thinking and then, in turn, use assessment fundamentals to make accurate inferences about the quality of thinking their learners demonstrate. Following this background, chapters 2 through 8 discuss each of the seven critical competencies necessary for success in a changing world. Chapter 2 delves first into the concept of *self-regulation*—the ability of students to learn how to learn and reflect on their strengths and challenges—as this ability is critical to all the competencies and essential for students to master if they are to become lifelong learners. Chapter 3 digs deeply into the complex skill of *critical thinking*. It discusses different ways teachers can choose to conceptualize critical thinking in the classroom and the ramifications this can have on the formative and summative use of assessments. Chapter 4 describes different types of *collaboration* and how to effectively assess this competency. It explores and acknowledges that collaboration is most often assessed alongside other competencies.

Chapter 5 identifies the keys to assessing *creative thinking* and problem solving, highlighting the importance of a shared understanding of creativity and the need for clear criteria so teachers can apply a collective approach to assessing creativity. Assessing *communication* is explored in chapter 6, which focuses on the technological developments of the modern world, their impacts on communication, and how teachers can assess modern communication in meaningful ways. Chapter 7 articulates a globally competent *digital citizenship* and the importance of teaching learners how to live productively and successfully in a digital world. Finally, chapter 8 explores how *social competence* is essential to creating a world in which all individuals, teams, and systems can thrive.

Each chapter defines the competency, describes how it is different now from past understanding, explains how to assess it by discussing criteria and other relevant issues, and offering ideas for measurement by providing tools and strategies for teachers. The chapters discuss instructional implications for each critical competency and then conclude with Pause and Ponder questions for reflection by individual educators, collaborative teams, schools, or whole districts or divisions. While presented separately, the competencies are interdependent, which allows for the design of meaningful, authentic, and relevant experiences.

This book is intended to generate lively dialogue and debate, identify radical new ways to engage and empower learners, and explore classroom cultures where all learners can and do succeed in big and small ways. When educators come to appreciate their learners' diverse characteristics—whether they are messy, compliant, defiant, organized, technology-obsessed, artistic, impatient, thoughtful, insightful, ornery, outrageous, awkward, or creative—these competencies can fully develop. When educators embrace the strengths of their learners, define critical competencies for the future, and develop new assessment tasks and practices to ensure students learn and grow in these competencies, learners will be prepared for a world not yet imaginable.

CHAPTER 1
HABITS OF THE MIND

Those who can synthesize well for themselves will rise to the top of the pack; those whose syntheses make sense to others will become invaluable teachers, communicators, and leaders.

—Howard Gardner

Each of the seven critical competencies outlined in the introduction—self-regulation, critical thinking, collaboration, creative thinking, communication, digital citizenship, and social competence—provides learners with the skills and adaptability required to live and work successfully in a constantly changing world. Underpinning each of the critical competencies are certain subject-neutral habits and skills. That is, each critical competency is universally applicable across all subject areas; in fact, for this reason some refer to the competencies as *cross-curricular*. Of course, there are differences in how learners apply the habits and skills underlying each competency within a specific discipline, but at their core, they are discrete skills learners can utilize in almost any context.

For teachers, this provides a real opportunity to emphasize the interconnectedness of different subjects. While some schools take a progressive approach to eliminate the traditional separate subject silos, many more—especially middle and high schools—still organize the school day around distinct subject areas. This traditional organization has often left teachers thinking primarily about the differences between what they teach and what others teach. Competencies, however, allow teachers to focus on similarities and overlap between and among subjects.

The critical competencies can have a unifying effect revealed through the alignment of these universal habits and skills across all subject areas. For example, almost every teacher at every level will have learners conduct some form of analysis. History teachers have learners analyze the validity of primary and secondary sources, while science teachers have learners analyze the results of an experiment. English teachers might have learners analyze the main characters in a short story, while mathematics teachers have learners analyze a problem to discern the appropriate strategy and solution. Beyond the traditional subjects, learners analyze different styles of music, their success in executing a recipe, their accents when speaking in a foreign language, or their fitness levels.

Analysis is just one aspect of critical thinking, but like analysis, all critical thinking is applicable across all disciplines. As such, teachers, in what appear to be separate subjects, can align their collective efforts to cultivate learners' abilities to analyze through a universal set of principles and thought processes that need only be contextualized within each discipline. What's important is that teachers collectively recognize the curricular overlap within the critical competencies and purposefully create a universal, relatively aligned approach to cultivating the critical competencies.

One of the biggest mental shifts educators must make in order to adopt a universal approach to cultivating the critical competencies is expecting all learners to achieve excellence. Teachers must believe all learners can learn how to think. Teachers must replace the notion that *some learners can't do it* as a preemptive instructional disposition with a core belief that all learners can—and will—learn to think critically, creatively, and collaboratively. If the critical competencies are, in fact, *critical,* then teachers, schools, and districts must ensure at least minimal proficiency with the skills and practices that will allow learners to thrive in both their current and future lives.

The position educators *can't* take is that the critical competencies are critical for all students except for those who take longer to learn, are English learners, have an exceptionality, or are subject to a whole host of other qualifying lenses through which the definition of success might be tamped down. *All* has to mean *all*—it means teachers approach instruction with the broadest sense of inclusivity. While it is no guarantee learners will actually reach teachers' lofty expectations, teachers can't approach the development of the critical competencies by thinking only the truly exceptional students can think critically or creatively.

Considering Thinking Now and Going Forward

There is no shortage of information in our rapidly changing world; rather, everyone now has *Google in their pockets*, as the saying goes. This unprecedented access to information fundamentally changes the nature of both teaching and learning. For teachers, dispensing knowledge is no longer their sole or even primary task since students can find what they require on their own in a far more efficient and perhaps even more effective way. The good news is this shift frees up teachers to push past knowledge acquisition—something many current curricular standards require—and instead immerse learners in the application of what they know and can do.

For some, this shift will be challenging, as it forces a reconceptualization of the teacher's role. The 21st century critical competencies emphasize using knowledge in meaningful, relevant, and nuanced ways. The Organisation for Economic Co-operation and Development's (OECD) Programme for International Student Assessment (PISA) 2015 survey, for example, broke new ground by focusing its assessment on *collaborative problem solving* (OECD, 2017c). According to the OECD (2017c), "The more interdependent the world becomes, the more it needs great collaborators and orchestrators. Innovation is now rarely the product of individuals working in isolation; instead, it is an outcome of how we mobilise, share and integrate knowledge" (p. 5).

Students now, ideally, are expected to think critically, creatively, or collaboratively about what they know; this repurposing of knowledge means *knowing* is still necessary, but is no longer the intended residual outcome of what happens in classrooms. What is most interesting about the 2015 PISA survey is that, according to the OECD's (2017c) examination of results, "Students who have stronger science, reading, or mathematics skills also tend to be better at collaborative problem solving because managing and interpreting information, and the ability to reason, are always required to solve problems" (p. 5). The net effect is teachers who maximize the efficient acquisition of prerequisite knowledge actually set up learners to be more effective collaborative problem solvers.

The emphasis on cultivating thinking skills via the critical competencies (see, for example, the Partnership for 21st Century Learning, n.d.) comes within an ever-evolving and increasingly complex global context. Human beings have always *thought;* however, the depth of thinking required for past generations seems pale in comparison to what is even minimally required for students today.

Harvard University professor Howard Gardner (2010) emphasizes at its core, education is still about how people think; he leaves no doubt that success in the future is tied to one's ability to cultivate the *five minds for the future*—the specific cognitive abilities people will need to seek and cultivate in the years ahead:

1. The disciplined mind
2. The synthesizing mind
3. The creating mind
4. The respectful mind
5. The ethical mind

Conceptually, the 21st century critical competencies are not new, but *are* more urgent than ever—a premise even Gardner (2010) acknowledges when he states, "one could have called for [the five minds] fifty or perhaps even five hundred years ago" (p. 10). The critical competencies are rooted in how learners *think*, which means the *five minds* serve as a universal foundation for the development of each critical competency. The *five minds* are both interrelated and interdependent, which means teachers need to teach learners how to "reconcile the tension between and amongst the five minds" (Gardner, 2010, p. 24).

Three of the five minds (the disciplined, synthesizing, and creating minds) are cognitive, while the other two (the respectful and ethical minds) relate to human dynamics. Together, the minds represent what Gardner (2010) believes is the way human beings will thrive in the future. While the cultivation of the minds will continue long into adulthood, teachers can and do play a significant role in laying a foundation for ways of thinking that more closely align learners with what is necessary to flourish in a world reinventing itself at an unprecedented pace. For some, these implications simply reaffirm some or all of the changes already established; for others, these implications represent a serious rethink of how students experience learning. The underlying assumption is that cultivation of the five minds begins in school, but continues long into adulthood, which means references to *students* could seamlessly be replaced with *adults*.

The Disciplined Mind

The disciplined mind has two distinct connotations. The first is learners will need to develop expertise in one or more disciplines. This has always been a significant part of the school experience, as a certain level of expertise will always be necessary to pass each subject. The other connotation of the disciplined mind is, in the strictest sense, *discipline*—since the pace of change is rapid and intense. Gardner (2010) writes that it will take discipline for people to maintain their level of expertise in any chosen field. Resting on one's laurels is simply not an option now or in the future. Expertise is never cemented, which means learning is never complete.

The implications of the *disciplined mind* for educators are twofold. First, knowledge still matters. As critical competencies began to emerge as a necessary shift, some educators worried that knowledge was being marginalized in the rush to establish schools for the future. However, knowledge was not being banished; it was simply being repurposed. The critical competencies must always be contextualized, which means learners will need to think critically or creatively *about* something. So, while it is necessary to repurpose knowledge as a *means* rather than an *end*, knowledge still matters, and teachers need to teach and assess it. Ensuring learners have a grounding in the essential knowledge within any discipline is how they will reach higher levels of thinking *and* demonstrate discipline-specific mastery. Only those with expertise in a chosen field can think critically, creatively, or collaboratively about what's possible beyond the status quo.

The second implication for teachers is in the realm of personal and social competence. Developing students as self-directed, motivated, and engaged learners will ensure they have the discipline to maintain their continual growth toward expertise. Learners will know they have a disciplined mind and disposition when they develop the habit of perpetual learning. A planned and purposeful focus on self-assessment and self-regulation will allow learners not only to recognize their level of expertise within a subject area but also to expand their ability to monitor their own discipline toward that expertise. Educators can teach, assess, and nurture behavioral attributes, characteristics, and habits in ways like more traditional subject-specific learning outcomes always have. While the emphasis within the disciplined mind may be the development of expertise, the parallel goal of *being* disciplined can also infuse the experiences of learners.

The Synthesizing Mind

There was a time when information was either in short supply or difficult to attain; now, it's just the opposite. According to Gardner (2010), the *synthesizing mind* can acquire, probe, and evaluate in continual cycles. Accessing information is no longer the issue; sifting through it is. The world has an abundance—maybe an overabundance—of information people need to grasp. Not everything found on the internet is credible, of course, which means sifting through and recognizing credible versus non-credible sources is essential. As well, the synthesizing mind can create coherence even when the amount of information available is potentially overwhelming. The interconnectedness of the five minds is illustrated through the connection between the disciplined and synthesizing minds. A level of expertise is required (disciplined) to create coherence (synthesizing), which means those who can synthesize can avoid having the minutiae of any discipline interfere with their ability to see the big picture.

The implications of the synthesizing mind for educators are that pushing beyond knowledge acquisition is essential; so, while it is necessary for learners to develop a level of expertise, the coherence within that expertise matters more. The direct connection to two of the critical competencies (critical and creative thinking) is obvious. Having learners think critically and creatively about a discipline has them *using* their expertise in original or thought-provoking ways. When learners analyze, critique, apply, conceptualize, or evaluate, they synthesize what they know and think it through on a deeper level. The elements of creative thinking are present since in most cases, synthesizing involves the creation of something original that brings the kind of coherence necessary to make meaning.

Additionally, cultivating the synthesizing mind can be a collaborative effort whereby learners create collective coherence through the synthesis of their combined expertise. The lines between the critical competencies blur since learners can collaborate to think critically and creatively. Each competency is enhanced when combined with the others, so while teachers, behind the scenes, need to be purposeful and plan how they teach, nurture, and assess each competency, the learner's experience is seamless and integrated. The synthesis process ideally involves collaborative teams thinking both critically and creatively to communicate something new for others to learn. That ideal may not always be possible, but it is important for teachers to continually look for opportunities to create this kind of cohesion with the critical competencies.

The Creating Mind

While the disciplined and synthesizing minds are primarily about mastery of existing subjects, Gardner (2010) notes all people—not just students—will continue to face situations and circumstances requiring a level of thought beyond careful or habitual practice. As Gardner (2010) writes, "It's not possible to think outside the box unless you have a box" (p. 17). Synthesis is not simply a procedural or formulaic exercise. If it were, then it wouldn't be difficult to rapidly develop; the creative side of synthesis is where the challenge and complexity lie. Gardner (2010) adds that if *discipline* is the depth and *synthesis* is the breadth, *creating* is the stretch.

The implications of the *creating mind* for educators are complex. Though educators can teach and assess creative thinking, one of the challenges is how to assess creativity without stifling it. When educators assess learners as having not been creative, does it result in them being less willing to be creative going forward? Educators must address the distinction between the mind and what is aesthetically pleasing. Gardner's (2010) emphasis on the creating mind guides teachers toward cultivating opportunities for learners to think with creative intent; creativity is not restricted to being artistic. Thinking with creative intent is found within every discipline and can rightly focus teachers on the front end rather than the back end. In other words, it is the level of originality in thought instead of how eye-catching the product is to the consumer.

Creative thinking will need contextualization since learners don't just *get creative* in the abstract. Teachers who maximize the opportunities to teach and assess the critical competencies are devising opportunities for engaging the three cognitive minds simultaneously. Educators should consider the level of utility of what learners create as they mature. Preschool and kindergarten students, for example, who think in creative, even outrageous ways, cultivate the ideal of pushing past the status quo to imagine something far beyond anything that currently exists, even if what they've imagined is not anywhere near plausible. For these learners, educators might de-emphasize utility since building the habit of thinking creatively is the primary goal. However, as learners mature, the impact of creativity maximizes when it results in a unique contribution to the collective thought.

Plausibility, which can be distinguished from being realistic, may increase in importance as learners begin to make significant contributions to how others examine a discipline. This is not a binary choice for teachers; there is a place for every kind of creative thought, but as the creating mind is cultivated in any discipline, a real contribution of original thinking can deepen expertise and expand coherence. Each of the three cognitive minds for the future contributes to the other two, so while there can be a place for abstract, subject-neutral creativity, the essential net result of the creating mind is a level of internal or external originality. Not every creative thought will necessarily make an external contribution; however, every creative thought will make an internal contribution to the learner because it represents a new way of thinking for the individual.

The Respectful Mind

The first of the two noncognitive minds is relatively self-explanatory: the world now and in the future will be better off if people can think of and act respectfully with others. Gardner (2010) says *character* is even more important than *intellect*. It's the human dimension that allows cognitive capacities to thrive and contribute to society in productive ways. The learner with a *respectful mind* is open to diverse perspectives, processes, and people. Giving the benefit of the doubt and avoiding prejudicial responses are what allow a respectful mind to flourish. The interconnectedness of the world, Gardner (2010) puts forth, makes it essential for people to come to respect those once feared, distrusted, or disliked, so while it is possible, of course, for respect to be lost, the respectful mind begins with the position that diversity is welcome, good, and necessary.

Teachers find the implications of the respectful mind in both the processes and results. First, the essentiality of the respectful mind will be most prominent during the collaborative process. Teachers would be wise to engineer a diversity of groupings to provide opportunities for learners to experience a wide range of perspectives and backgrounds. Those learners not only play a role in the development of the cognitive mind but also clearly influence the cultivation of the respectful mind. Maximizing learners' exposure to as much diversity in thinking as possible will serve to break down the real (or perceived) barriers to mutual respect. The bigger picture is the development of social competence which, for teachers, equates to an increase in intentionally and consistently implementing lesson and assessment design. The deliberate increase in learner-to-learner interaction brings a necessary focus on *how* they interact and whether their abilities to interact are improving with established criteria. Developing social competence is essential to any collaborative experience so students can learn to navigate the nuances of human interaction.

Learners develop respectful minds as they seek specific cognitive results. Collaboration will likely be contextualized, which means while the collaborative experience will be about *teaching collaboration*, the exercise of *being collaborative* will have a guiding cognitive purpose. As learners are exposed to others' disciplined, synthesizing, and creating minds, they can grow directly in those same areas themselves. For teachers, this means designing tasks that serve both cognitive and human development simultaneously. In this way, both collaboration and cognitive development have a symbiotic role in the classroom.

The Ethical Mind

Gardner (2010) suggests the *ethical mind* is a more sophisticated stance, allowing people to see and think abstractly about themselves. A reflective stance about the kind of person one wants to be characterizes the ethical mind; this decision is what drives ethical decision making. In a way, the ethical mind functions as a kind of moral compass that allows a person to act with both honesty and integrity.

Abstract attitudes don't typically develop until adolescence, which means preteen learners have a limited capacity to conceptualize the full extent of an ethical mind. That said, teachers can begin cultivating an ethical mind in two primary ways. First, teachers can engineer opportunities for learners to be *metacognitive* (or analyze their own learning and thinking processes). This thinking-about-thinking exercise, even if only focused on specific learning goals, begins to nurture learners' abilities to see themselves abstractly. Even kindergarteners can begin to develop the habit of self-reflection on both the cognitive and human dynamics sides of the five minds. Second, teachers can, as influential adults, model their own ethical minds by revealing their own reflections both as teachers (instructional decisions) and adults (a real dilemma). That is not to say teachers need to expose the most intimate parts of their lives; however, teachers can take the opportunity to appropriately model *how* they utilize an ethical mind to reveal the criteria one might use to make an ethical decision or assess the ethics of any situation.

Understanding Gardner's (2010) *five minds for the future* as specific cognitive abilities that people need to cultivate in the years ahead can provide teachers with a solid framework to articulate both the cognitive and human development outcomes of their 21st century focus on the seven critical competencies. With this in mind, teachers can begin developing the criteria and tools they need to both assess and measure thinking.

Assessing Thinking

Assessing thinking requires a purposeful and permanent shift away from traditional assessments. With ubiquitous access to information, teachers can do what many have wanted to do for decades: go deeper. Going deeper doesn't come without its challenges. Traditional assessments (such as recall questions) require finite answers with little interpretation on the part of the teacher; a learner is either right or wrong. Deeper, more complex questions offer many shades of *right* and allow learners to apply what they know to be more critical, creative, or collaborative in their thinking (Depka, 2017).

Essential Questions

Assessing thinking begins with *how* teachers design the tasks and opportunities to reveal learners' thinking. While there are certainly more robust and complex opportunities for learners to demonstrate their thinking, the foundation for a culture of thinking begins with the types of questions teachers ask learners. Traditionally, questions often focus on recalling information (whether important or trivial), which teachers use to measure how much a learner knows or has memorized. When information was not so readily available, memorization was a sign of how much a learner knew. Teachers often measured success in school on how much a learner could recall at a moment's notice.

Memorization today, for the most part, is unnecessary, which means teachers can now push past questions of *who*, *what*, and *when* toward questions of *why* and *how*. That said, the question starter alone does not guarantee a higher-level question;

however, it is a good first step for teachers to think about when constructing higher-level questions. In their book *Essential Questions: Opening Doors to Student Understanding*, authors Jay McTighe and Grant Wiggins (2013) write that it's time for teachers to focus on essential questions and enduring understandings so schools align with societal norms and expectations. Access to information makes memorization redundant, but *using* information to develop critical competency habits and skills is essential. McTighe and Wiggins's (2013) seven characteristics of essential questions serve to develop enduring understandings with the expected curricular standards:

1. Is *open-ended;* that is, it typically will not have a single, final, and correct answer.
2. Is *thought-provoking* and *intellectually engaging*, often sparking discussion and debate.
3. Calls for *higher-order thinking*, such as analysis, inference, evaluation, prediction. It cannot be effectively answered by recall alone.
4. Points toward *important, transferable ideas* within (and sometimes across) disciplines.
5. Raises *additional questions* and sparks further inquiry.
6. Requires *support* and *justification*, not just an answer.
7. *Recurs* over time; that is, the question can and should be revisited again and again. (p. 3)

Questions with many or most of these seven characteristics facilitate learners using their knowledge for more critical, creative, or collaborative endeavors. Helping learners use knowledge to *think* begins with teachers creating the opportunities for that thinking to occur.

Attempts to include essential questions in assessment lead teachers to ask more authentic questions more closely reflective of what an expert or professional in any discipline would be expected to consider. Authenticity can be viewed in two ways. First, many teachers use the term *authentic assessment* to frame more robust project- or problem-based learning experiences. Second, assessments can also be authentic when teachers focus on asking questions that cut to the core of a subject discipline or critical competency. The goal is for these authentic assessments to be *cornerstone tasks* (Wiggins & McTighe, 2005) that reflect genuine, real-world accomplishments set in authentic contexts; require application of learning; naturally integrate critical competencies; and recur across (and possibly through) grade levels (McTighe & Seif, 2010).

Figure 1.1 illustrates ways teachers can prompt learners to articulate their thinking through journal responses. In this case, the elementary students' journal entries are in response to a *maker session*, which is typically engineered within a dedicated space (often called a *makerspace*) designed for exploring, making, and learning frequently within a collaborative effort. The prompts provide a starting point for learners without overly prescribing what teachers expect them to write; the students choose which prompts they will respond to. As a result, while the questions appear to be binary, students are expected to explain the *why* behind their responses in the spaces provided. The key is to have learners articulate their thinking in authentic ways so it is transparent and easy for the teacher to assess.

Write about it, sketch it, give yourself some credit!

Students' names: _____

1.

2.

3.

Let's **C** what you can do!

Did you . . .

Combine your previous design idea with a new design idea?

Combine two existing designs to make a hybrid?

Change your design because something wasn't working?

Choose different materials to work with?

Choose a new plan for testing your design?

Source: © 2017 by Jennifer Moroz. Used with permission.

Figure 1.1: *Maker session journal competency prompts.*

Visit **go.SolutionTree.com/assessment** *for a free reproducible version of this figure.*

Using essential questions in conjunction with more engaging, real-world tasks gives students a deeper perspective into the context of their learning. The authentic application of knowledge, skills, and understandings is what the critical competencies allow students to do.

Authentic Tasks

Authentic tasks make learners think like those in a specific discipline, synthesize several interrelated aspects in that discipline, and intentionally connect the critical competencies. Curricular standards in most subject areas intentionally encourage this more authentic approach to learning. The Next Generation Science Standards (NGSS; 2016), for example, "identify scientific and engineering practices, cross-cutting concepts, and core ideas in science that all K–12 students should master in order to prepare for success in college and 21st-century careers" (p. 1). Authentic tasks in science will move students from simply *knowing* science to *thinking* like a scientist. To accomplish this, the NGSS outline practices and processes that reflect a more authentic experience. The following is a list of a few standards, practices, and processes from the Next Generation Science Standards (NGSS, n.d.) that serve to develop a deeper understanding of science.

> **Matter and its Interactions:** Analyze and interpret data on the properties of substances before and after the substances interact to determine if a chemical reaction has occurred. (MS-PS1–2)
>
> **Motion and Stability—Forces and Interactions:** Plan an investigation to provide evidence that the change in an object's motion depends on the sum of the forces on the object and the mass of the object. (MS-PS2–2)
>
> **Engineering Design:** Evaluate competing design solutions using a systematic process to determine how well they meet the criteria and constraints of the problem. (MS-ETS1–2)
>
> **From Molecules to Organisms—Structures and Processes:** Construct a scientific explanation based on evidence for how environmental and genetic factors influence the growth of organisms. (MS-LS1–5)

With verbs such as *analyze, interpret, investigate, evaluate,* and *construct,* the NGSS mirror what scientists do and allow teachers and learners to create more meaningful classroom experiences.

Educators striving to design tasks that encourage more authentic, real-world thinking often consider a problem-based approach to learning. The essence of *problem-based learning* (PBL) is learning that goes beyond short-term instructional instances and focuses on problematic scenarios that embody the major concepts learners need to understand and master (Barell, 2010). The complexity of PBL goes beyond right or wrong and forces learners to think through the relevant, potential solutions. With PBL, learners think critically, creatively, and (possibly) collaboratively about an *ill-structured* and *ill-defined* problem or scenario (Barell, 2010). These solutions may come in the form of a presentation or something tangible (project-based); however, the root of the experience is the expression of a plausible solution that allows a teacher to assess competency skills and the five minds for the future (Gardner, 2010).

The lack of a clear, universal PBL model has led to a wide variety of implementation models, making research challenging (Thomas, 2000). Whether called *problem-based*, *project-based*, or *expeditionary learning*, authentic PBL experiences appear to have the following five common characteristics or criteria (Thomas, 2000).

1. They are central, not peripheral to the curriculum.
2. They focus on questions or problems that drive learners to encounter (and struggle with) the central concepts of a discipline.
3. They involve learners in a constructive investigation.
4. They are learner-driven to some significant degree.
5. They are realistic.

All five criteria connect directly to the development of the seven critical competencies in this book because learning experiences that expect learners to *use* what they know will seamlessly infuse critical, creative, and collaborative thinking into their regular classroom routines.

At the heart of PBL is the investigatory process often known as *inquiry-based learning*. Inquiry-based learning ultimately taps into (and nurtures) learners' curiosity and intrinsic interests, while developing their critical-thinking skills (Barrow, 2006). Engaging students in an inquiry-based approach to learning can have a positive effect on student outcomes (Abdi, 2014). Although the research is not overwhelming, some studies (Pandey, Nanda, & Ranjan, 2011; Seyhan & Morgil, 2007) show a significant increase in achievement for students involved in an inquiry-based approach to learning. Again, the wide variety of what is referred to as *inquiry-based learning* has made thorough research in this area challenging (Friesen & Scott, 2013); one can surmise that the quality of the teacher-designed experiences plays a significant role in determining the residual effect of the inquiry process. However, research does seem to indicate that educators who incorporate authentic, high-quality tasks involving PBL and inquiry-based learning models into their assessments encourage higher-level thinking and application skills in learners, setting a firm foundation for the development of critical competencies.

Performance Assessments

The design and use of more authentic tasks will render more traditional methods of assessment invalid, irrelevant, or both. Once thought to be an add-on if time permitted or something to occasionally dabble in, the use of *performance assessments* is now an essential part of teaching and assessing competencies. Performance assessments are demonstrations of mastery that replicate the contextual application of knowledge (Lane, 2013) by linking school activities to real-world experiences (Darling-Hammond, Ancess, & Falk, 1995). According to University of Pittsburgh professor Suzanne Lane (2013), performance assessments are considered essential for three main reasons:

1. They allow for demonstrations of important and meaningful learning targets that cannot be easily assessed with other formats (Resnick & Resnick, 1992).

2. They serve as exemplars of tasks that stimulate and enrich learning rather than just serve as indicators of learning (Bennett, 2010; Bennett & Gitomer, 2009).

3. They help shape sound instructional practices by modeling to teachers what is important to teach and to students what is important to learn (Lane, 2010).

These characteristics, Lane (2013) notes, make performance assessments ideal for formative, interim, and summative assessments.

When designing performance assessments, teachers must be mindful of the assessment intent and clear on what content or processes the assessment is targeting. First, *intent* refers to the breadth and depth of the performance assessment. If the performance is meant to demonstrate a generalized mastery over a skill, process, or discipline (such as critical thinking), then teachers must ensure an adequate sampling of the skill, process, or discipline. If the demonstration is intended to be narrower (such as defining a specific issue), then adequate sampling is still required, though a narrower scope would allow greater depth. If the intent is formative, then the performance can take on an even narrower scope, as the teacher is likely examining a more specific underpinning for instructional purposes. Knowing the intent of the performance task will ensure teachers design tasks that elicit the necessary depth and breadth of evidence expected from the learner.

Teachers must also maintain clarity of the content and cognitive processes the performance assessment is targeting (Lane, 2013). Teachers should consider whether a performance assessment reflects an *open* or *constrained* cognitive process, as well as whether the assessment requires *rich* or *lean* content knowledge (Baxter & Glaser,

1998). Figure 1.2 illustrates this cross-section of content and cognitive processes in quadrants that help delineate the types of performance assessments teachers may design.

		Cognitive Process	
		Open	**Constrained**
Content Knowledge	**Rich**	Learners develop their own strategies for solving a problem. However, to do so, they require substantial content knowledge beforehand.	Learners follow a specific set of strategies for solving a problem and require substantial content knowledge beforehand.
	Lean	Learners develop their own strategies for solving a problem and only require a minimal amount of content knowledge to do so.	Learners follow a specific set of strategies for solving a problem and only require a minimal amount of content knowledge to do so.

Figure 1.2: *Content and cognitive processes for a performance assessment.*

Visit **go.SolutionTree.com/assessment** *for a free reproducible version of this figure.*

The quadrants in figure 1.2 allow for clearer articulation of what the teacher is not assessing. The following are the four combinations from figure 1.2 and the assessment design implications teachers would likely consider.

- **Open process, rich content:** The task likely targets both mastery of content and creative application in an authentic situation.

- **Open process, lean content:** The task likely targets the creative application of competencies in an authentic, transferable situation since learners require little content knowledge.

- **Constrained process, rich content:** The task likely targets both mastery of content and the specific application of competency skills in an authentic, discipline-specific situation.

- **Constrained process, lean content:** The task likely targets the specific application of competency skills in an authentic, transferable situation since learners require little content knowledge.

There is no hierarchy among the quadrants. The point is, teachers must have performance assessment design clarity to ensure the tasks are appropriately targeting what the teacher intends so that, in the end, what the teacher needs to assess is done so with validity and reliability.

By utilizing essential questions and developing authentic, real-world performance tasks, teachers will maximize the opportunities for learners to develop and refine their thinking skills so that the critical competencies become a natural part of how they learn. The more those opportunities are engineered, the more habitually thinking critically, creatively, and collaboratively will become. In turn, this will also shift the way teachers *measure* student success; traditional forms of testing will, at best, be incomplete; at worst, they will be obsolete.

Measuring Thinking

Measuring thinking goes beyond simply judging right and wrong. Rather, it requires clearly articulated criteria that describe both the depth and breadth of what learners must demonstrate. While these concepts and tools are not new, the content and criteria within them describe how teachers will measure thinking and other habits of mind.

Sophisticated Criteria

Anything can be measured—including higher-order thinking and critical competencies—provided teachers establish clear criteria. The upside for teachers and learners is the level of familiarity most have with performance rubrics, allowing for seamless application in the classroom. The downside is the performance criteria within the tool are likely less familiar, which means producing (for learners) and recognizing (for teachers) evidence of thinking could be more challenging. While some educators might wonder if they should measure competencies, it is necessary if school systems are going to continue to make substantive changes to curricular goals and outcomes that reflect the critical competencies for the 21st century. While not all jurisdictions have made these formal changes to date, the collective conversations in most places are about these critical competencies and how to best develop them in learners. Developing any attribute is impossible without assessment. Just as a coach can't develop athletes without assessment, teachers can't develop thinkers without assessment. In all cases, developing and growing any area begin with assessing the learner's current status to determine aspects of strength and aspects in need of strengthening.

Certainly, when it comes to measuring *thinking*, the criteria may be more sophisticated than the experiences of both teachers and learners. Since demonstrations of thinking are more authentic and robust than demonstrations of other skills, the criteria must reflect the same level of sophistication. When measuring critical thinking, for example, teachers may need to answer the following questions.

- Does the learner clearly identify the problem or challenge at hand?

- Does the learner analyze the current status and perspective of all stakeholders?

- Does the learner consider the strengths and limitations of all possible solutions?

- Does the learner examine each potential solution from the perspective of each stakeholder?

- Does the learner draw and communicate a reasonable, justifiable conclusion?

For example, take the first question (clearly identifying the problem at hand). The more sophisticated a problem is, the more layers learners will have to uncover, which means teachers have to be prepared to look for these layers as well. The more ill-defined a problem is, the more likely there will be implicit, embedded, and even subsidiary aspects of the problem that go beyond the first layer. As well, analyzing the perspectives of all stakeholders needs to be accurate and clear to ensure that potential solutions are respectful and accurate. Criteria have to match the sophistication of the presenting problem, which means binary right-wrong or yes-no criteria will be insufficient, at best.

When a learner demonstrates thinking through projects and other more authentic means, teachers need to work together to ensure they sharpen their collective skills at recognizing thinking. Most performance assessments articulate criteria in the form of a rubric to ensure consistent scoring inferences and transparent criteria; to establish a range of intended and acceptable responses; and to align with intended learning goals (Welch, 2006).

Teachers need to ensure consistent scoring inferences when it comes to measuring thinking. Calibrating against the success criteria for thinking will not only ensure consistency with inferences made among colleagues but also support collective expertise in recognizing thinking in the first place. While moving to more authentic, problem-based demonstrations is desirable and positive, it does come with the potential for what Samuel Messick (1994), who specializes in educational and psychological measurement, and cognition and personality, calls *construct irrelevant variances.* These variances are elements teachers inadvertently use as part of their scoring inferences, even though these elements are not articulated in the performance criteria. Neatness, punctuality of submission, or level of entertainment, just to name a few, are the kinds of construct irrelevant variances that can inadvertently compromise both the validity and reliability. Most often, these construct irrelevant variances are inconsistently utilized, which further compromises the reliability of the measure; if a measure is not reliable, it isn't valid. As the utilization of performance assessments grows on a larger scale following the Every Student Succeeds Act of 2015, ensuring validity and reliability will be an even greater priority, which can be done with purposeful, consistent, and collective efforts (Moon, Callahan, Brighton, & Tomlinson, 2002).

Rubrics and Scales

Implicit in the use of a rubric is *scalability*—the existence of several versions of correctness along a progression of quality. Learning goals, outcomes, or standards that are binary (yes or no) are not scalable, so a rubric would be inapplicable for assessments related to such goals. When measuring concepts such as thinking and competencies, however, scalability and the use of associated rubrics are indeed appropriate. Table 1.1 outlines the three most common types of rubrics, as well as their advantages and disadvantages.

Table 1.1: Rubric Types

Type	Description	Advantage	Disadvantage
Analytic	Breaks down the criteria into specific aspects of quality	Gives specificity as to what is strong and what needs strengthening; is excellent for formative assessment	Is challenging to create; can be cumbersome for summative assessment, especially when determining or recording an overall level of quality
Holistic	Provides a much broader, overall description of quality along several levels	Achieves reliability with scoring inferences much more easily; is excellent for summative assessment	Can be challenging for instruction and feedback purposes due to lack of detail
Single-Point	Breaks down the criteria into specific aspects of quality, but only describes the highest level of proficiency	Uses space beside each specific aspect for personalized comments on what is strong and what needs strengthening	Takes significantly more time to complete, which increases the turnaround time for feedback

Source: Adapted from Balch et al., 2016.

When teaching learners how to think via one or more of the critical competencies, it is advantageous to break down the process into its discrete elements. Figure 1.3 is an example of an *analytic* critical-thinking rubric teachers could use to determine which of a learner's critical-thinking elements are strong and which need strengthening. (Please note: This chapter's examples are merely to acclimatize readers with the general application of rubric fundamentals to critical competencies. Subsequent chapters will provide more detailed rubrics, along with detailed explanations on use.)

Aspect of Quality	Initiating	Developing	Achieving	Advancing
Explanation of the Issue	Minimally states and describes the issue with little specificity; significant gaps in information exist	Ambiguously states and describes the issue; some gaps in information evident	Adequately states and describes the issue; articulates most of the necessary information	Clearly states and thoroughly describes the issue; articulates all necessary information
Gathering and Analysis of Evidence	Minimally gathers the evidence and information and presents a limited view of the issue; superficially analyzes the quality of the available evidence for credibility and authenticity	Limitedly gathers the information and presents a narrow synthesis of the issue; minimally analyzes quality of the available evidence for credibility and authenticity	Sufficiently gathers the evidence and information and presents a complete synthesis of the issue; analyzes the quality of the available evidence for credibility and authenticity	Thoroughly gathers and presents evidence with an insightful synthesis of the issue; thoroughly analyzes the quality of the available evidence for credibility and authenticity

Figure 1.3: Analytic critical-thinking rubric.

continued ➔

Aspect of Quality	Initiating	Developing	Achieving	Advancing
Personal Hypothesis or Position	Presents a singular, limited (simplistic or unclear) view of the hypothesis or position	Presents a limited view of the hypothesis or position; addresses some alternate points of view, but needs to address some gaps in logic	Presents a diverse view of the hypothesis or position; clearly and logically addresses several alternate points of view	Presents a diverse and thorough view of the hypothesis or position; clearly and logically addresses a comprehensive wide range of alternate points of view
Justification and Assessment of Resolution and Its Implications	Offers limited justification and minimally examines the potential implications of the resolution	Supports justification and inconsistently examines the potential implications of the resolution	Supports justification and completely examines the potential implications of the resolution	Thoroughly supports justification and comprehensively examines the potential implications of the resolution

*Visit **go.SolutionTree.com/assessment** for a free reproducible version of this figure.*

Analytic rubrics are advantageous when specificity is the priority, which is most often the case with formative assessment. The advantage of using an analytic rubric through the formative assessment process is that learners know specifically which aspects of their critical thinking need further attention. The potential disadvantage of using analytic rubrics is that the level of specificity can make consistent scoring inferences more challenging.

On the other hand, a *holistic* rubric or *scale* is advantageous for summative assessments since reliability is the priority, especially when the teacher makes an overall judgment (Brookhart, 2013b). Figure 1.4 is an example of a holistic creative-thinking rubric.

Increased reliability is in rubrics containing fewer contributing variables or categories. The more categories, the greater the chance of misclassifying a student (Guskey, 2015). By scoring holistically, teachers can account for the margin of error when determining a learner's overall proficiency; two teachers *could* determine the same level for slightly different reasons, with the holistic process absorbing such inter-rater reliability differences.

Level	Holistic Description
Advancing	Process represents highly original creative thinking; shows great imagination, insight, and style; takes risks in form, approach, or content; imaginatively reframes the problem, enabling a compelling and powerful solution; may break rules or conventions to create a powerful new statement
Achieving	Process represents original creative thinking; shows effective imagination; uses a novel approach, demonstrating attention to detail; reframes the problem to enable a comprehensive and original solution; shows an effective blend of personal style and technical knowledge; combines familiar materials and ideas in new and imaginative ways; may bend rules or conventions to create something original
Developing	Process represents limited creative thinking; shows some signs of imagination, but in relatively conventional approach; reframes the problem in a safe or ordinary manner; shows a limited blend of personal style and technical knowledge; combines familiar materials and ideas in predictable and ordinary ways; mostly follows rules or conventions
Initiating	Process represents minimal creative thinking; shows minimal signs of imagination and is conventional and straightforward in approach; reframes the problem in a traditional manner; shows little personal style and technical knowledge; combines familiar materials and ideas in ordinary or inconsistent ways; exclusively follows rules or conventions

Source: Adapted from Wiggins, 2012.

Figure 1.4: Holistic creative-thinking rubric.

Visit **go.SolutionTree.com/assessment** *for a free reproducible version of this figure.*

A third option is the *single-point* rubric, which can take on the characteristics of either holistic or analytic rubrics. More often, teachers use single-point rubrics formatively. One of the main advantages of this rubric is the personalization of feedback. It is also more efficient to create (Balch, Blanck, & Balch, 2016). Figure 1.5 (page 36) illustrates a single-point rubric that utilizes the same criteria from figure 1.3 (pages 33–34) but with space for personalization. The criteria are only articulated at the most sophisticated or desired level; feedback is then either related to specific aspects of strength or what needs strengthening.

Clearly, the need to describe only the highest level of proficiency creates efficiency on the front end. However, the personalization of feedback does make using single-point rubrics more labor-intensive. While personalization is always preferred, teachers may not always have the time (most efficient) to provide that level of specificity. Thus, single-point rubrics are the most effective, but not always the most efficient of the rubrics. Utilizing single-point rubrics for self- and peer assessment can mitigate this efficiency issue.

Specific Aspects in Need of Strengthening	Advancing	Specific Aspects of Strength
	Explanation of the issue: Clearly states and thoroughly describes; articulates all necessary information	
	Gathering and analysis of evidence: Thoroughly gathers and presents an insightful synthesis; thoroughly analyzes the quality of evidence for credibility and authenticity	
	Personal hypothesis or position: Presents a diverse and thorough view, clearly, logically, and comprehensively addressing a wide range of alternate points of view	
	Justification and assessment of resolution and its implications: Thoroughly supports and justifies and comprehensively examines the potential implications	

Figure 1.5: Single-point critical-thinking rubric.

Visit **go.SolutionTree.com/assessment** *for a free reproducible version of this figure.*

Another option for teachers to consider is the frequency scale, specifically for the youngest learners. Rubrics articulate a progression of quality; however, it may not always be possible to ascertain several levels of quality. When demonstrations of thinking are not scalable, it may be possible for teachers to use a frequency scale to determine the level of consistency at which a student is able to think. Figure 1.6 illustrates how to use a frequency scale when assessing binary habits of the mind for the youngest learners.

Criteria	Rarely	Sometimes	Usually	Consistently
I can explain the problem or issue.				
I can get enough information to help me solve the problem.				
I make sure the information I use is trustworthy.				
I consider all sides of issues when deciding on a solution.				
I explain my solutions clearly.				
I support my decisions with facts and details.				
I consider the positive and negative effects of my decisions.				

Figure 1.6: *Critical-thinking frequency scale.*

Visit **go.SolutionTree.com/assessment** for a free reproducible version of this figure.

The use of a frequency scale is not necessarily an either-or decision. In most cases, thinking is scalable, which means more conventional rubric language will apply. However, the frequency scale does leave teachers with an alternative way to assess, should the distinction between levels of quality be challenging or too granular.

Assessment does not occur in a vacuum, so a focus on thinking will require a shift in instructional focus. If teachers are going to assess thinking, then they must teach it. The following section discusses instructional implications for deeper thinking.

Growing Deeper Thinking

Teaching *thinking* requires a context where the underlying belief is all students can learn to think deeply, plus a purposeful and more efficient effort to push past knowledge acquisition. While knowledge is still necessary, the shift required for instruction is the need to acquire the necessary foundation of knowledge and skills in a more efficient manner. Rather than accumulating vast amounts of knowledge, learners will think (either through the teacher or themselves) about what essential knowledge is necessary to think deeply. The knowledge learners acquire serves as the building blocks teachers ultimately scaffold up for a more thoughtful use of the knowledge

(Darling-Hammond et al., 2008) within the context of the critical competencies. Again, thinking requires context, as teachers must continually ask learners to think *about* something.

Knowledge, however, doesn't always have to come first; a kind of chicken-and-egg dynamic can emerge. Sometimes the acquisition of knowledge and skills does lead to deeper thinking, but sometimes deeper thinking leads to the identification of the necessary knowledge and skills, as is the case with most inquiry-driven processes. Instructionally, teachers are wise to let both play out naturally in the classroom. The advantage of starting with an inquiry-driven question—something learners are curious about—is that the relevance of the knowledge and skills is overt; learners understand more intimately *why* they must know certain concepts before they can develop certain skills. There is also an inherent efficiency in identifying what learners *must* know so they can think more deeply ahead of time. Beginning with thinking deeply to identify the necessary knowledge and skills could create instructional inefficiency, as some knowledge could be nothing more than tangential or irrelevant trivia.

The key is balance. Teachers know there are times when direct instruction is most efficient and effective to build a thinking foundation, and times when exploration and curiosity are what are most desirable. A continual commitment to either end of the instructional polarity (either the *sage-on-the-stage* or *guide-on-the-side*) is not optimal (Fullan, 2015). Balance matters because one side (sage) is more efficient, while the other (guide) might be more effective; being effective would be fine if time is unlimited, but it's not. When teachers have clarity about what, ultimately, they are trying to develop in learners, the instructional approach will also come clear. Teaching and assessing collaboration, for example, may have the teacher efficiently provide the necessary information more directly, while teaching and assessing inquiry-driven, critical-thinking processes might have the teacher allow students to determine what foundational knowledge and skills are necessary to think critically.

Conclusion

While many conversations center on 21st century *skills*, the wiser conversation would be about how 21st century *thinking* leads to the development of those skills. Access to information is almost ubiquitous, which allows for instructional efficiencies; however, the more sophisticated ways of *thinking* are necessary as the credibility and authenticity of that information become more opaque. The *five minds for the future* provide a solid framework for educators to articulate both the cognitive and human outcomes of their 21st century focus.

For their part, teachers need to ensure learners receive authentic opportunities to *think*, whether through more sophisticated, open-ended, and thought-provoking questions or inquiry-based learning sequences. Teachers must become habitual about eliciting evidence of thinking and then, in turn, use their assessment fundamentals to make accurate inferences about the quality of thinking learners demonstrate. While at times daunting, the opportunity to teach and assess thinking inherently creates opportunities for learners to use what they learn in more authentic and dynamic ways.

Pause and Ponder

On your own or as part of a collaborative teacher team, consider the following reflective questions.

1. What quote or passage encapsulates your biggest takeaway from this chapter? What immediate action (large or small) will you take as a result of this takeaway? Explain both to your team.

2. In what ways was your current view of critical competencies reaffirmed? In what ways was it challenged? Explain.

3. Of the *five minds for the future* (disciplined, synthesizing, creating, respectful, or ethical; Gardner, 2010), which one (or more) do you already purposefully cultivate in your classroom? Which one (or more) may be in need of more purposeful attention? Are any being ignored altogether?

4. In what ways do you or could you engineer opportunities for learners to think more deeply? How have you or could you utilize authentic assessments to elicit evidence of thinking?

5. Describe both the biggest successes and challenges you've had with performance assessment.

6. Which type of rubric (analytic, holistic, or single-point) do you tend to utilize most? Explain. How could you envision using the other two in both effective and efficient ways?

CHAPTER 2
SELF-REGULATION

The illiterate of the 21st century will not be those who cannot read and write, but those who cannot learn, unlearn, and relearn.

—Alvin Toffler

It's been argued in the court of public opinion that the one true lifelong skill is the skill of *self-regulation*, or learning to learn. The argument is logical: as the future changes rapidly and drastically, both employers and employees will forever be tasked with reinventing themselves and their organizations or their working conditions and technical tools. Learning will be necessary to survive across time and space for people of all ages and organizations in all industries. In other words, the skill of self-regulation is imperative for the success and well-being of everyone and every thriving entity.

The need for addressing a perceived gap in teaching self-regulation is recognized globally. Researchers Ruth Deakin Crick, Kai Ren, and Cristina Stringher (2014) note, "Internationally, learning to learn is emerging as a focus for school improvement and as a foundation for lifelong and lifewide learning" (p. 1). In 2006, the European Union identified *learning to learn* as one of its eight core competencies, and in 2013, the United Nations Educational, Scientific, and Cultural Organization (UNESCO) deemed the process of learning to learn as "a key domain that should be an entitlement for all children" (Crick et al., 2014, p. 1). The ultimate goal of education is to create a world full of lifelong learners, so it is crucial that "education should lead to more learning" (Cipollone, 2014, p. xiv). *Self-regulation* is not a single skill defined in simple steps; instead, it is a cross-cutting competency rich with a host of robust skills and processes working in tandem in timely and purposeful ways.

But where in the educational system are learners taught *how* to learn? With rare exception, most educators begin teaching learners *what* they are expected to learn without directing the learners' attention to the *process* of learning. When educators instruct learners on the process of learning, self-examination is virtually inevitable, and they end up discovering and ultimately defining their unique styles or processes of learning. In other words, when engaged in the learning process, a student should learn as much about the self as he or she does about the targeted content and skills. Cipollone (2014) states:

> Being aware of one's own learning processes and preferences, together with ways to improve them, is a key educational objective for present and future citizens living in a constantly changing environment, not only to be more adaptive, but also to extrapolate one's own meaning out of life experiences. (p. xiv)

It is incumbent on educators to make the learning process visible and available for all learners, arguably all the time.

Defining Self-Regulation

To *self-regulate* is to monitor one's own thoughts, beliefs, actions, and even reactions in response to given stimuli so the appropriate maneuvers ensure the most successful or preferred results. Educational consultant and author Susan M. Brookhart (2013a) defines *self-regulated learning* to be "when learners set goals and then systematically carry out cognitive, affective, and behavioral practices and procedures that move them closer to those goals" (p. 40). Self-regulated learning involves monitoring one's own beliefs, attitudes, and actions while constantly assessing one's personal level of proficiency of the concepts and skills, as well as effort and motivation.

Though self-regulation is most often explored within the field of motivation, the competency is broad and includes many interdependent skills ranging from cognitive and behavioral domains to affective domains. It turns out how a student feels *during* the learning is as important as the student's cognition *of* learning. Maintaining a sense of hope, fostering efficacy, and developing a growth mindset provide the backbone of a learner's intrinsic motivation.

While self-regulation is a competency in and of itself, it is also a focus alongside many of the other critical competencies. To master the competency of self-regulation, learners must develop the following five skills and dispositions in each of the domains, and teachers must create the conditions for students to self-regulate.

1. Cognition

2. Metacognition

3. Hope

4. Efficacy

5. Growth mindset

The list is provided sequentially, yet no one domain is more important than another. Equally if not more important, each of the five features of self-regulation requires forethought and care on behalf of teachers as they facilitate the development of these skills and dispositions. The list of five skills or dispositions is offered from the lens of what students need, but it would never be fair to assume students could develop these elements independently; rather, most students require instructional support from educators to develop and refine them.

Cognition

Learning is all about *cognition*—mental skills and comprehension. What does the learner think? What connections does the learner make? What information or skills does he or she retain? *Cognition* involves the act or process of knowing, and *knowing* involves the ability to make connections to the physical, social, emotional, or other relevant contexts surrounding the material, with the additional ability to consider and resolve potential problems or conflicting ideas.

When learning requires minimal challenge, a learner regulates without attention to his or her content expertise, current perceptions, and personal preferences and strategies to navigate the learning. However, when learners experience a challenging situation or one they don't readily understand, they require the ability to assess the situation and then employ a strategy or strategies to grasp the missing knowledge or skills. A learner's ability to self-regulate always begins with cognition.

Teachers help learners develop cognitive skills by providing them with discipline-specific content and skills; direct instruction on the processes and practices of critical thinking; robust questions; and meaningful, engaging, and challenging tasks. To do such work, teachers often employ instructional strategies, including advanced organizers, visual tools, metaphors or similes, hypothesis development and testing, and problem- or contradiction-based challenges. Learners are most likely to understand the partnership between self-regulation and cognitive development when teachers launch them into tracking their overall process and specific strengths and areas for growth as they learn and develop. This type of reflection is a key part of developing self-regulation (Brookhart, 2013a; Chappuis, 2015; Hattie, 2009).

Metacognition

While cognition involves striving to understand content and successfully applying skills, *metacognition* involves thinking *about* the thinking involved during cognition. The reflective aspects of metacognition are key to the core processes (such as self-selection of study skills, self-questioning, self-verbalization, self-assessment, and self-evaluation, to name a few) required for learners to monitor progress on their cognition and to scrutinize their degree of motivation to accomplish their goals. Metacognition leads to discovering new insights about the self as a learner *while* learning.

It's critical for educators to nurture metacognitive strategies during the learning process so learners "develop the ability to monitor and assess their own learning so that they recognize when they are learning and when they are not" (Heritage, 2007, p. 143). When preparing learners to be metacognitive, teachers engage them in the following levels of three-dimensional learning.

- **Level 1:** Discipline-specific content and context (for example, "Do I understand the life cycle of a plant? Is plant life at our school different than the plant life I find at home?")

- **Level 2:** Discipline-specific skills and competencies (for example, "Am I good at observation? Can I document what I observe the right way during my investigation of plant life?")

- **Level 3:** Generalizable observations of the learning process and personal experience (for example, "How interested am I in the life cycle of a plant? Is what I am learning matching my personal experiences with plant life? What strategies did I employ when I struggled to understand germination?")

At each level, teachers are guiding learners to observe their thoughts, strengths, weaknesses, interests, beliefs, and talents.

Hope

To *hope* is to look forward favorably with an assuredness that what is wanted can be achieved or that goodness can still be realized from a string of challenging events. True hopefulness is born of a sense of realism combined with faith and optimism; it is not based on idealistic and nonsensical wishes. Learners can only maintain hope in a system that allows them to rise above hurdles and still be rewarded with success in learning *and* in the resulting scores or grades.

Hope matters. Based on his extensive research about hope, former Gallup senior scientist Shane J. Lopez (2013) notes that hope is "a significant predictor of student success even when controlling for previous grades, intelligence, and other psychological variables (like engagement, optimism, and self-efficacy)" (p. 20). It turns out hope is a more powerful element in a learner's ability to self-regulate than previously thought:

> Of note, one study showed that low-hope students are three times more likely to be dismissed from school for poor grades. Another study, which pitted hope against ACT scores, found that hope is a better predictor of ongoing enrollment and graduation than this standardized entrance exam. (Lopez, 2013, p. 20)

In order for learners to remain hopeful, teachers must create a "learning rich culture [that] provides opportunities for risk taking, productive failure, and celebrated successes" (Erkens et al., 2017, p. 132). Previous experiences with celebrated successes and productive failure allow learners to navigate intellectual risk taking with a sense of hope for another positive outcome. In addition, the systems educators select and employ to evaluate learning (such as homework policies, grading practices, and reporting software programs) must allow for a learner's final grade to truly reflect the final outcome of a learning experience. If, for example, averaging scores is the grading practice, then a learner who failed early on the learning journey is likely to lose hope that success is even possible. Why continue to try if recognition of his or her final success will not be granted?

Efficacy

Efficacy is born of a personal faith in one's ability to accomplish goals and to control for desired results. Efficacious learners draw on their repertoire of past experiences, comprehend the context of the challenges before them, and still believe in their personal capacity to influence their own success while moving through the experience. Because of this, they have an evidence-based personal awareness that their efforts make a significant difference.

It is possible for learners to develop efficacy. According to Brookhart (2013a):

> The main basis on which students will build self-efficacy for an assessment is previous successes with similar tasks—a principle that still is one of the primary forces in good assessment design. Evaluations should emphasize the work—the student's performance and level of mastery of the task— rather than engagement. (p. 37)

Because maintaining a sense of efficacy is critical for a learner's success in self-regulating, educators will want to design tasks and feedback loops that acknowledge and incrementally build the learner's awareness of personal strengths.

Teachers help learners develop efficacy by highlighting strengths over weaknesses following every assessment experience. In addition to giving specific, diagnostic feedback on each assessment, teachers help learners seek trends and anomalies in their overall performance on specific skills and concepts. Finally, teachers help learners develop efficacy by engaging them in maintaining an open mind while exploring a host of strategies to tackle complex problems, noting along the way which strategies work best (and which don't) for each learner.

Growth Mindset

If hope is the light at the end of the proverbial tunnel to keep a learner motivated, and efficacy is the fuel with which to advance (positive energy and the self-confidence to apply effort), then a growth mindset is the engine (drive) of *The Little Engine That Could* ("I think I can. I think I can"; Piper, 1990). Author and educational consultant Dylan Wiliam (2013) notes that self-regulated learning is as "affectively charged" as it is "metacognitively governed" (p. 212). If the learner does not *feel* efficacious, hopeful, or competent, he or she will often make the decision to opt out. Wiliam (2013) acknowledges the ultimate decision making always sits with the learner, stating, "As a result of the appraisal, the student activates energy and attention along one of two pathways: (1) the *growth* pathway or the (2) *well-being* pathway" (p. 212). If growth does not seem feasible, a learner will opt to protect him- or herself on the well-being pathway. In order for a learner to choose the growth pathway, a growth mindset must foster assessment practices that build hope, efficacy, and achievement.

A growth mindset offers learners the drive to accept new and potentially risky challenges. Professor of psychology at Stanford University Carol S. Dweck (2006) notes a learner's perspective matters, stating, "*the view you adopt for yourself* profoundly affects the way you lead your life" (p. 6). If, for example, learners believe their intelligence is fixed and all their efforts will not alter predetermined outcomes, they are less likely to attempt to regulate for their own success in learning. If, however, they learn their efforts are a greater indicator of their overall success, and their attitudes, talents, interests, and even aptitudes are malleable, learners naturally strive for success. Toward that end, learners who maintain a growth mindset are not afraid to fail; they simply view failure as another learning opportunity to strengthen them personally in the long run (Dweck, 1999, 2006, 2007).

It is sometimes assumed high-achieving learners already have a growth mindset since they seem to behave in a manner that demonstrates a desire to learn. Unfortunately, these learners are just as prone to a fixed mindset as they wrap their identity in their past successes and avoid taking risks that might compromise their future grades. Dweck (2007) notes, "Adolescents often see school as a place where they perform for teachers who then judge them" (p. 38). Fear of a negative judgment blocks learners of all grade point average (GPA) ranges from taking intellectual risks.

Because a learner's ability to maintain a growth mindset is paramount to his or her success with intellectual risk taking, educators must strive to develop that mindset when engaged in instruction or assessment-like activities that involve generating evidence and, ultimately, evaluating results. Dweck (2006, 2007) advises educators to provide feedback that encourages continued efforts. However, feedback alone will not suffice. It's important to *show* learners how their efforts are directly linked to their overall improvements by using goal setting or tracking devices to monitor progress. More importantly, learners must be able to earn high marks even after they've made mistakes on the learning journey. If final grades do not represent the accurate level of proficiency a learner demonstrates at the end of the learning experience, then all of the positive reinforcements offered during the journey simply become empty promises in the eyes of the learner (Schimmer, 2016).

Considering Self-Regulation Now and Going Forward

It is unfortunately rare when schools or districts take time to teach students *how* to learn. Learners often enter kindergarten and are asked to learn as if they already know how to learn. It is uncommon for educators to teach the learning process or self-regulation strategies. So, in a traditional system, learners are expected to self-regulate by using marks, grades, or scores to make decisions about their instructional next steps. Unfortunately, because marks, grades, or scores are not always motivating to all learners, the commonly accepted strategy of hoping learners independently self-regulate has not worked. As a result, the chasm between those who know how to achieve and those who struggle to achieve in the classroom has only widened.

Sometimes educators attempt to engage learners in developing self-regulation habits but experience frustration when learners fail to direct their own efforts and control for their ultimate success. In such cases, it can be easy to blame the learners as being lazy, disinterested, or even unreachable. An alternative and more accurate perspective is that non-self-regulating learners are likely lacking any or all of the following.

- Awareness as to where they really are or where they need to be on their learning journey
- Hope that they will be able to overcome mistakes and still master concepts

- A toolkit of intervention strategies they can employ when struggling with challenging work

Or, if those components *are* in place and learners are still not self-regulating, then something in the system is interfering. At this point, it's an important first step to examine the beliefs and practices at the adult level, which may be unintentionally undermining the learners' ability or willingness to engage in regulating their own learning *before* examining (or blaming) the learners.

A self-regulated classroom is every teacher's dream. In a self-regulated classroom, all learners are invested in their learning and committed to success. Each learner engages in setting meaningful, focused academic goals and monitoring his or her own progress toward those goals. Each learner is reflective and can generate the accurate self-scores and peer feedback necessary to support the teacher's efforts in addressing any gaps in understanding. Each learner is metacognitive, self-aware, and able to isolate and even enhance the learning strategies or processes he or she must draw on in a given moment to reduce a discrepancy between what is and what should be in understanding or skill. Such a classroom would virtually run itself, freeing teachers to focus on robust content and dynamic instruction.

But the dream feels utopian, and teachers struggle to see how it's possible. The reality is often left up to the learners' own inclinations or tendencies. "That could only work if we had better students," teachers often say. The truth is, it can work, and it doesn't require better learners. It requires instruction that teaches students how to learn. It also requires examining and ultimately reconfiguring some of the policies, procedures, and beliefs that guide many schools and unintentionally undermine educators' best efforts to inspire learning. Teaching students how to learn is the core of self-regulation, and so finding ways to assess and measure it is central to giving self-regulation its deserved place at the forefront of what schools empower students to achieve.

Assessing Self-Regulation

Self-regulation is one of a few of the critical competencies that is best left self-assessed by the student, with diagnostic feedback provided by the teacher regarding the individual skills involved as well as the overarching process. The competency should not be awarded a final evaluative score in a gradebook as there is no overarching summative assessment of a student's ability to self-regulate. It could be argued that a data notebook, which would hold accumulated artifacts that demonstrate a student's capacity to self-regulate, could be graded, but it should be noted that the formative artifacts therein were generated in the *service* of measuring specific learning intentions on other summative assessments like reflecting on test results or setting goals for future accomplishments based on past achievement scores. Hence, it would be a mistake to reassess a student's capacity to self-regulate at the data notebook juncture.

However, there are processes that teachers use—such as teaching the process of self-assessment, developing student awareness of intervention strategies or preferences, providing feedback, and creating the conditions for continued learning through supportive grading practices—that can support both the teacher's *and* the students' capacity to assess self-regulation.

Self-Assessment

Self-assessment is a process learners use *while* they are learning to determine where they are on the learning journey, identify their strengths and assets, isolate their areas for improvement, and clarify their next steps, as well as the instructional maneuvers they will need to employ to reduce the discrepancy between where they are and where they need or want to be. Formative assessment experts (Chappuis, 2015; Hattie & Timperley, 2007; Wiliam, 2010) often refer to the three questions learners address during the learning process: (1) Where am I now? (2) Where am I going? and (3) How will I get there? When teachers engage learners in formative and self-assessment practices, they provide feedback and instructional supports to help learners address all three questions.

Self-assessment is the vehicle through which self-regulation is made visible, allowing educators to explicitly teach self-regulation. It is most often observed through self-ratings, goal setting, self-tracking, self-advocacy, and reflective comments. University of Auckland associate professor Gavin T. L. Brown and honorary research fellow Lois R. Harris (2013) note, "Perhaps the most powerful promise of self-assessment is that it can raise student academic performance by teaching pupils self-regulatory processes, allowing them to compare their own work with socially defined goals and revise accordingly" (p. 367). Brown and Harris (2013) assert that self-assessment is linked to improvements in students' (1) self-regulation, and likewise, (2) "motivation, engagement, and efficacy" (p. 368). Self-assessment can thus have a powerful impact on students' learning and confidence.

In order for learners to self-regulate, they must first assess their current level of comfort and proficiency. Wiliam (2013) says, "Simply informing students of their results produces small benefits, but when the feedback provides explanations or—even better—specific activities for reducing the gap between current and desired state, substantial increases in learning are possible" (p. 203). Learners cannot self-regulate if they cannot grasp an accurate picture of where they are relative to where they need to be. It's only after learners develop an accurate picture of where they are on the learning journey that they can get in the driver's seat to arrive at their final destination. The self-assessment process includes an array of activities outlined in table 2.1.

Table 2.1: Self-Assessment Activities

Purpose	Student Actions and Significance	Sampling of Teacher-Guided Activities to Support Student Actions
Answers: Where am I going?	**Clarifying the learning intentions (targets)** Without a clear vision, learners are unable to hit the target. Though teachers are advised to state clear learning targets, ultimately it is the learners who must clarify what they are expected to know and do. So, if learners are not provided a clear understanding of the learning intentions, they are subject to mystery learning and will likely miss the intended mark.	• Name learning targets or co-create targets through an inquiry-based approach. • Clarify terms. • Post targets everywhere—in the classroom, on assessments, on tracking forms, and so on. • Ask learners to define the targets in their own words and provide examples and non-examples of what that target means. • Ask learners to clarify which target they just worked on following an activity.
	Assimilating criteria In addition to the targets, learners need to understand quality and what it will look like. Without clear criteria, scoring feels subjective to learners and they are unable to accurately match the teacher's scores, so self-assessment will likely be inaccurate.	• Co-create criteria through examining exemplars. • Co-create rubrics or scales. • Provide examples and nonexamples. • Practice scoring to develop inter-rater reliability, learner-to-learner and teacher-to-teacher.
Answers: Where am I now?	**Seeking feedback** Feedback from the teacher, peers, or even themselves helps learners understand where they are relative to the learning intentions (targets and criteria). Without an accurate perspective, learners will fail to hit the final mark.	• Provide support materials, such as criteria, for quality feedback. • Set protocols for exchanging feedback. • Provide forms for recording and reflecting on feedback. • Teach learners the best ways to gather feedback and determine relevance of information.

	Responding to feedback Learners always have the power to embrace all feedback, accept parts of feedback, or ignore feedback. Teachers must teach the learner to respond to feedback wisely so he or she advances the learning him- or herself.	• Model strong and weak examples of sending and receiving feedback. • Teach learners to make strategic decisions regarding which feedback supports and which hinders continued learning.
	Scoring Learners can best self-assess when they frequently, independently, and accurately score self- and peer-generated work. When learners develop inter-rater reliability with teacher scoring, they more quickly control their own instructional decision making and drive their own improvement. When an entire class develops accuracy in self-scoring, peer evaluation provides a powerful support to teacher feedback.	• Continue to rehearse scoring of sample work to develop inter-rater reliability with teacher scoring. • Engage learners in scoring their own work before it is submitted—highlighting potential errors and noting questions within the body of the work. • Engage learners in comparing their scores to teacher scores and analyzing differences for increased accuracy with future scoring.
Answers: How can I succeed?	**Setting goals** Learner-generated goals direct a learner's purpose, focus monitoring efforts, and increase engagement in the learning process. Teacher-generated goals work for learners *if* teachers properly influence learners to *want* those goals.	• Provide goal-setting forms. • Engage learners in analyzing strong and weak goals. • Show learners how to use goals to monitor improvement from one assessment to the next. • Ask learners to write the goal at the top of relevant assessments and then highlight evidence demonstrating improvement of that goal.
	Monitoring progress An unmonitored goal becomes a wish. Goals have meaning when learners constantly compare their own current levels of proficiency against the desired state of proficiency (goal). Learners must continue self-assessing as they monitor progress.	• Provide data forms that allow learners to gather and track growth over time with visual tools. • Engage learners in analyzing errors and generating clarity on specific areas for growth.

Teachers help students learn to self-assess accurately by providing direct instruction on each of the self-assessment strategies listed in table 2.1. Individually, each strategy—clarifying the learning intentions, assimilating criteria, seeking feedback, responding to feedback, scoring, setting goals, and monitoring progress—requires considerable rehearsal and refinement, so ongoing practice and feedback are necessary. Learners' abilities to self-assess precede their capacity to apply the effort needed to reduce the visible discrepancies between where they are on the learning journey and where they need to be.

Intervention Strategies

Margaret Heritage (2007), assistant director for professional development at the National Center for Research on Evaluation, Standards, and Student Testing at UCLA, states, "When students recognize they are not learning, they have [to have] the strategies to do something about it" (p. 143). An *intervention* is the adjustment someone makes to correct errors or close gaps. So, for example, when a student realizes he or she is not understanding what is being read, then he or she employs one or more strategies—like rereading the section, looking for text clues, breaking challenging words into parts, looking key words up, or even searching for interpretations from other sources—to better grasp the text. External, teacher-generated adjustments are still necessary, but in the end, it's more powerful when learners strive to make their own corrections. Assessment experts Nancy Frey, Douglas Fisher, and John Hattie (2018) indicate it is possible to over-scaffold and under-support learners when employing interventions, no matter how appropriate or targeted those interventions might be:

> When we continually pair a particular strategy or tool with a text or problem, we rob learners of the decision-making skills they need to advance their own learning. Teachers of assessment-capable learners create opportunities for students to learn *how* to learn. (p. 49)

When teachers and learners work together to identify, employ, and test the effectiveness of intervention strategies, the results are not only amplified in that moment but also the learners gain important experiences to inform their own intervention strategies in the future.

Though scaffolded support and guidance might be required in the early stages of learning to learn, self-regulated learners must eventually willingly and independently engage in the following behaviors.

- Seeking and accepting new challenges in learning
- Identifying purpose, defining courses of action, and following through with a plan
- Applying prior knowledge and processes to construct new knowledge
- Accessing and utilizing information from a variety of sources

- Seeking and accepting feedback
- Engaging in disciplined problem solving for complex situations and resolving those same problems with ideal solutions

Teachers must find ways to explicitly teach and integrate such behaviors into their classroom learning through direct examples, guided practice, feedback, and rehearsal strategies. Such behaviors *can* be learned *if* teachers engage in identifying and celebrating student successes with each strategy. It is especially helpful when teachers call out the many different ways, styles, and strategies learners employ when self-assessing. Ultimately, though, it's important to remember that such strategies can only be activated to their fullest potential when learners maintain a growth mindset, a sense of efficacy, and the hope that all their efforts will be fully acknowledged through a final grade that demonstrates their final achievement.

Feedback

Feedback is an instructional intervention teachers employ to reduce discrepancies between where learners currently are versus where they ultimately need to be. Teachers use feedback to help learners make informed instructional decisions about what should come next in mastering knowledge or skills. However, not all feedback works equally well to support self-regulation. Hattie and Timperley's (2007) research identifies four specific types of feedback teachers tend to use and indicates which types of feedback are best when teaching learners to self-regulate. Table 2.2 provides the definition of each type of feedback as well as examples of what those types of feedback might look or sound like.

Table 2.2: Definitions and Examples of Hattie and Timperley's (2007) Four Types of Feedback

Can Hinder Self-Regulation	Can Promote Self-Regulation
Task feedback: Describes how well learners understand or perform specific tasks or projects *Examples* • "You earned a B+. Great story!" • "You have a D– on your science project." • "You earned 9 of 10 points." • "You earned 100 percent! Super job!"	**Process feedback:** Describes how well learners understand, manage, and perform the core processes; crosses multiple tasks and projects *Examples* • "When you are adding and you regroup like this . . . " • "When scientists draw conclusions, they make sure they have sufficient and reliable evidence. When I look at your work, I notice you have a lot of evidence, but how do you know it's all reliable?"

continued →

Self-feedback: What a teacher thinks of a learner or his or her character and affect (usually positive); virtually impossible not to be evaluative in nature; learner rarely converts into more engagement, commitment to learning goals, enhanced self-efficacy, or understanding of the task	Self-regulation feedback: How well learners manage learning literacy during the learning process (managing self-observation, judgment, and reactions as they navigate goal setting, generating targeted evidence, managing feedback, tracking progress, reflecting, and so on)
Examples	*Examples*
• "You are such a great student!" • "It's clear you truly struggle with mathematics."	• "What strategy did you use last time that worked?" • "What error are you trying to address? Is your approach working?"

Feedback aimed exclusively at a learner's product or even the character of the learner is actually detrimental to his or her ability or interest to self-regulate (Hattie & Timperley, 2007). With each of those types of feedback, the learner can find no pathway to grow or regulate him- or herself to make different instruction choices. On the other hand, feedback that analyzes learners' processes or learning strategies is much more likely to spur introspection and potential growth in self-regulation. In addition to the examples given in table 2.2, the following feedback processes can help learners self-regulate.

- Practice scoring samples of strong and weak work until learners achieve inter-rater reliability with the teacher (Chappuis, 2015).

- Engage learners in the constant practice of self- and peer feedback, striving to use measurement tools with accuracy.

- Use samples of strong and weak work to collaboratively diagnose errors and identify the strategies to fix them.

- Link learner feedback to the same language used in class discussions when diagnosing errors.

- Maintain an anchor chart of common errors and instructional fixes.

- Provide every learner with both success feedback and intervention feedback (Chappuis, 2015).

- Offer feedback that feeds forward.

- Provide feedback learners can use to revise a current project.

- Provide feedback learners can use to improve on future assessments.

- Provide feedback learners can use to improve their current self-regulation strategies.

- Provide feedback to continue the learning (for example, feedback that avoids doing the thinking for the learners; Chappuis, 2015).

- Focus on targeted areas that provide the greatest gains. Do not overwhelm learners with too much feedback.

- Have learners create a goal and a plan to address feedback.

- Have learners write their goal or feedback from a past assessment at the top of the next assessment. Then have them use highlighters to indicate the places they believe they have integrated the feedback and demonstrated growth.

When learners experience these feedback routines, they begin to value feedback as a genuine support mechanism for their continued learning. Wiliam (2013) states:

> ...to fully support student learning processes, feedback should also *focus on self-regulation, metacognition, attribution, self-efficacy,* and *goal orientation.* . . . In this manner, feedback can reinforce students' beliefs that they can always improve their work and that they can master new challenging goals and tasks, thus enhancing students' learning-goal orientation. (p. 220)

Such feedback is so powerful because it encourages self-regulated learners to solicit additional feedback—from the teacher, from their peers, and even from trusted or reputable sources outside the classroom.

Grades

Beyond devastating feedback (such as a personal attack on a learner's character or workmanship), it's likely grading is the single most significant educational practice to most quickly and permanently inhibit a learner's willingness to engage in self-regulation. Grading can prohibit productive failure and jeopardize hope and efficacy for learners trying to do the good work of self-regulation.

Grades are a teacher-centric tool used to communicate a level of achievement in a given moment in time. Some, and at times even many, educators have felt as if marks, grades, points, or percentages—some numerical or symbolic indicator of a level of proficiency—would suffice to motivate learners. The notion that some learners would *not* strive to get top marks seems illogical to many educators who themselves were likely successful, self-regulating learners in a traditional system that relied predominantly on grading systems to inspire achievement. But such indicators fail as motivating factors for far too many learners (Schimmer, 2016).

Authors Sir Ken Robinson and Lou Aronica (2015) state, "When we try to reduce something that is as magnificently messy as real learning, we always conceal far more than we ever reveal. Ultimately, grading gets assessment wrong because assessment is not a spreadsheet—it is a conversation" (p. 172). Robinson and Aronica (2015) highlight an unpleasant transition in grading over time—a shift from teachers creating a grade as a symbol to communicate about learning to the grade dictating what teachers feel they can and cannot do in the service of learning. The more traditional grading system, which often ignores improvement over time by averaging scores from the total experience, is *not* motivating to many students in 21st century classrooms. As outlined previously, a learner's hope disappears when early mistakes eliminate any possibility of success.

When educators want students to learn to self-regulate, they must align their grading practices to support these efforts. The following beliefs and practices may help improve self-regulation in learners.

- **Improvement matters:** Learners should have the ability to achieve top scores right up until the end of a unit of study.

- **Proficiency matters:** Records of proficiency must be included in an accurate reflection of where a student ended up in the learning.

- **Mastery matters:** Learners should re-engage and revise along the way so they are not only masterful in the content and skills being studied but also masterful at learning to learn.

If ever the process and practice of self-regulation fails to motivate and inspire learners, then an examination of the grading practices and policies might be the first place for teachers to begin. As Hattie (2009) states:

> The notion that increasing achievement is a function of our efforts and interest is critical to success—there is no point, for example, in investing in study or preparation if we do not believe that our efforts can make a difference. (p. 48)

The cap, or ceiling, many learners feel in their capacity to make a difference in their results may be less the result of the learners' sense of ability and more a consequence of the evaluative system they are trying to operate in. Teachers should attempt to set up learners for success by creating an evaluative grading system that most readily allows for self-regulation.

There should not be a final evaluative score in a gradebook as there is no overarching summative assessment for a learner's ability to self-regulate. One could argue a data notebook would accumulate artifacts demonstrating a learner's capacity to self-regulate, like formative artifacts learners generate by measuring specific learning intentions on other summative assessments, such as reflecting on test results or setting goals for future accomplishments based on past achievement scores. The following section provides tools and strategies to help educators measure self-regulation.

Measuring Self-Regulation

Self-regulation is a learner-owned process. It is best handled with assessment *as* learning processes. In other words, learners do not formally measure self-regulation; instead learners diagnose *what is* and dialogue about *what could be*. Self-regulation is explored in relationship-based conversations: learner to teacher, teacher to learner, learner to learner, and especially, learner to self. Because discussing self-regulation involves making oneself vulnerable, tremendous care must be taken to nurture and support the learners' risk taking. Safety is required.

Evidence of self-regulation in the classroom shows up in the artifacts learners create at each stage of the learning process. Those products—a learner's goals, a tracking form of what happened, a self-assigned score, a reflection of how the learning altered the learner—are about the *self*, so the teacher should not measure or evaluate them. Instead, any teacher evaluations should be on the academic work produced *in response to* the learning intentions—the papers, projects, or performances—whether or not learning happened. Those academic measures provide the results learners need to better understand their ability to self-regulate. Academic measures are the goalposts in the learning ballgame. If the entire effort of teaching self-regulation is to empower learners to monitor and ultimately measure their own efforts, then it is both redundant and contradictory to also evaluate their endeavors. The goal is to help learners improve their self-regulation processes to support continued learning.

Data notebooks are not required for self-regulation; they simply serve as an organizational method to store information. If used appropriately, data notebooks can also help learners reflect on how their own regulation processes are improving over time. However, self-assessment protocols and reflective tools are necessary to help learners become metacognitive of their processes, even if they are not all organized in one location.

Precursors to Measuring Self-Regulation

A precursor to launching self-regulation processes is to ensure the culture is suitable for the investment of time and energy. Learners must have hope that success is possible if they are going to attempt to regulate for their own success. It helps when schools take an honest look at how learners perceive their chances for success. Hope survey data in figure 2.1 can open up dialogue schoolwide and help staff carefully monitor their own culture and policies.

The answers to the reflection questions following the data analysis will likely open new avenues to investigate; namely, what policies, procedures, and classroom practices the school might need to reconsider if it wants to serve as a beacon of hope for all its learners. Educators might also benefit from taking the hope survey to determine their own readiness and perceptions for building a culture that promotes risk taking and high achievement.

Another precursor activity to engaging students in self-regulation is to help them recognize themselves as *learners.* It might seem odd to suggest students don't always view themselves in that vein, but many feel as though they are simply moving through required motions and they haven't stopped to observe themselves learn, taken stock of their natural strengths, identified their preferred strategies to support learning, recognized their behaviors and preferences when under stress, and so on. Figure 2.2 (pages 60–61) offers a reflective inventory students can take to begin to understand their own learning thumbprint, or what coauthor Cassandra Erkens (2016) calls "the individual's *learning DNA* (desires, needs, and assets)" (p. 156).

If learners keep a data notebook, the learner's DNA inventory could serve as a preface. Inviting learners to update their inventory periodically with different colored pens or pencils can help them remain metacognitive about their learning DNA as they expand their understanding through continued learning experiences.

Self-Assessment Processes

The true work of self-assessment, however, involves using academic evidence to inform decisions about oneself relative to the learning intentions, and then making decisions about instructional maneuvers to improve. Students who are self-regulating their learning do need to focus internally on their thoughts and feelings so they can get to know themselves as learners. With a clear awareness in place, learners can better navigate pending challenges by anticipating their responses and taking a proactive stance toward success early in the process.

There are many different reflection templates, effort trackers, and data notebooks educators may use or adapt when measuring self-assessment processes.

Reflection Templates

It's powerful when learners can reflect on their performance following an assessment. Some reflection forms are really blueprint templates of the assessment itself. Figure 2.3 (pages 62–63) provides a sample self-reflection template complete with student responses. To use such a form effectively, two things must happen: (1) class

Directions for learners: Circle the answer that best describes your belief about each statement.

Yes	No	1. I have been successful in school in the past.
Yes	No	2. I have been successful outside school in the past.
Yes	No	3. I will be successful in school in the future.
Yes	No	4. I will be successful outside school in the future.
Yes	No	5. I have goals for my future.
Yes	No	6. I will be able to get the knowledge and skills I need to pursue my goals.
Yes	No	7. I have access to many resources to help me when I am challenged.
Yes	No	8. I can think of many ways to solve problems.
Yes	No	9. I can identify and rely on my personal strengths.
Yes	No	10. I have strategies to compensate for any limitations or challenges I face.

Directions for educators: Provide the hope survey to a group of learners (an individual classroom, a grade level, a department, or the whole school) to take anonymously in order to gauge the degree of hopefulness present or needed. Analyze the aggregated data by using questions like the following to explore the data.

Questions 1–4:

- Is there a significant difference between when learners feel hopeful outside school versus in school? Is there a reason for concern?
- Is there a difference between learners' degree of hopefulness in the past versus the future? Is there a reason for concern?

Questions 5–6:

- Are our learners goal oriented?
    - If so, are there things we do to support that?
    - If not, are there things we could be doing to support that?

Questions 7–10:

- Do our learners feel efficacious and resourceful when tackling challenges?
    - If so, are there things we do to support that?
    - If not, are there things we could be doing to support that?

Questions 1–10:

- When we look at the findings as a whole, what are we doing well to increase hope for our students in the learning experience?
- When we look at the findings as a whole, are there things we might need to do to increase the degree of hopefulness our students have when learning?
- What other insights or observations do we have?
- What are our immediate action steps based on our results?

Figure 2.1: Hope survey.

*Visit **go.SolutionTree.com/assessment** for a free reproducible version of this figure.*

My Learning DNA (Desires, Needs, Assets) Inventory

Directions: This learning DNA inventory will help you and your teacher get to know your learning preferences. Please complete it to the best of your ability, then share it with your teacher. Hold on to it throughout the school year, adding, modifying, or deleting entries as you encounter new learning opportunities.

My Desires:

My future goals and aspirations are _____.

My favorite activities and hobbies are _____.

My favorite topics are _____.

My favorite space to learn is _____ because

_____.

My Needs:

I would like to continue to grow in my understanding of or ability to _____.

One thing that challenges me is _____.

I get stressed when _____.

When I am stressed, I need to _____.

When I am studying, I like it to be some place _____.

My Assets:

I am interested in learning _____.

I am interested in doing _____.

My talents and personal gifts are _____.

One thing I have learned about myself is _____.

I know if I am to be a successful learner, I have to _____.

Strategies I use to help me be successful when I need to study are _____.

Strategies I use to help me be successful when I am confused are _____.

Volume								
	Quiet							Loud
Light								
	Dim							Bright
Social Interactions								
	Private							Public
	Just me alone in a room (in a coffee shop, for example)							A room full of people

Figure 2.2: *My learning DNA inventory.*

Visit **go.SolutionTree.com/assessment** *for a free reproducible version of this figure.*

discussions *during* the learning, which helps all learners isolate and understand the most common errors made on each learning intention and, (2) the teacher scoring the assessment by placing a mark next to an error (percentages and grades are not required yet) and returning the marked assessment to the learner with the reflection form for analysis.

Imagine that figure 2.3 (pages 62–63) provides the architectural blueprint behind an assessment that Ben took. Ben gets his test back and sees that the teacher has highlighted any item that was wrong. Ben then uses figure 2.3 to analyze his own results. The item number references the number of the assessment itself, and the target listed references the learning expectation behind the item (for example, question one on the assessment was about describing the law-making process). Ben looks at his assessment to see where the teacher placed dots indicating errors and puts an *X* next to any item marked wrong on the reflection form. Next, Ben tries to determine what he did wrong to earn the dot on the assessment. Finally, Ben does the mathematics in the Results section and makes a decision (with teacher rules in place about how many need to be correct) about next steps. The teacher then provides Ben with potential resources to support his continued learning in sections where he must re-engage in the learning based on evidence that suggests the target is not yet mastered.

Social Studies   **Ben**

Our standard: Learners will describe the process of making laws, carrying out laws, and determining if laws were violated.

Item	Target 1	Wrong (X)	Type of Error or Mistake	Results
1	I can describe the lawmaking process.			I have <u>5</u> of 5 correct. What will you do?
4	I can describe the lawmaking process.			____ Keep working
5	I can describe the lawmaking process.			<u>X</u> Done
7	I can describe the lawmaking process.			
9	I can describe the lawmaking process.			

Resources to support target 1: social studies book, pages 97–100 and election lab worksheets

Item	Target 2	Wrong (X)	Type of Error or Mistake	Results
2	I can explain the role of citizenship as it relates to enacting laws.			I have <u>2</u> of 5 correct. What will you do?
3	I can explain the role of citizenship as it relates to enacting laws.	X	Concept error: law	<u>X</u> Keep working
6	I can explain the role of citizenship as it relates to enacting laws.	X	Reading error: "always"	____ Done
8	I can explain the role of citizenship as it relates to enacting laws.			
10	I can explain the role of citizenship as it relates to enacting laws.	X	Reasoning error: evaluate	

Resources to support target 2: social studies book pages 92–96 and community surveys

Reflect on your learning by completing the following statements based on which items you got right or wrong.

- My strength (the things I got right) is learning target 1, which means I can describe the lawmaking process.
- My area for growth (the things I got wrong and will work to fix) is learning target 2, which means I need to work on explaining the role of citizenship as it relates to enacting laws.
- My learning goal for next steps is to learn more about and understand the role of being a citizen as it relates to enacting laws.
- Strategies or activities I will use to meet my goal include the resources on pages 92–96, so I can revise my responses and fix the answers I got wrong.

Figure 2.3: *Example of a self-reflection following a pencil-and-paper assessment.*

When learners fill in reflection forms and see the patterns and trends in their data, they should complete the following important statements to help them self-regulate.

- My strengths (the things I got right)
- My areas for growth (the things I got wrong and will work to fix)
- My learning goal for next steps
- Strategies or activities I will use to meet my goal

The most important part of the entire process is completing these reflection statements because a learner can then understand what comes next in the learning. Learners modify the process to accommodate performance assessments that use proficiency levels (instead of correct answers) and to accommodate primary students with pictures and metaphors (instead of numbers). Figure 2.4 (page 64) provides an example of a form a primary learner might use to monitor his or her progress with proficiency levels.

Learners can use a self-reflection form in multiple ways. For example, they could use the form to peer edit or self-score. The form could also be filled in prior to a teacher's score and submitted with the original work. Or, the learner could fill in the appropriate box after the teacher scores the work. No matter how learners use such forms, the power of the reflection always rests in having the learner *see* his or her current proficiency level and then make plans to support continued success.

Effort Trackers

Effort matters, so it's important that teachers help students to notice how their own effort made a difference in the final product. But effort is virtually impossible

Initiating	Developing	Achieving	Advancing

Color in the picture that matches your work.

- I am good at _____.

- I am still learning _____.

- Next, I have to _____.

- I will try _____ to see if I can improve.

Figure 2.4: *Elementary student-reflection template for use following a pencil-and-paper assessment.*

*Visit **go.SolutionTree.com/assessment** for a free reproducible version of this figure.*

for a teacher to measure accurately, so it's helpful to provide learners with tools they can use to monitor their own effort. Self-monitoring increases awareness and can alter the outcome for the better because effort makes such a powerful difference in a learner's ultimate success. Figure 2.5 is a tool that learners can use to self-monitor their own level of effort.

When teachers want to build the case that effort matters, they can ask learners to self-assign effort scores (a single data point just for effort) for an entire unit of study and then invite them to compare the aggregate effort data with their final achievement data or grades for that same unit. Yet another strategy is to make the conversation a classwide learning opportunity by making the following comparisons for the previous unit of study.

- Average of class effort scores

- Average class grades

- Range of the top ten grades (completely anonymous) across the entire grade level and the correlating effort scores (for example, "The top ten scores on our last assessment ranged from 20 to 25, and the students who earned those marks scored mostly 4s with a

My Effort Tracker

Directions: Use the effort tracker after completing a unit of study or a performance assessment. Score your personal effort (1 = rarely; 2 = sometimes; 3 = most often; 4 = consistently). If your score is a 1 or 2 in any category, identify actions you could take to improve in the left-hand column. If your score is a 3 or 4 in any category, identify the strategies, resources, or skills you used that might help someone else be successful too.

Improvement Ideas	Advancing				Celebrations Worth Noting
	Interest: I demonstrate a genuine desire to learn.				
	1	2	3	4	
	Challenge: I strive to take intellectual risks, knowing that sometimes I might fail, but I will always still learn.				
	1	2	3	4	
	Expectations: I set high expectations for myself and then challenge myself to meet or exceed those expectations.				
	1	2	3	4	
	Readiness: I am always prepared for class and for each assigned task.				
	1	2	3	4	
	Initiation: When given a task, I get started right away.				
	1	2	3	4	
	Persistence: I seek alternative strategies to help me push through difficult moments or experiences until I complete the task at hand.				
	1	2	3	4	
	Engagement: I actively engage in class discussions and team projects, striving to be a positive influence on others.				
	1	2	3	4	

Figure 2.5: *Effort tracker.*

*Visit **go.SolutionTree.com/assessment** for a free reproducible version of this figure.*

small handful of 3s on the effort self-assessment inventory. Every top assessment score was matched to a top effort score.")

- Range of the lowest ten grades (completely anonymous) across the entire grade level and the correlating effort scores (for example, "The lowest ten scores on our last assessment ranged from 9 to 13, and the students who earned those marks scored mostly 1s and 2s on the effort self-assessment inventory. So, every low assessment score was matched to a low effort score as well.")

Please note: the comparisons should always be anonymous, with no individual learner's data ever revealed in the process. Providing data across the entire grade level or across all the same courses disperses the anonymous data even further so peers do not recognize any learner's data.

Data Notebooks

Sometimes teachers help learners maintain data notebooks or portfolios as tools to provide necessary evidence. Data notebooks usually hold an array of tracking forms. A *tracking form* is a tool learners use to track a single target over time or a small group of targets in a unit of study. It's always best if tracking forms include visual tools so the trajectory of growth is visible. Following is an array of visual tracking tool examples. These figures are a means to show the trajectory of growth over a period of time.

Bar graphs (see figure 2.6), run charts, and other simple variations of these visual tools help learners monitor growth over time. These tools work well with right and wrong answers, but only with equivalent data. When the data are not equivalent (for example, when a student earns 7 of 7—the best he or she could do—on a formative assessment but the bar graph goes up to 10), the learner will see a gap where none exists.

Day	Number Correct	Graph
Monday	7	
Tuesday	12	
Wednesday	10	
Thursday	18	
Friday	20	

Figure 2.6: Example of a bar graph for tracking progress.

Progressive bars (see figure 2.7) allow learners to document the scores they achieve for a specific standard or competency revisited multiple times. Learners can fill in the name (for example, homework or draft one) or the type of the assessment (for example, formative assessment). Learners use lighter colors or different symbols to delineate which items were self- or peer scored, and darker colors or different symbols to isolate teacher scores on summative projects or tests (summative assessment). The goal is to reach the highest level.

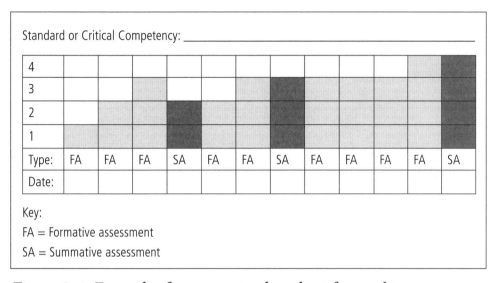

Figure 2.7: *Example of a progressive bar chart for tracking progress over time.*

Spider graphs (see figure 2.8, page 68) are simply a variation of using progressive bars, but spider graphs accommodate multiple targets on a single assessment. Learners use spider graphs within a single unit of study to note progress on all of the targets in that unit.

When using a spider graph, learners fill in their proficiency scores on each bar with each assessment. Then, by connecting each data point with a line, the learner's progress *web* emerges; using different colors over time also allows for tracking growth with a number of targets.

The goal of every self-assessment process is to lead learners toward improvement. Using more formal tools for planning improvement can solidify and enhance the reflective work learners do when answering the *what-comes-next* questions following each assessment. Figure 2.9 (page 68) offers a more comprehensive set of questions to guide learners in planning their next steps. Such a tool is helpful when learners are striving to grow between units of study on important skills or critical competencies.

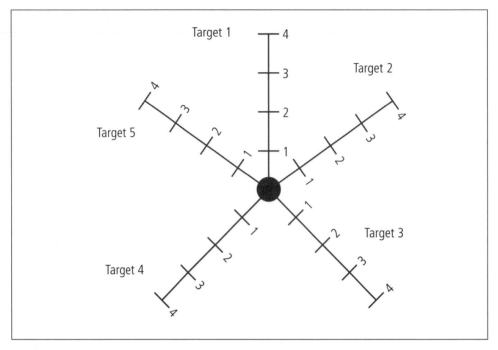

Figure 2.8: Example of a spider graph for tracking progress.

My Improvement Plan

What are the instructional decisions I can make at this juncture? Check all that apply.

☐ Seek a little additional feedback or support to get confirmation I am close to achieving mastery.

☐ Re-engage in learning and then reassess to guarantee mastery.

☐ Seek consultation.

☐ Participate in new instruction.

☐ Engage in actively practicing key concepts and skills.

☐ Enrich or enhance my current understanding.

Which targets have I mastered? Use data to validate assertion.

What evidence do I have that I have mastered those targets?

Which targets have I yet to master? Use data to validate the assertion.

What evidence will I seek to validate I am on my way to mastering targets?

What strengths do I bring to the task? What strategies have worked for me in the past when I faced challenges?

What new strategies will I try and how will I know when they are working, or what will I do if they are not working?

Figure 2.9: Questionnaire for improvement planning.

*Visit **go.SolutionTree.com/assessment** for a free reproducible version of this figure.*

If teachers want to engage learners in a dialogue about their self-regulation efforts, they can use a rubric (see figure 2.10, pages 70–71) or a scale (see figure 2.11, page 72). Both tools use similar language. The rubric focuses on the strengths of individual criteria, whereas the scale focuses on the comprehensive aspects of a single level of proficiency.

Both the rubric and scale provide language teachers can use to support dialogues with learners regarding their efforts to regulate their own learning. Learners can use both tools (with possible modifications for age-appropriate vocabulary) to self-score their efforts. Teacher should not use either tool to *evaluate* learners regarding their ability to self-regulate, and most certainly should not end up anywhere near a report card.

Growing Self-Regulation

Tools are only a small part of the overall process teachers must use to develop self-regulated learners in their classrooms. So much depends on the classroom culture, the opportunities to learn from mistakes, and the types of conversations teachers generate about learning as students are immersed in it. Teachers can teach content and weave in conversations about how students are learning as they proceed, or they can start with focusing on learning and use content as the vehicle to help students explore the learning process.

The seemingly slight switch in vernacular—from *learning content* to *using content to learn how to learn*—is actually a dramatic switch in the classroom. Content is no longer the end goal in the second version. Learning to learn is the end goal, and content is the vehicle to help learners understand the process, monitor their experience, and achieve the academic gains necessary. Jean Piaget, the famous Swiss psychologist who created a widely accepted theory of cognitive development, says, "Each time one prematurely teaches a child something he could have discovered himself, that child is kept from inventing it and consequently from understanding it completely" (Piaget, 1970, p. 715). Teachers should avoid learning *for* the students, instead encouraging them to be self-aware on their journeys of learning to learn. Once learners understand *how* to learn and experience success with regulating their own processes, there will be no limit on where they'll go on their lifelong journey.

	Initiating	Developing	Achieving	Advancing
Seeks and Accepts New Challenges in Learning	Engages in teacher-led learning	Expresses curiosity and is willing to follow a tangential lead to gain information or attempt something the teacher has not established	Actively seeks and accepts challenges within the identified area of study that stretch personal knowledge and skills and that exceed the teacher-required parameters	Actively seeks and accepts challenges within a self-identified area of study that stretch personal knowledge and skills and that exceed the teacher-required parameters
Identifies a Purpose, Charts a Course of Action, and Follows Through	Adopts the provided purpose and follows the predetermined course of action	Accepts the provided purpose and creates a course of action with some personal preferences on the best way to advance the learning, and then follows through	Identifies a purpose for self within the context of study, charts a course of action that will support achieving the purpose, and follows through, revising until the purpose is satisfied	Identifies a purpose for self within a self-selected area of study, charts a course of action that will support achieving the purpose, and follows through, revising until the purpose is satisfied
Identifies and Employs an Array of Strategies to Navigate Challenge	Utilizes strategies offered as teacher recommendations	Seeks and utilizes optional strategies identified through additional reading or that classmates share	Articulates and employs an array of favored strategies, self-monitoring for effectiveness, and drawing conclusions or documenting what works best for future use	Articulates and employs favored strategies; actively strives to learn and incorporate additional challenging or uncomfortable strategies; and self-monitors for effectiveness, drawing conclusions or documenting what works best for future use

	Initiating	Developing	Achieving	Advancing
Seeks and Incorporates Feedback	Accepts feedback when offered	Seeks feedback from a trusted peer; may or may not implement it	Seeks feedback from a variety of sources—including those with alternative perspectives—and strives to incorporate it	Intentionally solicits alternative perspectives and dabbles in modifying work in significant ways, then seeks additional feedback and reflects before selecting the best option
Persists	Attempts a challenge but gives up if the challenge is too frustrating	Attempts a challenge and completes the task but is satisfied with a focus on completion and little attention to quality	Tackles a challenge with strong commitment, using multiple strategies to overcome the hurdles; finishes with attention to detail, revising until final project accurately addresses all of the intended criteria	Tackles a challenge with passion, attempting new and possibly uncomfortable strategies to overcome the hurdles; ensures final product is *publish ready* with attention to detail, revising until achieving excellence

Figure 2.10: Self-regulation rubric.

Visit go.SolutionTree.com/assessment for a free reproducible version of this figure.

Advancing	Actively seeks and accepts challenges within a self-identified area of study that stretch personal knowledge and skills and that exceed the teacher-required parameters
	Identifies a purpose for self within a self-selected area of study, charts a course of action that will support achieving the purpose, and follows through, revising until the purpose is satisfied
	Articulates and employs favored strategies; actively strives to learn and incorporate additional challenging or uncomfortable strategies; and self-monitors for effectiveness, drawing conclusions or documenting what works best for future use
	Intentionally solicits alternative perspectives and dabbles in modifying work in significant ways, then seeks additional feedback and reflects before selecting the best option
	Tackles a challenge with passion, attempting new and possibly uncomfortable strategies to overcome the hurdles; ensures final product is *publish ready* with attention to detail, revising until achieving excellence
Achieving	Actively seeks and accepts challenges within the identified area of study that stretch personal knowledge and skills and that exceed the teacher-required parameters
	Identifies a purpose for self within the context of study, charts a course of action that will support achieving the purpose, and follows through, revising until the purpose is satisfied
	Articulates and employs an array of favored strategies, self-monitoring for effectiveness, and drawing conclusions or documenting what works best for future use
	Seeks feedback from a variety of sources—including those with alternative perspectives—and strives to incorporate it
	Tackles a challenge with strong commitment, using multiple strategies to overcome the hurdles; finishes with attention to detail, revising until final project accurately addresses all of the intended criteria
Developing	Expresses curiosity and is willing to follow a tangential lead to gain information or attempt something the teacher has not established
	Accepts the provided purpose and creates a course of action with some personal preferences on the best way to advance the learning, and then follows through
	Seeks and utilizes optional strategies classmates identify or through reading to use in addition
	Seeks feedback from a trusted peer; may or may not implement it
	Attempts a challenge and completes the task but is satisfied with a focus on completion and little attention to quality
Initiating	Engages in teacher-led learning
	Adopts the provided purpose and follows the predetermined course of action
	Utilizes strategies that are offered as teacher recommendations
	Accepts feedback when offered
	Attempts a challenge but gives up if the challenge is too frustrating

Figure 2.11: *Proficiency scale for self-regulation.*

Visit go.SolutionTree.com/assessment for a free reproducible version of this figure.

Conclusion

There is much research in the area of self-regulation. For example, Brown and Harris (2013) note that while the extent of the gains vary, and the studies vary in their approach and overall conclusions, "there is empirical evidence that self-assessment of a task or self-confidence in the quality of the work will generally improve academic performance across a range of grade levels and subject areas" (p. 381). Teaching self-regulation makes for better students and better learning experiences.

Moreover, self-regulation is a critical competency for learners of all ages, in and out of the school setting. Teaching everyone how to self-regulate also makes for a more sustainable society. Learning is truly a lifelong endeavor. Society is dependent on adults who not only continue their own learning but also constantly strive to deepen and improve their own capacity to learn how to learn.

Pause and Ponder

On your own or as part of a collaborative teacher team, consider the following reflective questions.

1. Why might helping students maintain a sense of hope and develop a sense of efficacy be so important to the work of self-regulation?

2. What do you already do that supports developing self-regulation as a core competency in your classroom or school?

3. What would you have to teach students if you wanted them to learn how to self-assess? What are the components of self-assessment that would require instruction?

4. What strategies can you use to help students develop inter-rater reliability with your teacher scoring so that their self-assessments are reliable?

5. What strategies can you use to help students monitor their own progress?

6. What two or three things could you begin to do immediately to help learners in your classroom or school develop self-regulation skills, beliefs, and processes?

7. What classroom or school policies or practices might negatively affect hope in the learning process?

8. What would you need to do to truly *empower* learners to make their own instructional decisions?

CHAPTER 3
CRITICAL THINKING

The basic idea undergirding the study of critical thinking is simple—to determine strengths and weaknesses in one's thinking in order to maintain the strengths and make improvements by targeting the weaknesses.

—Linda M. Murawski

While critical thinking has long been a valued outcome of education, newly emerging state, provincial, and national standards put a premium on this invaluable competency. Critical thinking is now the focus of learning, and content is used in the service of teaching learners to think. The list of critical-thinking skills is endless; whether learners are analyzing, hypothesizing, comparing, evaluating, synthesizing, defending, inferring, or predicting, they're thinking critically. The real advantage for teachers and learners alike is that each of those skills is subject-neutral, making them universally applicable across almost every subject area.

The good news is that teachers are not starting from scratch when it comes to assessing critical thinking; most *thinking* activities teachers currently use are still applicable. The fundamental shift is not in redefining what the skill or disposition is; rather, it is about engaging learners in creating new knowledge through skills rather than using the skills to manipulate a body of given information. By and large, teachers can hit the ground running as they shift the emphasis of instructional outcomes.

Again, knowledge is being repurposed as a *means* so learners can *think critically* within the context of discipline-specific challenges.

Defining Critical Thinking

Most attempts to define critical thinking in a singular or narrow set of terms minimize both the depth and breadth of what critical thinking is (Murawski, 2014). While some may focus on the *critical* aspect of critical thinking by emphasizing the *critique* of the current state (Biesta & Stams, 2001), the American Philosophical Association offers a broader definition that includes such actions as interpretation, analysis, evaluation, and even inferencing (Facione, 1990). For the purpose of this book, *critical thinking* comprises a large set of skills and dispositions—including analysis, synthesis, and evaluation—that help learners make informed, self-regulatory judgments; solve problems; or understand and explain concepts more deeply. But simply *defining* this construct is only the beginning. In order to instruct learners in this critical competency, teachers, teacher teams, and schools must decide whether critical thinking should be taught as a generalist or a specific skill.

There is little consensus about whether critical thinking is a set of generic skills that apply across subject domains or whether these skills depend on the subject domain and context within which educators teach and apply (Ennis, 1989; as cited in Abrami et al., 2015). Psychological views of critical thinking tend to lean toward the *generic-traits* approach (that aspects of critical thinking are generalized, discrete skills), while philosophical views believe critical thinking has *contextual traits* that always involve thinking about some specific context, even if generic skills happen to apply across more than one discipline (Abrami et al., 2015). The *generalist* view of critical thinking, then, would have discrete skills being easily transferable, so once learners know how to think critically, they can readily and consistently apply this thinking across multiple settings and disciplines. The *specifist* view would have critical-thinking skills be subject-specific—a historical analysis, for example, would be very different from a literary analysis, even though *analysis* is the root of both processes. In the specifist view, critical-thinking skills are context-dependent instead of easily transferable.

The implication for schools is that any proclamations about *developing critical thinkers* would require at least a consideration of which perspective will serve as the school's foundation, even though a balanced approach is likely most favorable. If schools take the generalist approach, then educators could easily teach critical-thinking skills in a stand-alone class on critical thinking (Royalty, 1995; Sá, West,

& Stanovich, 1999). Another generalist approach would be to develop a protocol for the process in every class. A generalist approach would look similar across disciplines, whereas a specifist approach would require educators to teach and assess critical-thinking skills individually, within the context of specific subject domains (Halliday, 2000; Smith, 2002).

Balance is most favorable since schools could take a generalist approach when identifying the skills and dispositions of a critical thinker, but then a specifist approach in having educators teach those generic skills throughout specific-subject domains to ensure teachers prioritize the contextualization of those critical-thinking skills and dispositions. Defining critical thinking—and its associated skills—is not meant to narrow the scope of what is possible for learners; it is meant to bring some necessary clarity to a somewhat abstract concept.

Considering Critical Thinking Now and Going Forward

While the *skills* of critical thinking are what most educators tend to think of when conceptualizing this critical competency, the *dispositions* of a critical thinker are equally important to identify and develop. Not only do critical thinkers utilize a discrete set of skills, they develop a disposition that has them *behave* as critical thinkers (Ennis, 2011). Table 3.1 (page 78) offers Tusculum College adjunct professor Linda M. Murawski's (2014) examination of critical-thinking skills, critical-thinking behaviors, and the residual outcomes.

The biggest takeaway for teachers is to realize that critical thinking is not just what learners will *do*, it is who they will *become*. As with any other skill that students develop, the repetition of quality opportunities for learners to apply critical-thinking skills can help them develop both a procedural fluency with the skills themselves as well as an automaticity in how they perceive and then respond to the world. In other words, by continually applying critical-thinking skills, learners will become critical thinkers.

This automaticity of critical thinking, along with its dispositional tendencies, is what separates the more current view of critical thinking from what it was often in the past. In the new paradigm, it is preferred that learners emerge as partners and key decision makers in their own experiences, allowing them to create relevance while exploring those areas and topics that naturally pique their curiosity. As a result, modern instruction of critical thinking is focusing on two issues in particular—(1) student-driven critical thinking and (2) skills that transfer beyond the classroom—when developing students to succeed in this critical competency in the real world.

Table 3.1: *Potential Impacts of Critical-Thinking Skills and Behaviors*

Critical-Thinking Skills	Critical-Thinking Behaviors	Outcomes
• Distinguishes fact from opinion • Seeks multiple perspectives • Recognizes assumptions • Identifies bias and persuasion • Evaluates arguments for relevance and accuracy • Weighs data appropriately • Uses multiple sources rather than a single source • Balances logic and emotion • Uses diagrams to visually represent processes and thinking	• Asks questions that further understanding • Doesn't draw conclusions too hastily • Considers all sides of an argument • Uses criteria to evaluate information • Can "push back" effectively • Recognizes other people's agendas • Explores multiple perspectives • Adjusts assumptions in light of new evidence • Understands how conclusions were drawn • Identifies what's known and what isn't	• Makes well-thought-out decisions based on a sound rationale and evidence • Revises information, conclusions, and decisions as new information comes to light • Reflects a systems thinking rather than silo approach with decisions • Evaluates information based on evidence, logical inference, and informed guesses • Presents ideas and plans in a coherent and well-thought-out fashion

Source: Murawski, 2014.

Student-Driven Critical Thinking

More and more, teachers are turning to inquiry-based models of learning, where learners engage in a kind of investigatory process that begins with a driving question to shape and define what to explore. Learners, within the context of one or more subject disciplines, will define an existing problem or something about which they are naturally inquisitive. From there, learners will identify the fundamental knowledge and skills necessary to understand the depth and breadth of their investigation. The International Baccalaureate (IB) Middle Years Programme (MYP), for example, is geared toward having students (ages eleven through sixteen) explore through an inquiry process (International Baccalaureate Organization, n.d.). In the program, each year MYP students:

- Engage in at least one collaboratively planned interdisciplinary unit that involves at least two subject groups

- Complete a long-term project, where they decide what they want to learn about, identify what they already know, discover what they will need to know to complete the project, and create a proposal or criteria for completing it

MYP projects are student centered and age appropriate, and they enable students to engage in practical explorations through a cycle of inquiry, action, and reflection (International Baccalaureate Organization, n.d.).

Likewise, the curricular standards lean heavily toward an inquiry-driven, critical-thinking experience for learners. The Next Generation Science Standards (NGSS) were developed in part to "better prepare high school graduates . . . with strong science-based skills—including specific content areas but also skills such as critical thinking and inquiry-based problem solving" (NGSS, 2012). The Common Core State Standards (CCSS) were developed to, among many outcomes, utilize rigorous content so students will apply knowledge through higher-order-thinking skills (CCSS Initiative, n.d.). As well, the College, Career, and Civic Life Framework (C3) was designed to enhance the rigor of the social studies disciplines; build critical thinking, problem solving, and participatory skills to help students become engaged citizens; and align academic programs with the CCSS for English language arts and literacy in history/social studies (National Council for the Social Studies, n.d.). These standards make it clear that critical thinking is a necessary component for mastering content and process expectations.

At its heart, critical thinking will now and forever be about developing critical thinkers, which is why nurturing student curiosity is essential. Setting up learners to create and then explore meaningful questions is relatively easy since teachers can manufacture activities that require analysis or investigation. However, developing the habits and dispositions of critical thinkers is more challenging since learners need to be involved in determining the direction of their exploration. Developing the necessary habits and dispositions of critical thinking—to view the world through the lens of a critical thinker—requires that learners think and act as those in specific disciplinary fields act; they need to learn to think like scientists, writers, historians, mathematicians, artists, musicians, and so on.

Positively, subject-specific critical-thinking opportunities infuse many mandated curricular standards. The goal isn't necessarily to have learners specialize too early in their school experience; thinking like a scientist, for example, doesn't require that one become a scientist. Learners will still have a well-rounded experience, as teachers still have the responsibility of thoroughly covering the standards; after all, it is the standards that provide the substance behind the learners' exploration. Inquiry-based, curiosity-driven learning is not just a free-for-all where learners, on a whim, go in whatever direction they feel like. Rather, the curricular standards ensure a quality learning experience that underpins the notion of student-driven learning. Essentially, standards provide the structure for meaningful investigations, while student-centered, inquiry-based processes provide the substance.

Skills That Transfer Beyond the Classroom

Another differentiator between the former paradigm of critical thinking and the modern paradigm is the focus on how critical thinking transfers beyond the walls of the school. Because critical thinking is now an end, not a means, and the focus is on developing critical thinkers for life (not just during school), the most desirable result would be for learners to approach their daily lives as critical thinkers. Eventually, the use of critical-thinking skills and habits will be pervasive throughout learners' life experiences. The goal is for learners, for example, to be able to analyze the information found on the internet, hypothesize about the best possible action should they find themselves lost, or understand how to weigh the pros and cons of a particular social dilemma they may find themselves in.

Teachers can accelerate the transferability of these habits and skills when they purposefully set up or allow learners to explore the usefulness of these skills in all situations. As established earlier, context and content still matter in that learners with a greater understanding of the context (for example, how to detect authenticity on the internet) and content (for example, they are expert enough to spot misinformation) will be more apt to use the skills and habits to their advantage. That said, once a learner is a critical thinker, the transferability is more likely.

Expertise will always be needed. As learners get older, graduate, and begin to specialize, they will develop a level of expertise that makes critical thinking more habitual. Learners who, for example, see themselves headed for an engineering program in college will likely develop expertise in physics and calculus, allowing them to explore their future field more deeply. Still, their habits as critical thinkers can, and hopefully will, transfer to other areas.

Assessing Critical Thinking

Assessing critical thinking requires teachers to pay close attention to both the specific elements of critical thinking and the larger process of thinking critically about significant authentic challenges. As universal fundamentals of assessment are applied to critical thinking, teachers must balance both formative and summative practices as they carefully prepare and lead students toward demonstrating critical thinking at sophisticated levels. The unpacking of critical thinking into specific individual skills to assess formatively, the repacking of critical thinking to assess holistically and summatively, and the assessing of critical thinking on a larger scale allow teachers to create a more enriched, effective, and efficient approach to utilizing assessment practices to develop critical thinkers.

Unpacking Critical Thinking

While critical thinking can sound like a singular moment or event, it is actually a series of practices and processes purposefully sequenced, though not always in a linear fashion. While assessing critical thinking in its totality is ultimately the goal, the fundamental principles of a balanced assessment system still hold true. Assessing critical thinking—like any skill—happens by developing specific actions, practices, and processes. By unpacking critical thinking into its specific elements, teachers can begin to scaffold the experiences that lead to thinking critically on a larger scale.

The formative and summative purposes of assessment still matter, which means teachers need to be clear on the specific critical-thinking standards they intend to verify. If, for example, teachers are specifically assessing whether students can identity and define a specific problem, then teachers may create some practice experiences (formative) before verifying (summative) a learner's ability to identify and define a problem. If, however, the larger process of thinking critically is in play (that is, inquiry-based exploration), then exercises for identifying and defining a specific problem may be more formative in purpose (since the larger process of thinking critically is the ultimate goal). Each school, district, or jurisdiction will need to determine the level of desired proficiency, as that will influence the formative and summative assessment purposes. If, for example, schools are going to generalize about a learner's ability to think critically, then the specific aspects of critical thinking (such as defining the problem, gathering evidence, synthesizing trends, and drawing conclusions) will be isolated as more formative experiences. If, however, the intent is to develop proficiency at the more granular skill level, then a balance of formative and summative experiences would be more appropriate. To be clear, assessing and evaluating are necessary to develop learners into critical thinkers.

By unpacking critical thinking into its more granular underpinnings, teachers can create a purposeful learning progression that leads learners from the simplest to most sophisticated forms of critical thinking, much in the same way teachers would for any academic learning outcome. In fact, many of the learning outcomes and standards already have critical-thinking skills built in. The NGSS (NGSS Lead States, 2013), for example, expect learners to develop proficiency on the following eight specific science and engineering practices.

1. Asking questions (for science) and defining problems (for engineering)

2. Developing and using models

3. Planning and carrying out investigations

4. Analyzing and interpreting data

5. Using mathematics and computational thinking

6. Constructing explanations (for science) and designing solutions (for engineering)

7. Engaging in argument from evidence

8. Obtaining, evaluating, and communicating information

Each of these eight practices is a critical-thinking skill. A teacher then unpacks each practice into a subsequently more granular level to help learners know specifically what each practice entails. Figure 3.1 illustrates the specific skills that underpin the practice of analyzing and interpreting data.

Science and Engineering Practice	Unpacked Skills and Practices
Analyzing and interpreting data	• Gathering data • Organizing and presenting data (for example, in tables or graphs) • Making sense of data • Evaluating the quality of the data • Deriving meaning from the data • Making data-based decisions or solutions

Figure 3.1: *Unpacking the practice of analyzing and interpreting data.*

Each of the unpacked skills and practices is not intended as the *end* of instruction; however, educators should teach and assess each in order to know the specific skills learners are competent in, as well as those in need of strengthening. Each of the underpinnings can be initially developed in isolation; for example, teachers can work exclusively on organizing data. As practices repeat and grow in sophistication, teachers can expect learners to begin putting skills together (for example, gathering, organizing, and presenting data). Thus, if teachers are going to develop critical thinkers, there needs to be a purposeful and specific effort to identify the unpacked habits and skills that make up what it means to think critically.

Repacking Critical Thinking

If learners are going to begin thinking like those within a specific discipline do, they will need to authentically integrate specific critical-thinking skills to allow for a more robust experience. Conducting an authentic, inquiry-based investigation is a natural way to comprehensively experience the practices and processes of critical thinking. Unpacking and assessing specific critical-thinking skills may be advantageous for those at the beginning stages of understanding what it means to think critically, but repacking critical thinking allows teachers to put it all together in a rich, multifaceted experience.

When focused on a science investigation, for example, teachers could ask learners to explore all eight science and engineering practices and conduct an entire inquiry-driven project; this is of particular importance because the intent of the science and engineering practices is skillful integration. If learners wanted to investigate the positive and negative aspects of genetically modified food, for example, they would follow all eight practices in their entirety to draw their conclusions. Social studies teachers may ask learners to explore how urban and regional planners balance political, social, economic, and environmental impacts. An argumentative essay could expect learners to argue the plausibility of navigating civil discord with discourse in the service of thwarting civil war. Whenever teachers ask learners to *think* at a level of depth that requires them to derive an original solution, plan, or decision, teachers can assess the critical-thinking process in its entirety.

Ultimately, the focus on critical competencies is about replicating realistic experiences, which means pushing past specific curricular outcomes is most desirable. Teachers could ask high school students, for example, to decide whether their city should invest in expended roadways or expanded transit options to address traffic issues. This exercise would allow learners to formulate a question, develop a hypothesis, conduct an investigation to explore all sides of the issue, gather and evaluate relevant data, make an interpretation of those data, and then draw a plausible conclusion. As teachers engineer exercises at the most local level, learners can begin to feel as though what they are learning is deeply connected to their experiences outside school.

Assessing Critical Thinking on a Larger Scale

Beyond local issues, teachers can ask learners to think critically about global issues that impact the world around them. Population crises, food shortages, resolving political conflicts, and other social justice issues allow learners to lean into what matters to them. Obviously, the best-case scenario is for learners to explore their own curiosity about the world. However, even if the critical-thinking opportunity is sourced from the teacher, it can provide an incredibly rich learning opportunity. Teachers could ask learners to consider the fluctuation of oil prices and the impact on countries around the world, women's rights worldwide, the benefits and drawbacks of global free trade, the viability of renewable energy, or the social policies that impact poverty. The possibilities are endless, and the point is to get to a place where teachers can assess critical thinking on a larger scale to help learners see that critical thinking is not an isolated incident but rather, a process of *doing and being.* As a reminder, learners will need foundational knowledge and skills to think critically, so once again, knowledge is acquired for a purpose. However, the goal is for learners to *use* that knowledge as a foundation for more synthesized decisions that will, in all likelihood, have more than one correct solution or response. This is what adult experts in their chosen fields face each day.

A focus on big-picture critical thinking requires a big-picture approach to assessment that may push the envelope of more traditional assessment norms. While assessing critical competencies will not require a complete overhaul of the collective approach to assessment, there are some aspects educators would be wise to question to create a more relevant assessment system. Renowned educator, author, and speaker Douglas Reeves (2010) suggests 21st century assessments should lean toward being nonstandardized, blend both individual and team results, and be more public than private.

First, while assessing critical thinking, teachers will most likely need to use constructed-response items or performance assessments, instead of the ever-popular selected-response assessments to gauge learner proficiency. In other words, what learners *do* to show their critical thinking need not—and should not—be standardized. Allowing for at least some personalization, especially in an inquiry-driven environment, will build relevance and alignment. As Reeves (2010) points out, "Variation is neither good nor bad, but merely reflective of the complexity of the tasks and processes entailed in authentic assessment of 21st century skills" (p. 309). This will require teachers to become even more skilled at making scoring inferences, since using repetition for learning is likely.

As well, allowing for some team-based results (via a collaborative process) is, as Reeves (2010) points out, more reflective of society as a whole. Reeves (2010) suggests, "When students enter the world of work, society, and life in the 21st century, their hyper-competitive habits of mind will be sadly out of place" (p. 310). Finding the balance between individual and team-based results is key, as this is not an all-or-nothing endeavor. Simply put, teachers can and should make room for a team-based approach to assessing critical thinking, which is explored more intimately when discussing collaboration in chapter 4 (page 105).

Finally, Reeves (2010) suggests a more open, or public, approach to assessment because "it is not cheating to know the questions in advance of the test; rather, it's the only thoughtful and responsible thing to do" (p. 310). To push past trivia to more thoughtful, deeper assessment opportunities, making assessment a collaborative effort between the teacher and the learner where the questions or prompts are co-constructed or known ahead of time is necessary; trying to guess what the assessment will entail is short-sighted and unfair. Instead of dwelling on memorizing information or procedures, learners will (hopefully) have advance access to knowledge so they can use the assessment to think critically about issues and draw conclusions. Once again, this style of assessment is more reflective of what is true in modern society. Access to knowledge is no longer the challenge; rather, thinking critically with knowledge is.

Measuring Critical Thinking

Measuring critical thinking is complex; it requires teachers to pay close attention to both the specific elements of critical thinking, as well as the larger process of thinking critically about greater issues. Anything can be measured; however, not everything can be tested, so measuring critical thinking requires more performance-based assessments than traditional test formats.

When considering these strategies, please note that measuring critical-thinking skills and dispositions will require more robust criteria to allow for consistent scoring inferences among teachers. The diversity learners can and will present in their thinking makes it more necessary for teachers to establish clear criteria squarely focused on what is being assessed. This also allows for Reeves's (2010) non-standardized, collaborative, and open-assessment process. Additionally, this section will discuss the many ways teachers can contextualize critical thinking according to subject and age-appropriateness as they strive to measure it.

Measuring Specific Skills

Measuring the specific skills of critical thinking will require specific criteria that ensure transparency when measuring finite skills. Figure 3.2 (page 86) presents clear and specific criteria for the example in figure 3.1 (page 82). When teachers are scaffolding learning, it is essential for specific skills to be obvious to learners. To be clear, teachers do not require analytic rubrics for every finite or specific skill, as this might create a sort of "death by rubric" conundrum. Rather, while making criteria transparent is non-negotiable, it may not always be necessary to use such a robust format. That said, analytic rubrics do have some inherent advantages.

The analytic rubric in figure 3.2 presents a progression of quality or consistency at a granular level most advantageous in the early stages of developing the finite skill of analyzing and interpreting data. Teachers then simply highlight areas of strength and areas in need of strengthening so learners are keenly aware of what comes next in developing their approach to data. It is also possible that the tool itself has a finite shelf life; for example, early on, the granular specifics are necessary, while later, as

	Initiating	Developing	Achieving	Advancing
Gathering Data	Rarely gathers an appropriate amount of evidence	Sometimes gathers an appropriate amount of evidence	Usually gathers an appropriate amount of evidence	Consistently gathers an appropriate amount of evidence
Organizing and Presenting Data	Displays significant omissions or inaccuracies that interfere with the overall understanding of what is presented	Often displays omissions or inaccuracies that interfere with the overall understanding of what is presented	At times, displays some minor omissions or inaccuracies, but nothing that interferes with overall understanding	Consistently displays well-organized data, presented in a logical way that makes it easy to understand
Making Sense of Data	Recognizes only the most straightforward patterns and big ideas	Recognizes some patterns and a few big ideas	Recognizes important patterns and the crucial big ideas	Recognizes insightful patterns and the inconspicuous big ideas
Evaluating the Quality of the Data	Knows that critiquing the quality of evidence is important, but rarely does it with any kind of precision; challenged to recognize why evidence lacks credibility	Understands the importance of critiquing the quality of evidence, but only does it under the most obvious circumstances; explains why evidence lacks credibility when it's glaring	Critiques the quality of evidence to ensure accuracy, relevance, and validity; often explains why evidence lacks credibility	Critiques the quality of evidence to ensure accuracy, relevance, and validity; thoroughly and consistently explains why evidence lacks credibility
Deriving Meaning From the Data	Draws only the most obvious and overly simplistic conclusions; some inaccurate	Draws somewhat accurate, but often vague, inferences and conclusions	Draws accurate, but sometimes narrowly focused inferences and conclusions	Draws accurate and comprehensive inferences and conclusions
Making Data-Based Decisions or Solutions	Rarely justifies decisions or solutions with accurate and relevant information; identifies few new insights and ignores the limits of most other possible decisions or outcomes	Sometimes justifies decisions or solutions with accurate and relevant information; identifies narrow insights and superficially acknowledges the limits of most other possible outcomes	Often justifies decisions or solutions with accurate and relevant information; explains new insights and recognizes the limits of most other possible decisions or outcomes	Consistently justifies decisions or solutions with accurate and relevant information; thoroughly explains new insights and recognizes the limits of all other possible decisions or outcomes

Figure 3.2: Analytic rubric for the practice of analyzing and interpreting data.

Visit go.SolutionTree.com/assessment for a free reproducible version of this figure.

learners move to more complex demonstrations, the specific criteria regarding one aspect of a critical-thinking process may be unnecessary.

Figure 3.3 presents the same criteria as figure 3.2, using a single-point format that allows teachers to provide more specific feedback. Remember, the choice of every tool has both strengths and limitations. The rubric in figure 3.2 is labor-intensive to create but more efficient to use; figure 3.3 is the opposite. There is not a perfect tool, so every teacher must decide which tool is most likely to optimize the assessment and feedback process for learners.

Specific Aspects in Need of Strengthening	Advancing	Specific Aspects of Strength
	Gathering data: Consistently gathers an appropriate amount of evidence	
	Organizing and presenting data: Consistently displays well-organized data, presented in a logical way that makes it easy to understand	
	Making sense of data: Recognizes insightful patterns and the inconspicuous big ideas	
	Evaluating the quality of the data: Critiques the quality of evidence to ensure accuracy, relevance, and validity; thoroughly and consistently explains why evidence lacks credibility	
	Deriving meaning from the data: Draws accurate and comprehensive inferences and conclusions	
	Making data-based decisions or solutions: Consistently justifies decisions or solutions with accurate and relevant information; thoroughly explains new insights and recognizes the limits of all other possible decisions or outcomes	

Figure 3.3: *Single-point rubric for the practice of analyzing and interpreting data.*

*Visit **go.SolutionTree.com/assessment** for a free reproducible version of this figure.*

Teachers need not solely provide feedback in written form. While the rubrics in figure 3.2 (page 86) and figure 3.3 (page 87) provide a feedback structure, nothing would prevent the teacher, especially with figure 3.3, from providing feedback orally. Another option, particularly in cases where learners peer assess, would be to post the rubric in a Google Doc so other students could contribute their feedback. If the demonstration of critical thinking is public (for example, online), feedback can be sourced from beyond the classroom. Obviously, this type of *open feedback* would need to be vetted by the teacher or controlled within a safe online environment (for example, with students from other schools in the same grade); the idea is not to open our students up to anonymous, counterproductive, or even hurtful comments, but rather to solicit helpful feedback. The possibilities are endless, but the structure of articulating clear criteria is still necessary.

Measuring the Process of Critical Thinking

While focusing on granular skills is essential, the desired result of any approach to critical thinking is for a learner to think critically throughout the entire process— from start to finish of an issue, a problem, or a challenge. Figure 3.4 (pages 90–91) presents an analytic rubric that focuses on the bigger picture of critical thinking.

Clearly these are criteria for fairly sophisticated learners; teachers will need to adapt the criteria according to the age of their learners and the subject discipline. Teachers are also encouraged to adapt figure 3.4 because it doesn't represent an exhaustive list of what critical thinking is. Teachers, schools, and districts need to decide the focus and depth and breadth of their critical-thinking efforts. Regardless of which criteria teachers, schools, and districts select, the point is to make them transparent so learners know what they are expected to do. There are times when the process may be more open to allow learners to explore their interest and passions; at other times, the process is more closed due to certain principles to which learners must adhere (for example, in science investigations). Establishing clear criteria should never turn critical thinking into a clinical, step-by-step exercise; rather, it should be synthesized with the other competencies described in this book.

Figure 3.5 (pages 92–93) presents criteria geared toward an inquiry-driven learning experience. What is particularly noteworthy is the progression from knowledge and thinking to communication and application. Also, it's worth noting the synthesis of the critical competencies in the inquiry-driven project. Communication is included as a criteria category, while creative and critical thinking are blended together. The specifics of this rubric allow learners to see overtly what is expected of them in totality of the project. Rubrics are never thorough in explanation; some teaching and contextualizing are required. That said, transparency lets learners know what their inquiry projects entail, and the use of exemplars guides their understanding, increasing the likelihood they will internalize those criteria.

On the other hand, grading might be a challenge when using a rubric like the one in figure 3.5. If, for example, the inquiry-based project is reduced to one score, grade, or level, teachers must decide ahead of time how to synthesize all aspects of quality to determine a singular level. In most cases, the aspects of quality are not of equal value or weight, so teachers or teacher teams would need to clarify how to rate a learner overall—achieving or advancing. Even when the level of recording is more specific (for example, when giving individual scores for each aspect of knowledge and understanding, thinking, communication, and application) there would need to be some clarification, especially when more than one aspect is included in the criteria. For example, the teacher would need to resolve how to deem a learner initiating through advancing in communication.

This level of complexity, while necessary when using analytic rubrics, is the reason why some teachers favor a holistic approach to grading. While specificity is needed when assessing formatively, the summative purpose of assessment requires reliability since how teachers determine overall proficiency levels requires alignment. As a general rule, the more categories there are, the greater chance there is of misclassifying a learner (Guskey, 2015). Figure 3.6 (page 94) is an example of a holistic critical-thinking rubric.

According to Peter and Noreen Facione (2011), this holistic rubric is designed primarily to assess verbal presentations or written reports. However, teachers could easily adapt this rubric for use in assessing other demonstrations or projects. The key is to look at the demonstration of learning in its totality and not treat each bullet point as a checklist. When considering demonstrations of learning holistically, all the criteria are considered together to make one overall judgment of quality. The reliability issues resolved are twofold. First, the reliability among teachers (the inter-rater reliability) is likely to increase with only four categories. Second, the internal reliability of individual teachers (the intra-rater reliability) increases as the rubric becomes less daunting and complex in making consistent distinctions between the four levels.

	Initiating	Developing	Achieving	Advancing
Formulates or Reformulates a Vital Problem, Question, or Issue	Restates the problem, question or issue without summary or synthesis	Summarizes the problem, question, or issue with some aspects confused or incorrect; nuances and key details missed; superficial or overlooked context	Clearly and precisely formulates or reformulates the vital aspects of the problem, question, or issue in context	Clearly and precisely formulates or reformulates the vital aspects of the problem, question, or issue, identifying integral relationships essential to analyzing the problem, question, or issue in context
Gathers, Assesses, and Analyzes Relevant Information, Data, or Evidence	Provides simplistic, inappropriate, or unrelated information, data, or evidence for the problem, question, or issue; repeats information or data without question; dismisses evidence without adequate justification	Provides superficially appropriate information, data, or evidence; provides selective information or data, largely unexamined for accuracy, relevance, and completeness	Provides appropriate information, data, or evidence that are thorough, fully analyzed, and reported; questions information, data, or evidence and sources for accuracy, relevance, and completeness	Provides extensive information, data, or evidence with further insight into the problem, question, or issue; fully analyzes and evaluates information, data, or evidence and sources for accuracy, relevance, completeness, and point of view
Arrives at Well-Reasoned Conclusions, Solutions, and Implications	Provides a simplistic solution or absolute conclusion attributed to an external source; demonstrates little to no consideration of implications	Demonstrates industrial habits of mind that present conclusions as relative to each other, with simplistic solutions and a superficial examination of implications	Exemplifies strong habits of mind by providing plausible solutions, consideration of assumptions, reasoned judgment, and conclusions based on evidence; considers implications beyond the immediate situation	Exemplifies strong habits of mind by providing plausible, coherent working theories, well-reasoned judgment, and conclusions based on evidence; provides an examination of different viewpoints, an analysis of assumptions, a discussion of how things might be otherwise, a thorough examination of implications, and a consideration of ambiguities

Integrates Other Disciplinary Perspectives	Provides limited evidence of differing disciplines or perspectives; ignores viewpoints from other disciplines or treats them superficially or misrepresents them	Acknowledges different disciplines and perspectives but does not incorporate them into analysis; analyzes a viewpoint from another discipline thoughtfully and mostly accurately	Provides interpretation, analysis, and synthesis with some integration of other disciplines and perspectives; calls on viewpoints from more than one other discipline to understand the problem, question, or issue more fully	Provides powerful and illuminating interpretation and judgment requiring the use of a variety of disciplines and perspectives; calls on viewpoints from a wide range of disciplines to fully understand the problem, question, or issue in deeply textured ways
Communicates Effectively	Works alone to answer questions related to the topic	Shares ideas with others related to the topic to build collective understanding	Interacts with others in figuring out complexities related to ideas about the topic	Engages in considerable, rigorous interaction with others in figuring out complexities related to ideas about the topic; coherently communicates ideas to promote improved collective understanding of the topic

Source: Adapted from Galileo Educational Network, 2008.

Figure 3.4: Critical-thinking rubric.

Visit go.SolutionTree.com/assessment for a free reproducible version of this figure.

	Categories and Expectations	Student-Friendly Language	Initiating	Developing	Achieving	Advancing
Knowledge and Understanding	Knowledge of content	Demonstrates knowledge of concepts	Demonstrates limited knowledge of concepts	Demonstrates some knowledge of concepts	Demonstrates good knowledge of concepts	Demonstrates thorough knowledge of concepts
	Understanding of concepts	Shows understanding of concepts (for example, discusses concepts and answers questions)	Shows limited understanding of concepts	Shows some understanding of concepts	Shows good understanding of concepts	Shows insightful understanding of concepts
Thinking	Use of creative and critical-thinking processes	Creates a product that reflects learning and the key concepts; uses creative or critical-thinking processes with effectiveness	Uses creative or critical-thinking processes to create a final product and reflects on learning with limited effectiveness	Uses creative or critical-thinking processes to create a final product and reflects on learning with some effectiveness	Uses creative or critical-thinking processes to create a final product and reflects on learning with considerable effectiveness	Uses creative or critical-thinking processes to create a final product and reflects on learning with a high degree of effectiveness

Category	Criteria		Limited effectiveness	Some effectiveness	Considerable effectiveness	High degree of effectiveness
Communication	Expression and organization of ideas and information in oral, written, and visual forms	Expresses and organizes ideas and information with effectiveness, which may be shared in a variety of formats	Effectively organizes ideas in presenting results of inquiry with limited effectiveness	Organizes ideas in presenting results of inquiry with some effectiveness	Organizes ideas in presenting results of inquiry with considerable effectiveness	Organizes ideas in presenting results of inquiry with a high degree of effectiveness
Communication	Communication for different audiences and purposes	Communicates for different audiences and purposes with effectiveness (for example, videos, pictures, discussion, and written information)	Presents findings of inquiry for different audiences with limited effectiveness	Presents findings of inquiry for different audiences with some effectiveness	Presents findings of inquiry for different audiences with considerable effectiveness	Presents findings of inquiry for different audiences with a high degree of effectiveness
Application	Use of conventions, vocabulary, and terminology	Uses vocabulary and terminology related to the concepts in an inquiry-project presentation	Uses vocabulary and terminology in an inquiry project with limited effectiveness	Uses vocabulary and terminology in an inquiry project with some effectiveness	Uses vocabulary and terminology related to an inquiry project with considerable effectiveness	Uses vocabulary and terminology related to an inquiry project with a high degree of effectiveness
Application	Making connections within and between contexts	Makes connections between the project and the world outside the school (real life)	Makes a limited number of connections between the project and the world outside school	Makes some connections between the project and the world outside the school	Makes a variety of connections between the project and the world outside the school	Makes a wide variety of connections between the project and the world outside the school

Source: Adapted from © 2016 by Thom Markham.

Figure 3.5: Inquiry-driven project rubric.

Visit go.SolutionTree.com/assessment for a free reproducible version of this figure.

Level	Holistic Description
Advancing	Consistently does all or almost all of the following: • Accurately interprets evidence, statements, graphics, questions, and so on • Identifies the salient arguments (reasons and claims), pros, and cons • Thoughtfully analyzes and evaluates major alternative points of view • Draws warranted, judicious, and non-fallacious conclusions • Justifies key results and procedures, and explains assumptions and reasons • Fair-mindedly follows where evidence and reasons lead
Achieving	Does most or many of the following: • Accurately interprets evidence, statements, graphics, questions, and so on • Identifies relevant arguments (reasons and claims), pros, and cons • Offers analyses and evaluations of obvious alternative points of view • Draws warranted, nonfallacious conclusions • Justifies some results or procedures, and explains reasons • Fair-mindedly follows where evidence and reasons lead
Developing	Does most or many of the following: • Misinterprets evidence, statements, graphics, questions, and so on • Fails to identify strong, relevant counterarguments • Ignores or superficially evaluates obvious alternative points of view • Draws unwarranted or fallacious conclusions • Justifies few results or procedures, and seldom explains reasons • Regardless of the evidence or reasons, maintains or defends views based on self-interest or preconceptions
Initiating	Consistently does all or almost all of the following: • Offers biased interpretations of evidence, statements, graphics, questions, information, or the points of view of others • Fails to identify or hastily dismisses strong, relevant counterarguments • Ignores or superficially evaluates obvious alternative points of view • Argues using fallacious or irrelevant reasons and unwarranted claims • Does not justify results or procedures, and fails to explain reasons • Regardless of the evidence or reasons, maintains or defends views based on self-interest or preconceptions • Exhibits closed-mindedness or hostility to reason

Source: Adapted from Facione & Facione, 2011.

Figure 3.6: *Holistic critical-thinking scoring rubric.*

*Visit **go.SolutionTree.com/assessment** for a free reproducible version of this figure.*

Measuring Critical Thinking for Younger Learners

Younger learners—in grades K–2—can think critically too. While teachers may need to simplify and focus their criteria for younger learners, the need to present clear criteria is still essential so learners understand they are developing skills in a critical competency.

Jennifer Moroz, assessment curriculum coach in School District No. 57, Prince George, British Columbia, develops assessment rubrics to align with the critical competencies that are part of the new curriculum in British Columbia. Figure 3.7 (page 96) shows how learning is communicated during the process of rehearsal and production of musical theater based on the Fraser-Cariboo Gold Rush. Single-point rubrics provide scaffolding for specific feedback related to the proficient descriptors of learning endeavors. The *Core Connections* space is the journal component in which students share their journey with respect to the critical competencies.

Although the journal is a reflective piece, students access both personal and social awareness as well as critical thinking. For example, students evaluate commonly held values in 1860 by comparing their own lives with that of a woman or man in the mining community simply by embodying that character. Students intuitively use communication competencies to hone their speaking skills and physical presence and to impart their factual knowledge of that time period to the audience. This is an example of how more than one critical competency (in this case *critical thinking* and *social competence)* are seamlessly connected.

Figure 3.8 (page 97) is an example of a K–2 critical-thinking rubric geared toward project-based learning. This rubric uses images to illustrate a learner's natural progression of achievement. Teachers would be wise to utilize images most learners would find familiar.

Using images can assist younger students who may have limited to no academic language proficiency; any sequence of images can work, as long as they illustrate a natural progression of sophistication. The other option is to use a frequency scale (see figure 3.9, page 98), since the criteria can be a binary choice. If learners have completed several projects or demonstrations, the frequency scale has an advantage in summative reporting because it communicates the consistency with which younger learners are able to think critically. Figure 3.9 is an example of how teachers can adapt the K–2 PBL criteria from figure 3.8 for a frequency scale.

Coordinated Competency Assessment, Grades 3/4

Social Studies 4, Arts Education 3, English Language Arts 3/4

Musical Theater Production: *The Fraser-Cariboo Gold Rush*

Student Name:

Big Idea: The pursuit of natural resources has played a key role in changing the land, people, and communities in Canada.

SS, AE: Prepare a presentation using selected communication forms (drama/dance) to support the purpose of the presentation.

Endeavor(s):					Core Connections
Rehearse script dialogue to convey story about the Cariboo Gold Rush; present play to audience.					**Acquire, interpret, and present information.**
On My Way			Proficient		Here are **two interesting facts** I've learned about the Fraser-Cariboo Gold Rush:
Emerging	Beginning	Developing	Applying	Extending	
				Next Steps	Here are **two ways** that I presented those facts to the audience through drama and dance:
		a. Is able to rehearse and deliver lines in script to portray a character in the Gold Rush			
		b. Is able to rehearse and perform square dance to demonstrate understanding of time and place			

SS: Construct narratives that capture attitudes, values, and worldviews commonly held by people at the time; ELA 3/4: Plan and create a variety of communication forms for different purposes and audiences.

Endeavor(s):					Analyze and Critique
Share characters' motivations and attitudes by providing an "actor's interview."					Here are two ways my character in the play is DIFFERENT from me:
On My Way			Proficient		
Emerging	Beginning	Developing	Applying	Extending	
				Next Steps	Here are two things that are the SAME about my character and me:
		a. Is able to clearly describe his or her character's role in the play to the audience in the context of the Cariboo Gold Rush (1860) by answering the following questions: What is your character's main struggle? How does your character solve his or her problem? Where and when does your character live?			

Source: © 2017 Jennifer Moroz. Used with permission.

Figure 3.7: Coordinated competency assessment for musical theater production.

	Initiating	Developing	Achieving	Advancing
I can explain why we are doing this project.				
I can ask questions about the project.				
I can use information I get from different places.				
I can say why an idea is a good one.				
I can use feedback from my friends and teacher to improve my work.				
I can explain my idea using facts and details.				

Source: Adapted from Buck Institute for Education, n.d.

Figure 3.8: *Critical-thinking rubric for project-based learning (K–2).*

Visit **go.SolutionTree.com/assessment** for a free reproducible version of this figure.

	Rarely	Sometimes	Usually	Consistently
I can explain why we are doing this project.				
I can ask questions about the project.				
I can use information I get from different places.				
I can say why an idea is a good one.				
I can use feedback from my friends and teacher to improve my work.				
I can explain my idea using facts and details.				

Source: Adapted from Buck Institute for Education, n.d.

Figure 3.9: Frequency-based critical-thinking rubric for project-based learning (K–2).

Visit **go.SolutionTree.com/assessment** *for a free reproducible version of this figure.*

Those who teach learners in grades K–2 should use clear and transparent performance criteria so learners understand what is expected of them, regardless of whether what is being assessed is a product or a process. In doing so, learners are likely to internalize performance criteria, allowing them to also develop competence at self- and peer assessment.

Measuring Critical-Thinking Dispositions

While the view of critical thinking so far has had a more skill-based focus, it is important to acknowledge the dispositional view of critical thinking and how to assess it. Although the lines are admittedly blurry, recall that critical-thinking *skills* are what learners do, while critical-thinking *dispositions* represent who they *are*. Figure 3.10 illustrates how critical-thinking dispositions are rated along a frequency scale. Since dispositions manifest as habitual, behavioral actions or responses, the use of a frequency scale is more favorable since many of the dispositions are binary.

Figure 3.10 is not meant to be an exhaustive list of dispositional characteristics; the nature of the critical-thinking activities and other factors, such as the age of the learner or subject, determines which dispositions learners most consistently demonstrate. It does, however, provide a potential list of what teachers could look for as they engineer opportunities for learners to develop their critical-thinking habits. Schools and districts will need to contextualize the specifics, but what is universal is the need to nurture and measure critical-thinking dispositions so they become a habitual way of responding to situations or challenges students encounter.

	Rarely	Sometimes	Usually	Consistently
I ask questions to further my understanding of the challenge.				
I consider the strengths and limitations of all sides of an argument.				
I use criteria to evaluate the credibility of the gathered information.				
I draw logical and measured conclusions.				
I can recognize bias in other people's positions.				
I can adapt and adjust my position when new information emerges.				
I am open and honest about my own potential biases.				

Figure 3.10: *Critical-thinking dispositions rubric.*

Visit **go.SolutionTree.com/assessment** *for a free reproducible version of this figure.*

Incorporating Self- and Peer Assessment

Researchers frequently tout self-assessment as a positive experience that leads to increased achievement and personal awareness (Brown & Harris, 2013). Self-assessment teaches learners to be self-regulatory, which has the residual effect of raising achievement (Andrade, 2010; Ramdass & Zimmerman, 2008). Being more self-regulatory draws on important metacognitive competencies (Zimmerman, 2002), so learners self-observe, self-assess, self-judge, self-react, self-motivate, and maintain self-control.

Research on peer assessment is equally compelling (Topping, 2013). Learners have much to tell one another about how they can improve the quality of their work. Teachers who are purposeful about developing a culture of peer assessment not only enable learners to be active participants in their own development but also create an efficiency for accessing feedback. There is significant value in having learners be assessors of one another's work in a cooperative setting to the point where the high value of peer assessment is considered one of the most important revelations to emerge from the educational research in the modern era (Wiliam, 2011).

All educators know that self- and peer assessment can also apply to critical thinking. With any self- or peer assessment exercise, teachers must guide learners to make proper judgments and decisions about their own or others' work. Learners will find making scoring inferences difficult if they are not taught *how* to recognize quality, so from the outset, teachers should teach learners how to recognize both strengths and what needs strengthening in their own and others' learning. Becoming an independent, active learner is the preeminent goal.

Creating self- and peer assessment opportunities within the realm of critical thinking creates a kind of circular experience. Self- and peer assessments increase learners' achievement with critical thinking, and self- and peer assessments *are* critical thinking. This is not to suggest that simply having learners engage in self- and peer assessment is all that's necessary to teach critical thinking; however, it does create one more opportunity for learners to think critically—it's a kind of simultaneous "means-and-end" experience. The advantage of using self- and peer assessment to teach critical thinking is that for most learners, the task will be less abstract than critical thinking within a project or demonstration. Even if the focus is on assessing their own or others' knowledge-based content, learners can begin to think critically about how they or others are progressing. Ultimately, self- and peer assessment can have learners think critically about their own and others' critical thinking.

As teachers adapt their assessment and measurement of critical-thinking skills, certain modifications will naturally need to occur in their instruction. The following section discusses implications for instructing critical thinking.

Growing Critical Thinking

Emerging research indicates critical thinking is most effectively taught through dialogue and authentic instruction (Abrami et al., 2015). These techniques "are not an exhaustive list of promising ingredients, but they are a useful starting point for thinking about the challenges teachers face" (Abrami et al., 2015, p. 304). Further, learners can develop critical-thinking skills at all grade levels and across virtually all subject areas (Abrami et al., 2015). The key is *intentionality*. So many of the instructional experiences teachers utilize are not new; what is new is the purposeful approach to teaching learners to think critically.

Dialogue

One important instructional strategy necessary for developing critical-thinking skills is increased dialogue in the classroom. Dialogue is clearly not a new concept to classrooms, but what learners discuss or debate might be. Likewise, the residual effect of that dialogue—thinking critically—may also be new. When teachers create opportunities for whole-class, in-group, or between-group discussions and debates, they cultivate an environment where learners expect critical thinking. The opportunities for learners to present an idea, support their position, actively listen, analyze contradictory positions, rethink their stance, and potentially revise their position are critical-thinking experiences that occur in real time; these experiences allow teachers to take advantage of teachable moments—when affirmations and corrections are not delayed.

Dialogue need not be restricted to oral conversations; learning through technology is a real advantage. Debates can also occur in written form, and certainly in the age of social media there are opportunities for real (asynchronous or synchronous) dialogue and debate. Obviously, social media provides the best and worst of what online debates can be like, so teachers should engineer these opportunities with the utmost care and attention to detail. However, there is great potential for debates to occur across schools, districts, states, and even countries. The analysis of current events or problem-based dilemmas (to name just two) allows for a rich and robust conversation that can occur from a variety of sources at a variety of times. The iterations of debate and dialogue are endless.

Authentic Instruction

As discussed previously in this chapter, authentic instruction includes tasking learners with project- or problem-based learning experiences. However, it need not always be such an epic endeavor. The gist of any authentic instruction is to replicate, as best as possible, the authentic experiences those who work in a specific field might experience. The three criteria of educators Fred M. Newmann, Dana L. Carmichael, and M. Bruce King's (2016) Authentic Intellectual Work framework—(1) construction of new knowledge, (2) disciplined inquiry, and (3) value beyond school—apply to instruction as well as assessment design. With authentic instruction, teachers strive to engage learners in discipline-specific experiences; learners employ genuine processes and skills as they create meaning within a field of study. Activities such as case studies, role plays, or simulations provide learners with a contextualized learning opportunity that *feels* more authentic than simply reading or listening to a third-party account.

This move toward authentic experiences in many cases will involve only some slight adjustments to what teachers ask learners to do. In the minutiae of authenticity, teachers may still require learners, for example, to solve equations. Engineers, plumbers, and a whole host of other professionals must solve equations; however, these equations always involve authentic problems. Plumbers, for example, may need to calculate the pressure differential between two different sized pipes. Obviously, learners are not scientists, historians, authors, or programmers. However, they can still have their learning contextualized with a level of authenticity that neutralizes any feelings of disjointedness between what teachers are asking learners to do and what is *real* in the subject-specific discipline. This increased authenticity reveals the repurposing and application of knowledge that are at the heart of what the critical competencies entail.

Conclusion

The depth and breadth of critical thinking make it challenging to narrow its focus into a neat and tidy, finite set of skills. In addition to comprising many complex cognitive processes and skills, critical thinking is also a disposition learners assume as a default response to complex challenges. While critical thinking is not new per se, what is new is the prioritization and prominence of critical thinking as a purposeful, specified outcome of instruction. Schools that find the balance between the generalists' and the specifists' views will find a way to take a school- or districtwide approach to critical thinking while ensuring its contextual application and nuance are not lost.

Critical thinking is embedded in many curricular standards documents. Critical thinking as an *end* is fairly ubiquitous, which means teachers can repurpose knowledge to facilitate critical thinking. That said, a more modern approach puts learners at the center of critical thinking, which gives teachers greater opportunities to create learner-centered, inquiry-based investigatory experiences.

Assessing critical thinking requires some forethought, as teachers need to be clear about how narrow or wide the scope will be, and how to scaffold from a finite to a more broad-based focus. The unpacking and repacking of critical thinking (along with a balance of formative and summative purposes of assessment) will give teachers a foundation on which to approach the various desired levels of sophistication. With critical thinking, the cliché, "think big, but start small" is most applicable.

Pause and Ponder

On your own or as part of a collaborative teacher team, consider the following reflective questions.

1. What quote or passage encapsulates your biggest takeaway from this chapter? What immediate action (large or small) will you take as a result of this takeaway? Explain both to your team.

2. In what ways was your current view of critical competencies reaffirmed? In what ways was it challenged? Explain.

3. Do you lean toward a more generalist or specifist view of critical thinking? How does your view of critical thinking influence your decisions for instruction?

4. How have you or could you take advantage of your current curricular standards to intentionally develop learners as critical thinkers? How have you or could you create a parallel focus on content acquisition and critical-thinking skills development?

5. How have you or could you develop a learner-centered approach to developing critical thinkers? What practices, processes, and tools allow learners to self- and peer assess critical-thinking skills and dispositions?

6. What specific critical-thinking skills or dispositions receive more attention in your classes? Why do you emphasize those skills and dispositions?

7. What success and challenges have you had with teaching and assessing critical thinking on a larger scale (such as project-based learning or inquiry-driven investigations)?

CHAPTER 4
COLLABORATION

Collaboration gives the freedom to come out from the narrow scopes of life to the field of endless possibilities.

—Amit Ray

Collaboration is a critical competency essential to thriving in an interconnected and interdependent global context. Facebook inspired Salesforce to create the Chatterbox app as a way for its employees, colleagues, and customers to track progress, share ideas, and collaborate (Ibarra & Hansen, 2013). Salesforce CEO Marc Benioff watched with interest and excitement as he realized this forum provides invaluable insight and knowledge about the company that was not often accessible because not all employees were involved in larger company decisions. Shortly after this observation, Salesforce management was planning an off-site retreat. Benioff suggested his team invite everyone to virtually participate using Chatterbox. The retreat started off as it had in the past—with two hundred managers in the room—but this time there was a virtual audience of over five thousand. After a slow start in the online dialogue, Benioff posted a comment "noting what he found interesting about what was being said and adding a joke to spice it up" (Ibarra & Hansen, 2013, p. 3). The post ignited the company's virtual conversation, which was incredibly productive, and prompted dialogue long after the retreat ended. This new form of cutting-edge technology inspired collaboration. It is a rich example of the incredible potential collaboration has to empower people and generate new and innovative ideas.

The rapidly expanding literature on teamwork and collaborative problem solving suggests these skills are becoming increasingly more important to the health and sustainability of a global economy, environment, and technological landscape (Ibarra & Hansen, 2013; Weiss & Hughes, 2013). Teamwork and collaborative problem solving are among the most frequently mentioned 21st century skills learners need to thrive in their future endeavors (Casner-Lotto & Barrington, 2006; Wildman et al., 2012). Employers and policymakers point to the importance of teamwork and collaboration skills in the current and future workplace. Educational systems are starting to recognize the importance of teaching those skills, for example, through authentic or real-world experiences (Fiore et al., 2017). However, education's history with group work (or collaboration) leaves much to be desired; parents, families, and even some educators are suspicious of its implementation and application in the classroom. It's time to clarify and modernize the understanding and application of collaborative thinking in the classroom.

Defining Collaboration

Collaboration is the ability of individuals to engage in a systematic process in which teams work together interdependently to create something new, solve problems, analyze existing patterns and systems, or advocate for change. This interdependence requires capitalizing on the strengths and expertise of each team member to improve individual and collective results around a meaningful purpose. The nuances of collaborating well include the following aptitudes.

- **Displaying curiosity:** Inquire and ask questions to clarify, connect, and generate ideas.

- **Listening:** Actively hear, paraphrase, and summarize others' ideas to deeply understand alternative or competing perspectives.

- **Contributing:** Offer new, radical, and sometimes unpopular views.

- **Committing to work through conflict:** Productively engage in and move through conflict—do not avoid it or unnecessarily incite it for the sake of argument.

- **Consensus building:** Find ways to compromise—balancing practicality and orthodoxy—to provide innovative solutions.

- **Observing:** Observe nonverbal cues and verbal words and actions to productively and honestly navigate dialogue, conflict, and conflicting ideas.

- **Focusing on strengths:** Capitalize on the strengths of individual group members; presume positive intentions.

- **Focusing on goals:** Keep the overall goal front and center over an individual need to be "right."

- **Knowing what to do when you don't know:** Embrace uncertainty with questions and a commitment to pursue information and next steps.

- **Synthesizing:** Explore and persevere to synthesize large amounts of information or competing perspectives; blend ideas to co-create and innovate.

- **Sourcing:** Discern the reliability of information through interrogating sources, such as authors' perspectives, organizations, funding sources, and other potential areas of bias; assess its reliability, realistic potential, and competing and contradictory reports that counter the sources' main argument.

These skills offer a foundation and starting point for learners and teachers to define effective collaboration. Defining the tasks across grade levels and disciplines allows learners to use these skills.

In 2015, the Programme for International Student Assessment (PISA) launched a new form for assessing collaborative problem solving (Fiore et al., 2017). These computer-based tasks were designed to assess a learner's collaborative problem-solving skills. To create a clear picture of what criteria or skills learners engage in to do this effectively, they created a matrix (Fiore et al., 2017). Figure 4.1 (page 108) describes the complexity of collaboration and problem solving by identifying twelve skills using both collaboration and problem solving as larger categories (Fiore et al., 2017). The matrix is another tool to guide the criteria teachers and learners identify and use as they engage in multiple types of collaborative tasks for various purposes (Fiore et al., 2017).

As learners engage in tasks that require collaboration and problem solving, they get feedback, self-assess, and eventually master these aptitudes. If schools are to truly respond to the call for learners to cultivate effective collaboration skills, then assessing the skills and providing learners multiple opportunities to practice are essential. This begins with a clear vision for what collaboration looks and sounds like, and how the current understanding of collaboration is different than what the next generation of collaboration means.

	(1) **Establishing and Maintaining Shared Understanding**	**(2)** **Taking Appropriate Action to Solve Problem**	**(3)** **Establishing and Maintaining Team Organization**
(A) **Exploring and Understanding**	(A1) Discovering the perspectives and abilities of team members	(A2) Discovering the type of collaborative interaction to solve the problem, along with goals	(A3) Understanding roles to solve problems
(B) **Representing and Formulating**	(B1) Building a shared representation and negotiating the meaning of the problem (common ground)	(B2) Identifying and describing tasks to complete	(B3) Describing the roles or team organization (communication protocols or rules for engagement)
(C) **Planning and Executing**	(C1) Communicating with team members about the actions to perform	(C2) Enacting plans	(C3) Following rules of engagement (for example, prompting other team members to perform their tasks)
(D) **Monitoring and Reflecting**	(D1) Monitoring and repairing shared understanding	(D2) Monitoring results of actions and evaluating success in solving the problem	(D3) Monitoring and providing feedback and adapting the team organization and roles

Source: Fiore et al., 2017, p. 11.

Figure 4.1: *Matrix of collaborative problem-solving skills.*

Considering Collaboration Now and Going Forward

A common feeling of dread often emerges when remembering the all-too-familiar concept of *group work*. Whether it was a group member taking over the whole project, one not pulling his or her weight, or another continually talking while avoiding the work (or a combination of any or all of these things), the "group-project-gone-bad" scenarios are often a source of angst or frustration for parents and learners alike. "Can I do the project on my own?" is a refrain teachers often hear from learners who anticipate potential challenges when working with others. Despite its potential to elicit a negative visceral reaction, collaborating to solve problems and create innovative ideas—to navigate through conflict and find solutions to pressing problems—can no longer be an afterthought or a hoped-for byproduct of group work. In such cases, collaboration was simply a means to an end, like when doing group work to explore the purpose of cells. In this example, the group work serves as an instructional strategy to learn content, or *collaboration 1.0*. In collaboration 1.0, group work isn't essential to learning the concept; individuals could independently complete the task to learn the concept, but the power of talking to others to learn is tapped in this model. Such a practice, common in traditional classrooms, aims to use collaboration as a means to helping students learn a concept. The other two forms of collaboration—*collaboration 2.0* and *collaboration 3.0*—focus on learners developing deeper collaboration and communication skills.

Collaboration 2.0 moves beyond learners simply working in groups to learn a concept to working together to develop their collaboration skills. This meaningful purpose may involve solving a realistic problem, discovering a pattern in a system or set of behaviors or phenomena, or designing something new to make life more efficient or effective or for the greater good. However, the end goal is to develop collaboration skills and an aptitude for collaborating.

There are many factors involved in effective collaboration. Some are outside the control of any one person's collaboration skills because there are always multiple collaborators who bring different sets of attitudes and behaviors that make collaboration unpredictable. So, someone who is an effective collaborator must be able to read the situation and respond productively to these differences, which includes working through conflict. Retired businessman Bart Becht posits, "The chance for new ideas is much greater when you have people with different backgrounds (and experiences). The chance for conflict is also higher—and conflict is good per se, as long as it's constructive and gets us to the best idea" (Becht, 2013, as cited in Ibarra & Hansen, 2013, p. 7). Collaboration 2.0 poses a meaningful task but focuses on learners developing the aforementioned aptitudes of collaboration: displaying curiosity, listening, contributing, committing to work through conflict, consensus building, observing, focusing on strengths, focusing on goals, knowing what to do when you don't know (learning to learn), synthesizing, and sourcing.

Collaboration 3.0 requires people to work on common problems or issues together to find innovative solutions or patterns that one person would not be able to solve or discover. As Fiore et al. (2017) state:

> Collaborative problem solving involves two different constructs—collaboration and problem solving. The assumption is that collaboration for a group task is essential because some problem-solving tasks are too complex for an individual to work through alone or the solution will be improved from the joint capacities of a team. (p. 2)

Collaboration in its most sophisticated form involves learners working together with other learners in their class or school, local and global organizations, or outside experts to provide new solutions or innovations to pressing issues. Ibarra and Hansen (2013) substantiate this need for collaboration that brings together different people and organizations in the *Harvard Business Review*: "Global virtual teams are the norm, not the exception. Facebook, Twitter, LinkedIn, videoconferencing, and a host of other technologies have put connectivity on steroids and enabled new forms of collaboration that would have been impossible a short time ago" (p. 2). Advancements in technology provide learners access to people and problems in efficient ways, allowing a new iteration of what it means to collaborate. Table 4.1 summarizes the different types of collaboration and identifies criteria one might use to assess proficiency and provide feedback to learners as they gain mastery in collaboration at all three levels.

This new, globally connected reality requires more advanced collaboration. For individuals and communities to thrive, there is a need to tap into individual differences in ideas, backgrounds, experiences, and expertise to generate innovative solutions to pressing problems and to create more efficient and effective innovations. To achieve collaboration 3.0, there are some implications for assessment—both in terms of how teachers should assess and what they can measure.

Table 4.1: *Different Iterations of Collaboration—Purpose and Criteria*

Purpose	Criteria
Collaboration 1.0 **To Help Students Learn a Concept**	Applying content standards and team behavior expectations • Staying on task • Respectfully contributing ideas • Listening

Collaboration 2.0 **To Develop Collaboration Skills**		Contributing to the team's work • Being curious and generating ideas • Contributing ideas Interacting with team members • Listening • Committing and working through conflict • Seeking to understand another point of view (curiosity) • Building on ideas of team members • Coming to consensus—being willing to give and take and come to a solution that benefits the overall focus Keeping the team on track • Ensuring participation • Building on ideas • Observing nonverbal actions and verbal cues and responding productively • Keeping the focus and overall goal in front of the team • Making sure any individual's need to be right doesn't hijack the team's focus Having knowledge, skills, and abilities • Considering the counterargument or perspective • Synthesizing ideas to generate an innovative, effective solution • Knowing what to do when you don't know (or the team does not know)
Collaboration 3.0 **To Facilitate Creative Problem Solving or Productivity**		Exploring and understanding • Comprehending the problem • Clearly articulating the nature and components of the issue Representing and formulating • Seeking quality, credible, and reliable sources to research and fully understand all aspects of the problem and potential solutions Planning and executing • Clearly communicating and articulating the solution offered with a well-thought-out and thorough explanation of the process and evidence • Displaying creativity; presenting solutions that put multiple ideas together in new ways to produce a viable solution Monitoring and reflecting • Responding to, connecting to, and building on team members' ideas • Observing individual team members' problem solving and the team itself to determine the effectiveness of the process and generated solutions Applying all or parts of collaboration 2.0

Visit **go.SolutionTree.com/assessment** *for a free reproducible version of this table.*

Assessing Collaboration

The *how* of assessment involves designing tasks and experiences that elicit the type of evidence necessary to measure the intended learning. Assessing collaboration requires a new conception of what it means to gather evidence, as much of the gathering is through observation, self-assessment, and peer assessment. Observation is a core mechanism for understanding the effectiveness of collaboration (in general) and how proficient any individual collaborator is on a set of predetermined criteria. For observation to be effective, teachers and learners must work together to develop a shared understanding of the various skills, or aptitudes, involved in collaboration. Teachers must then consider how to develop the task; whether they will observe collaboration or utilize self- or peer assessment; and how they intend to communicate results.

Developing a Shared Understanding of Collaboration

To gain a shared understanding of collaboration, learners and teachers must co-construct what quality collaboration looks like, sounds like, and even feels like. Teachers should start with the core aptitudes in this chapter (pages 106–107) and select a few on which to focus. Younger learners also participate in describing what it means to be an effective collaborator, and teachers can tap pictures and symbols to articulate these qualities. As teachers and learners continuously practice achieving the agreed-on criteria through different collaborative tasks, observation will become even more reliable and accurate. Figure 4.2 provides a template to use to start these conversations.

Criteria	Your Thoughts as the Learner (Complete this column individually or in pairs.)	Observable Attributes of This Characteristic
Displaying curiosity: Inquire and ask questions to clarify, connect, and generate ideas.		
Listening: Actively hear, paraphrase, and summarize others' ideas to deeply understand alternative or competing perspectives.		
Contributing: Offer new, radical, and sometimes unpopular views.		

Committing to work through conflict: Productively engage in and move through conflict—do not avoid it or unnecessarily incite it for the sake of argument.		
Consensus building: Find ways to compromise—balancing practicality and orthodoxy—to provide innovative solutions.		
Observing: Observe nonverbal and verbal words and actions to productively and honestly navigate dialogue, conflict, and conflicting ideas.		
Focusing on strengths: Capitalize on the strengths of individual team members; presume positive intentions.		
Focusing on goals: Position the overall goal over an individual need to be right.		
Knowing what to do when you don't know: Embrace uncertainty with questions and a commitment to pursue information and next steps.		
Synthesizing: Explore and persevere to synthesize large amounts of information or competing perspectives; blend ideas to co-create and innovate.		
Sourcing: Discern the reliability of information through interrogating sources—authors' perspectives, organizations, funding sources, and other potential areas of bias; assess its reliability, its realistic potential, and competing and contradictory reports that counter the sources' main argument.		

Figure 4.2: Co-constructing criteria with learners.

Visit **go.SolutionTree.com/assessment** *for a free reproducible version of this figure.*

A teacher may decide to focus on only a few criteria (first column in figure 4.2, pages 112–113) for any given collaborative task. He or she may ask learners, in pairs, to describe each characteristic of each criteria (second column). Then, the class as a whole generates a list of characteristics one might observe when this attribute is strong or lacking (third column). When learners are in the beginning stages of learning to collaborate, they will benefit from sentence starters to help them navigate conflict, build on other collaborators' ideas, or provide alternative or counterperspectives. The teacher is responsible for generating this shared understanding of quality collaboration through his or her ongoing instruction and feedback processes. These clear descriptions of criteria are essential if the forms of assessing collaboration (observation, self-assessment, and peer assessment) are to be accurate.

Developing the Task

Assessing collaboration effectively and accurately requires teachers to make some key decisions when developing the task. Consider the following steps and questions to guide your decision making when designing a high-quality scenario and task for collaboration.

1. **Set the purpose:** What is the purpose of the collaboration?

    a. *Collaboration 1.0*—To learn or explore a concept (an instructional strategy)

    b. *Collaboration 2.0*—To learn to collaborate effectively

    c. *Collaboration 3.0*—To collaborate to solve a complex problem, make decisions, or produce something

    d. *Both collaboration 2.0 and 3.0*—To both learn to effectively collaborate and solve a complex problem

2. **Determine the knowledge domain (literacy, mathematics, science, community):** What are the content standards learners must acquire as they engage in this collaborative task? What are the content and problem-solving skills needed to engage with this problem? Identify the content standards and develop the criteria for solving the problem. Most likely, this is where to integrate other critical competencies—including critical thinking, communication, digital citizenship, social competence, and creativity. Learners may need to tap into each of these competencies, but for brevity, focus on the most essential skills on which to assess and provide feedback, and then expect learners to show a predetermined level of proficiency or mastery.

3. **Decide on the number of team members:** How many members are on the team? Who is on the team? Are there external partners? How will members communicate? These questions help determine the best way for teachers to compose teams.

4. **Establish roles and responsibilities:** Will the teacher assign roles, or will they emerge as the team determines its focus and how to move forward in collaborating? Will one team member have a different kind of status than another—for example, will one member be the leader who guides more of the decision making or process than another? Will it be a shared role? In some countries, one doesn't question a leader or superior. If one member is the leader, there may need to be some learning around what this role means. Will everyone have equal decision-making power?

5. **Elect goals for team members:** Will each team member have the same goal or task, or will there be different goals and tasks for various team members? In some cases, each member may explore or research a different issue or play a different role, so the end product is not the goal but the member's collaboration and contribution to the overall picture are what the teacher targets to measure.

6. **Choose the collaboration structure:** How will the teacher structure the collaboration? How will teams or groups be organized? Who will participate? There are many choices for how to organize collaboration. The purpose of the collaboration and the standards or learning objectives learners must acquire naturally lend themselves to certain structures. Choose a model that will be most effective given what learners need to accomplish. If collaboration 2.0 is the goal and learners need to learn how to navigate through conflict and build on ideas, then the structure of the group can be more flexible and can take on many forms. The following are a few options.

    a. *School or external teams*—Some tasks require learners to work in teams that include external partners from a business or organization. In this case, virtual access will typically be essential.

    b. *School teams*—Some learners or teams might collaborate with other schools' learners or teams.

    c. *Common task teams*—Teachers may organize some tasks so each team has a similar task and each group has similar roles. Often in this case, learners are expected to gain the same essential skills and content standards.

d. *Partial to whole teams*—Each team or group of learners has a different task essential to the whole (or one large and complex problem). This type of task is *interdependent*. Each team is dependent on other teams to create the whole picture and provide solutions to the problem. As a result, each team collaborates internally and then those teams must communicate to put all the parts together. This may or may not also include external partners.

e. *Differentiated teams*—Each team has a different task; most often, learners choose the task by interest or passion. Sometimes the teacher presents the teams with various challenges, and they choose one to pursue.

f. *Jigsaw*—The teacher can use this form of collaboration in any type of situation where there are multiple resources to examine. In one version of the jigsaw, each member of the team is responsible for a different aspect of the problem, task, or information. Each team member explores one aspect of the problem, reviews information from various sides of an argument, or studies a specific topic. In another version of the jigsaw, the first groups formed become the expert teams. "Expert" teams work together to learn or study different assigned topics. Then, new groups form with members consisting of one person from each of the first "expert" teams. Each member on this new team shares what he or she has learned, including areas for further study, key questions, and key points. Depending on the overall task, the collaboration may end there. Or, collaborative teams may move forward with this learning to a more complex task that usually requires posing solutions or designing something.

7. **Define the task as independent or interdependent:** An *interdependent* task is impossible to solve independently. Various people or teams may contribute different parts of the puzzle, but to come up with a viable solution or generate a creative or effective product, the parts (or people) must work together. Team members may each participate, but one person could solve an *independent* task.

8. **Predesign the task (static or dynamic):** A *static problem* does not change throughout the time the team is working to solve it. A *dynamic problem* evolves, and the design of the task may involve introducing a new element or an emerging challenge that changes the course of the team's collaboration throughout the process. These challenges are great options

for teachers to predetermine when one of the goals is observing how learners monitor and adjust through the collaborative process. With an authentic problem, these challenges and new information naturally occur.

9. **Determine the parameters of the task (well defined or ill defined):** A *well-defined problem* has a right or wrong answer, and members use very clear information and skills to solve it. An *ill-defined problem* has many potential solutions, and members must explore various arguments or sources with a variety of perspectives; often there are dilemmas that make one decision advantageous for one group and perhaps a little tougher for another. Because ill-defined problems are generally authentic, often organizations or businesses are willing to work in collaboration with schools for learners to work on these problems.

10. **Establish the communication medium:** How will the collaboration take place? Will the team meet face-to-face? If online, will they use a text chat feature, do a video chat, or a combination of both? Collaboration is a skill in itself, and the teacher may also assess or target other competencies such as communication and critical thinking during the collaboration. While the teacher may integrate these other competencies, he or she should assess them individually if, in fact, they are a purposeful outcome of the collaborative effort.

11. **Choose whether or not to challenge collaborative problem-solving abilities and styles:** Collaboration is unpredictable, and issues often arise that the team must manage. The teacher should decide if he or she will predetermine some "curve balls to throw" in order to assess the group members' ability to respond to and maneuver with conflict or surprises. For example, the teacher may change the task midway or introduce a challenge not present at the beginning of the collaboration. It's also feasible for the teacher to ask one team member to do something such as be unresponsive, provide an incorrect content idea, or be disruptive, coordinating, independent, or domineering. During these "curve ball moments," the teacher should observe how learners respond and consider: To what extent are learners able to do a workaround? How do learners handle a team breakdown? This is most effective when engaging in collaboration 2.0, as the main purpose is to assess collaboration skills.

Figure 4.3 (pages 118–120) provides a guide of the elements to consider when designing the task.

The Aquarium Unit	
Design Element	**Planning**
Set the purpose.	The purpose is to assess learners' collaborative and problem-solving skills. This is a combination of collaboration 2.0 and 3.0. Collaborating to make decisions: • **Curiosity**—Inquire and ask questions to clarify, connect, and generate ideas. • **Consensus building**—Seek to understand others' points of view and find ways to compromise—balancing practicality and orthodoxy—to provide innovative solutions (or, in this case, the best solution possible). Problem solving: • **Explore and understand**—Articulate the nature and components of the issue. • **Represent and formulate**—Clearly communicate and articulate the solution offered with a well-thought-out and thorough explanation of the process and evidence.
Determine the knowledge domain (such as literacy, mathematics, science, community).	Science: • The learner can apply the scientific method. This means he or she can identify controlled variables and manipulate them based on analyzing results from multiple trials. • The learner can describe factors that contribute to a healthy aquarium environment.
Decide on the number of team members.	There are two members of the team: the learner and an electronic agent, Abby.
Establish roles and responsibilities.	The electronic agent and the learner are equal partners and share in making decisions and coming to consensus on each trial (to get the best possible aquarium conditions).
Elect goals for team members.	The teacher will assess the learner's collaboration and problem-solving skills. The learner must respond to the electronic agent's ideas and ask the agent for his or her thoughts. If the learner does not, the agent automatically offers the ideas, but the learner does not show evidence of those particular collaboration skills (curiosity and consensus building).
Choose the collaboration structure.	One learner chats online with Abby, an electronic agent. Each is responsible for different conditions in the aquarium, so it is a jigsaw structure. The learner is responsible for water, scenery, and lighting, while the electronic agent is controlling food, fish population, and water temperature.

Design Element	Planning
Define the task as independent or interdependent.	The task is independent because although the learner works with an electronic agent (partner), either could solve the task independently.
Predesign the task (static or dynamic).	The task is static. It will not change. The student scoring form for collaboration and problem solving (see figure 4.4, pages 122–123) is an example of what learners and teachers might use to score their progress on the task. Learners may check where they see themselves, and teachers may affirm or provide counter-evidence. If the goal requires a summative score, teachers may use the scale to identify a standards-based mark such as advanced, meets, approaching, and beginning. Or, if the teacher needs to assign a letter grade, he or she may reassign categories to indicate the letter grade for each column such as A, B, C, and not yet.
Determine the parameters of the task (defined or ill defined).	The task is well defined. The learner and Abby decide how to find the best conditions for fish to live in an aquarium. In this task (OECD, 2017b), the learner collaborates with the electronic agent through open-ended response in the form of the chat box. The learner also selects conditions for the aquarium from a series of choices and provides open-ended responses to analyze the results. The computer generates a general rating on the quality of the aquarium as Abby and the learner identify the conditions in the aquarium. Based on the rating, Abby and the learner change the conditions to get the best results possible in the allotted time frame. Segment 1: The student interacts with Abby to understand what he or she controls and what the task is. Segment 2: The pair begins to establish the conditions for the first trial. Segment 3: The pair talks about the rating generated from their conditions and sets up new conditions. Segment 4: The pair runs up to five trials (the limit) to get better conditions. This final segment also includes reflection on the effectiveness of the collaboration. The learner and Abby have five trials to find the best conditions for the fish to live in the aquarium. The learner works with Abby to select conditions to test. There is an automatically generated result, and Abby and the learner work to analyze it and then come up with a new set of conditions.

Figure 4.3: Collaborative-planning guide example.

continued ➔

Establish the communication medium.	The teacher determines the learner and electronic partner will use the online chat to dialogue and access both video and text online materials.
Choose whether or not to challenge collaborative problem-solving abilities and styles.	The electronic agent will introduce some conflict in the form of disagreeing with an idea and providing an inaccurate response. The goal of this conflict is to see how the learner navigates through it.

Source: Adapted from OECD, 2017b.

*Visit **go.SolutionTree.com/assessment** for a free blank reproducible version of this figure.*

Observing, Self-Assessing, and Peer Assessing

Once teachers and learners co-construct what it means to effectively collaborate, and the teacher decides the task, he or she can begin assessing the learners' collaboration. Observation (of a collaborative task in action), self-assessment, and peer assessment provide the most effective and efficient way for teachers to gather evidence of a learners' collaborative skills.

Self-assessment is evidence that provides the teacher insight into the effectiveness of the collaboration. Self-assessment is an essential skill for learners to develop as they start to recognize and articulate where they are doing well and what needs work. Learners' self-assessment becomes more accurate as they form a clearer picture of what it means to collaborate and develop the language to describe what works and why, what went wrong and why, and how to get better. However, it is essential to combine this self-assessment information with teacher observations and other learners' observations, as well as the collaborators' reflections. Multiple perspectives on effectiveness will provide a much more valid assessment of the quality of the collaboration.

Learners' observations, for example, might come from highly structured tasks where one or more learners document the frequency of desired behaviors during a collaborative experience (such as the number of academic transitions employed, challenging questions asked, or references made to preparation materials). Documented learners' observations can add to the teacher's reflections of the experience as well as the peer reflections of the collaborative group's collective effort to improve.

Likewise, reflections from other collaborators can inform the teacher's assessment and provide a fuller picture as the teacher tries to measure individual and group effectiveness. For example, if one learner takes over the group and does most of the work or dominates the conversation, that learner may inaccurately reflect that other members did not pull their weight. It is possible that learner may not have given other members an opportunity to engage or offer ideas. In effect, that one learner, while appearing to do all the work, may have actually shut down collaboration because he or she wanted to control the outcome and ensure everyone follow his or her lead.

Peer assessment, when implemented well, has great power to foster a collaborative culture where everyone is contributing their strengths in ways that generate new ideas and empower each individual. However, peer assessment can lead learners astray if there is not a clear understanding of what quality collaboration looks like. Brown and Harris (2013) find that much of the feedback learners receive is from their peers, and most of that peer feedback is inaccurate. While an important and helpful form of evidence, if learners do not execute it carefully and teachers intentionally model it, peer feedback can be misleading. It is important, just as with self-assessment, for the teacher to generate a common understanding, dialogue, and descriptions of criteria prior to conducting a peer assessment, and to check in on learners' perceptions to increase accuracy, which inevitably are essential to help learners improve their collaboration.

The learner scoring form for collaboration and problem solving (figure 4.4, pages 122–123) is a self-assessment tool to guide learners to reflect on their collaboration and problem-solving skills. Learners can apply this tool in various situations. This reflection is invaluable to both the teacher and learner. Teachers can review a learner's reflections with their own observations to understand more fully where a learner is strong and where he or she needs work. This form also helps learners understand the qualities of effective collaboration and problem solving and promote focused goal setting as learners engage in subsequent tasks.

Communicating Results

There are numerous ways to communicate results. One way to report collaboration results is to determine the overall score using a criterion-based rubric, like the one in figure 4.5 (pages 123–124), and select the most frequently marked category or descriptor.

Alternatively, teachers could utilize a points-based model. Figure 4.6 (page 125) depicts a grading template that assigns points to indicate proficiency level. This type of grading model works well when each criterion is equally important. When using this tool, teachers must take care to ensure the points, which they often need to convert to percentages, reflect an accurate picture of proficiency and not just a simple algorithm. Teachers may find it helpful to use a scale up to ten points (rather than four points) when later converting the score to a percentage of proficiency. For example, when two out of four correct is changed to a percentage, it is only 50 percent, which inaccurately reflects proficiency when the middle score is closer to 70 and not 50. In figure 4.6, basic competency earns seven of ten points, not five, making the percentage more reflective of proficiency.

Student: _____ Date: _____

Directions: Assess the frequency of your use of each of these skills. Provide examples in the Notes row for both collaboration and problem solving. Then, reflect using the questions following the table. The teacher will then provide comments, confirming the assessment or providing another perspective.

	Unsure	Sometimes	Usually	Consistently and Effectively
Collaboration				
Curiosity:				
• Inquires and asks questions to clarify				
• Inquires and asks questions to connect ideas and understand the team members' roles				
• Inquires and asks questions to generate ideas				
Notes:				
Consensus building:				
• Seeks to understand others' points of view				
• Finds ways to compromise				
• Uses those compromises to provide a viable solution				
Notes:				
Problem Solving				
Explore and understand:				
• Shows understanding of the nature of the problem				
• Shows understanding of the components of the problem				
Notes:				

Represent and formulate:			
• Clearly communicates and articulates the solution offered with a well-thought-out and thorough explanation of the process and evidence for each trial			

Notes:

Learner Reflection Questions:

1. What was your biggest strength during this collaborative task? (Please choose from the criteria in the table.)

2. What was your biggest challenge?

3. How did you attempt to overcome this challenge? To what degree were you successful?

4. If you could do this task again, what would you do differently?

Source for criteria: OECD, 2017b.

Figure 4.4: Collaboration and problem-solving student scoring form.

Visit **go.SolutionTree.com/assessment** *for a free reproducible version of this figure.*

	Initiating: Rarely with evidence of effectiveness	**Developing:** Occasionally with evidence of effectiveness	**Achieving:** Usually with evidence of effectiveness	**Advancing:** Consistently with evidence of effectiveness
Collaboration				
Curiosity:				
• Inquires and asks questions to clarify		X		
• Inquires and asks questions to connect ideas and understand the team members' roles			X	
• Inquires and asks questions to generate ideas			X	

Figure 4.5: Scoring using a standards-based model.
continued ➔

	Initiating: Rarely with evidence of effectiveness	Developing: Occasion-ally with evidence of effectiveness	Achieving: Usually with evidence of effectiveness	Advancing: Consistently with evi-dence of effectiveness
Consensus building:				
• Seeks to understand others' points of view			X	
• Finds ways to compromise			X	
• Uses those compromises to provide a viable solution				X
Overall collaboration score: Achieving				
Problem Solving				
Explore and understand:				
• Shows understanding of the nature of the problem		X		
• Shows understanding of the components of the problem		X		
Represent and formulate:				
• Clearly communicates and articulates the solution offered with a well-thought-out and thorough explanation of the process and evidence for each trial			X	
Overall problem-solving score: Developing				

Visit **go.SolutionTree.com/assessment** *for a free reproducible version of this figure.*

	Not Yet (Not observed)	7 points (At a surface level)	8 points (Most of the time)	9 or 10 points (Consistently with evidence of effectiveness)
Collaboration				
Curiosity:				
• Inquires and asks questions to clarify		7		
• Inquires and asks questions to connect ideas and understand the team members' roles			8	
• Inquires and asks questions to generate ideas				9
Consensus building:				
• Seeks to understand others' points of view				10
• Finds ways to compromise				9
• Uses those compromises to provide a viable solution			8	
Collaboration: 51 of 60				
Problem Solving				
Explore and understand:				
• Shows understanding of the nature of the problem			8	
• Shows understanding of the components of the problem			8	
Represent and formulate:				
• Clearly communicates and articulates the solution offered with a well-thought-out and thorough explanation of the process and evidence for each trial				10
Problem Solving: 26 of 30				

Figure 4.6: *Collaboration and problem-solving scoring in a points-based model.*

*Visit **go.SolutionTree.com/assessment** for a free blank reproducible version of this figure.*

Measuring Collaboration

It is essential for learners and teachers to continue to develop their understanding of the qualities of effective collaboration as the collaborative task unfolds. The co-construction process (see the section Developing a Shared Understanding of Collaboration on page 112) is one way to ensure the validity of the measurement and accuracy of the feedback before, during, and after collaboration.

Teachers should do the following before collaboration begins.

- Clearly describe the nature of the collaboration, such as 1.0 (to learn or explore a concept), 2.0 (to develop collaboration skills), 3.0 (to make a decision, solve a problem, or produce an innovation), or any combination of the three.

- Provide criteria for the collaboration skills learners will need to develop or co-construct these criteria with learners. Look at different collaboration scenarios and ask learners to critique those examples for strengths and ways to improve. Ask learners to describe what kinds of feedback teachers and peers might offer individuals in the scenario. Ask learners to reflect on their understanding of what they are like as collaborators.

Teachers should do the following during collaboration.

- Have learners conduct observations. While this is optional and not always feasible at the learner level, it is helpful both from a metacognitive perspective (for learners) and from a data-gathering perspective (for teachers) to task learners with observing and recording evidence of a specific, isolated feature. For example, while engaging in a collaborative experience, the teacher could ask one learner to record the specific citations studied while learning the content, and another learner to record the number of times learners asked each other questions. Sometimes, especially early in the learning process, the metacognitive feature of self-monitoring and documenting the new skills can support learners in grasping the content and skills more quickly. Always record and share the evidence, as it can supplement (either through endorsing or challenging) the teacher's observations.

- Have learners engage in self-assessment. Ask learners to reflect informally on what worked and what needs work at various points throughout the collaboration. Use the shared criteria so learners can provide specific examples about what worked and what was challenging. Also, provide open-ended moments so the criteria can change if the nature of the task is leading collaboration that way; it is important to allow this flexibility and adjustment to happen.

- Have learners conduct peer assessment. Ask learners to reflect on the effectiveness of their entire collaboration and what is working and what is not. This allows the teacher to understand the level of understanding each individual has in assessing effective collaboration and to give instruction if there are misunderstandings.

- Intentionally guide reflection on specific aspects of collaboration. For example, if the teacher wants students to learn how to deal with conflict, ask them to reflect on various ways to handle conflict.

- Refine the criteria as the collaboration unfolds. It is one thing to predetermine criteria and have a picture of what it looks like. However, applying the criteria provides another view of clarity and often leads to clear language and descriptions of what collaboration looks like.

- Use checklists, rubrics, and reflection forms to conduct in-the-moment checks so learners (and the teacher) can provide midcourse corrections to make the collaboration as effective as possible.

Teachers should do the following after collaboration.

- Provide opportunities for self-assessment. Ask learners to reflect on their perceptions of their own collaboration skills. Use a rubric or descriptions generated over the course of the project so there is a clear picture of quality.

- Provide opportunities for peer assessment. Ask learners to reflect on individuals in the collaboration and provide specific examples.

- Provide an overall description of the level of proficiency on the agreed-on criteria.

Despite collaboration being dependent on various members, the measurement must be as accurate as possible to reflect an individual's development and engagement in collaboration. Rubrics, checklists, and scoring criteria are essential and comprise the cornerstone of fair and accurate feedback and reporting. The following sections will present tools to provide clarity surrounding collaboration criteria, learner self-assessment tools, peer assessment tools, and tools for fairly and accurately scoring collaboration.

Tools to Provide Clarity for Collaboration Criteria

While teacher collaboration and student co-construction may develop the detailed descriptions of collaboration, it is helpful to have a guide for what to consider. Figures 4.7 and 4.8 offer tools to share with learners so they clearly understand the expectations. Use these tools in part or whole to guide clarity of expectations before collaboration, for feedback and self-reflection during collaboration, and for grading after collaboration.

Rubrics describe the expected quality and provide descriptions along a continuum to articulate varying degrees of proficiency. At their best, rubrics describe the qualities present versus what is lacking. Rubrics are best refined as they are applied so teachers can obtain precise descriptions of the qualities at each level of proficiency. The ultimate goal of a rubric is to provide clear collaboration criteria that learners and teachers can understand easily.

Criteria	Initiating	Developing	Achieving	Advancing
Staying on Task	I need lots of reminders to focus on the task.	I need some reminders to stay focused on the task.	I stay on task and can refocus on my own.	I stay on task and respectfully redirect the group to stay on task.
Listening	I tend to blurt out ideas and forget to listen to others' ideas.	I sometimes hear others' ideas.	I hear others' ideas and can paraphrase their thoughts.	I listen to others' ideas to understand what they are saying. I can summarize their ideas and contributions before sharing my own ideas.
Contributing	I blurt out my ideas or agree with others even when I have a different thought.	I offer ideas that reiterate others or are redundant.	I contribute ideas that add to the focus of the dialogue.	I offer new ideas, building on others' ideas and providing a different view that pushes the conversation deeper.

Figure 4.7: *Scoring criteria for collaboration 1.0.*

Visit **go.SolutionTree.com/assessment** *for a free reproducible version of this figure.*

Criteria	Descriptors
Contributing to the Team's Work	• Contributes an equitable amount of work • Contributes quality work • Commits and follows through • Supports or "fills in" for teammates when needed
Interacting With Teammates	• Seeks input and shows interest in teammates' work • Facilitates communication among teammates; shows enthusiasm • Asks for feedback and uses it to improve • Listens to teammates • Shares information and ideas
Keeping the Team on Track	• Notices team's actions or words that change where the team is and may impact its success • Is clear on what each team member's role and work are • Offers suggestions for improvement when the team gets off track
Expecting Quality	• Desires and believes in quality work from the team • Encourages quality
Having Relevant Knowledge, Skills, and Abilities	• Has specific skills and knowledge to engage in the team's task • Performs multiple roles on the team • Knows how to learn skills and gain knowledge to engage in the team's task (particularly, if not initially unknowledgeable and unable to demonstrate the skills)

Source: Adapted from Ohland et al., 2012.

Figure 4.8: *Scoring criteria for collaboration 2.0 with descriptors.*

*Visit **go.SolutionTree.com/assessment** for a free reproducible version of this figure.*

Figure 4.9 (pages 130–131) is an example of a collaboration rubric teachers can use over time. Learners may also track their progress over time on one or more of the criteria. As learners engage in collaborative tasks, they reflect on their strengths and next steps.

Rubrics provide descriptions of quality in order to guide students in developing a more sophisticated understanding of collaboration. Sharing rubrics with learners and asking students to use rubrics to assess anonymous samples of collaboration help learners develop a more sophisticated understanding of what it means to collaborate. When students can make accurate observations of quality and not-so-quality collaboration, their self- and peer assessment will be more accurate and meaningful. As students and teachers use the rubrics, the language is refined to be more concise, clear, and accurate.

Standards	Initiating	Developing	Achieving	Advancing
Exchanging ideas (paraphrasing, responding, and offering insights and ideas) I can exchange ideas. This means I can build on the ideas that others offer by using their words or paraphrasing their ideas before I add my own. When I add my own ideas, I can qualify what I mean and justify that I am accurate by using the evidence from outside sources to show that I am connected to the quality work of other experts.	• Responds when prompted • Contributes, but ideas are disconnected or loosely connected to the general flow of the conversation	• Paraphrases are stilted or clumsy, often copying the exact words of the previous speaker • Offers ideas but minimal support for them • Engages mostly by listening; personal contributions are minimal	• Paraphrases to clarify, build on, or challenge another • Paraphrases previous responses smoothly so the listener feels heard but not parroted • Validates personal responses using sufficient support for ideas (like examples and clarifying terminology) • Prompts continued civil discourse with open-minded, logical answers • Shares personal beliefs and ideas in a respectful and inviting way that welcomes input from others	• Paraphrases based on the emerging themes from the overall conversation (not just the words of the previous speaker) • Synthesizes and articulates insights emerging from the collective wisdom of the group • Embeds ideas in references from multiple sources to lend credence to ideas
Referencing background preparation (paraphrasing, quoting, and citing materials) I can come prepared. This means I can refer to the things I studied and materials I prepared for a discussion. I will read and research in advance of the discussion, and I will show my preparedness by citing the evidence that I encountered when I was preparing.	• May or may not be able to provide examples from background preparation if asked • May provide evidence, but it is insufficient or irrelevant for supporting the conversation	• Talks in general about evidence and examples to support the collaboration	• Uses evidence from background materials to rationalize personal thoughts and contributions • Easily and readily employs quotes and paraphrases from reference materials to support claims • Locates appropriate references to respond to questions or statements from peers	• Makes connections to materials that were provided during the planning phase, as well as materials from previous learning (for example, earlier units of study)

Propelling or maintaining focus in the conversation (questioning, answering, transitioning, and redirecting) I can propel and maintain the focus in a conversation. This means I can pose questions and respond to others in a way that invites the conversation to continue or go deeper, but always to stay on the same topic.	• When prompted, offers a statement or question • Offers statements or questions that do not promote an ongoing exchange of ideas	• Questions are planned or staged and employed at times or in ways that do not help the group move forward from the current point of discussion	• Offers genuine, thoughtful questions as a mechanism to explore someone else's contribution or to elicit information from a group member • Responds directly to the questions asked with clear and concise answers • Uses academic transitions to navigate the flow of the conversation and link disparate ideas • Employs redirection strategies or cues when the conversation drifts off topic • Guarantees all members are on task and the key points addressed	• Connects ideas from multiple team members • Invites team members to participate and build on others' ideas
Employing agreed-on rules and roles I can follow the identified rules to guide our discussion, and I can use my assigned role to help the conversation remain on track.	• Must be reminded of the rules and roles while engaged • Requires prompting or cuing to recall the rules	• Employs the assigned role	• Uses the rules of the selected discussion structure to support healthy dialogue among all team members • Employs the assigned role to help facilitate the work of the team • Monitors self and others for adhering to the rules and roles of the discourse	• Effectively keeps the group on track and ensures rules and roles are working smoothly

Figure 4.9: Sample collaboration rubric.

Visit go.SolutionTree.com/assessment for a free reproducible version of this figure.

Learner Self-Assessment Tools

Learner self-assessment tools are essential for developing self-regulation. Learners benefit from pausing and reflecting on their progress, reviewing observations from teachers and their peers, and identifying their strengths and next steps in order to move their collaboration skills forward. Figure 4.10 provides guidance in helping learners self-assess on a list of criteria. This self-assessment could happen before, during, or after collaboration, depending on how familiar and experienced the learners are in executing these skills. Figure 4.11 (pages 134–135) allows learners to track their progress and reflect on how to get better. Finally, figure 4.12 (page 135) provides open-ended prompts to guide exit tickets that teachers ask learners to complete to get feedback on how collaboration is going. The feedback gained from these questions can help the teacher provide more instruction and feedback to increase the level of collaboration occurring.

Criteria	I need clarification on what this means and looks like.	I am working on it but need ideas in order to get better.	I do this sometimes but need to work on doing this more intentionally.	I do this often and can articulate examples.	I do this consistently, with evidence of effectiveness.
Displaying curiosity: Inquires and asks questions to clarify, connect, and generate ideas					
Listening: Actively hears, paraphrases, and summarizes others' ideas to deeply understand alternative or competing perspectives					
Contributing: Offers new, radical, and sometimes unpopular views					
Committing to work through conflict: Productively engages in and moves through conflict—does not avoid it or unnecessarily incite it for the sake of argument					
Consensus building: Finds ways to compromise—balancing practicality and orthodoxy—to provide innovative solutions					

Observing: Observes nonverbal and verbal words and actions to productively and honestly navigate dialogue, conflict, and conflicting ideas				
Focusing on strengths: Capitalizes on the strengths of individual group members; presumes positive intentions				
Focusing on goals: Positions the overall goal over an individual need to be right				
Knowing what to do when you don't know: Embraces uncertainty with questions and a commitment to pursue information and next steps				
Synthesizing: Explores and perseveres to synthesize large amounts of information or competing perspectives; blends ideas to co-create and innovate				
Sourcing: Discerns the reliability of information through interrogating sources—authors' perspectives, organizations, funding sources, and other potential areas of bias; assesses a source's reliability, its realistic potential, and competing and contradictory reports that counter the source's main argument				

Figure 4.10: *Learner self-assessment for tracking progress on collaboration 2.0.*

*Visit **go.SolutionTree.com/assessment** for a free reproducible version of this figure.*

Use the following scale to reflect on your collaboration skills before, during, and after the collaborative task.

4—Consistently in ways that move the group forward

3—Often in ways that help the group

2—Sometimes, but needs reminders or gets the group off track at times; may take over the group so others don't have the opportunity to contribute

1– Needs work in order to productively contribute to the group (may feel shut down or uncomfortable contributing)

Criteria	Before	During	After
Displaying curiosity: Inquires and asks questions to clarify, connect, and generate ideas			
Listening: Actively hears, paraphrases, and summarizes others' ideas to deeply understand alternative or competing perspectives			
Contributing: Offers new, radical, and sometimes unpopular views			
Committing to work through conflict: Productively engages in and moves through conflict—does not avoid it or unnecessarily incite it for the sake of argument			
Consensus building: Finds ways to compromise—balancing practicality and orthodoxy—to provide innovative solutions			
Observing: Observes nonverbal and verbal words and actions to productively and honestly navigate dialogue, conflict, and conflicting ideas			
Focusing on strengths: Capitalizes on the strengths of individual group members; presumes positive intentions			
Focusing on goals: Positions the overall goal over an individual need to be right			
Knowing what to do when you don't know: Embraces uncertainty with questions and a commitment to pursue information and next steps			

Synthesizing: Explores and perseveres to synthesize large amounts of information or competing perspectives; blends ideas to co-create and innovate			
Sourcing: Discerns the reliability of information through interrogating sources—authors' perspectives, organizations, funding sources, and other potential areas of bias; assesses a source's reliability, its realistic potential, and competing and contradictory reports that counter the source's main argument			

Figure 4.11: *Learner self-assessment form for collaboration skills before, during, and after collaboration.*

Visit go.SolutionTree.com/assessment for a free reproducible version of this figure.

Name: _____ Date: _____

Members of my team:

1. What is working well in your collaboration?
2. What have you accomplished?
3. What conflicts have emerged?
4. How have you resolved them?
5. What part of your collaboration needs work? Do you need help in moving forward?
6. Is there anyone on your team you are worried about? Explain the situation.
7. What questions do you have?

Figure 4.12: *Reflective questions for learners.*

Visit go.SolutionTree.com/assessment for a free reproducible version of this figure.

Peer Assessment Tools

While peer assessment should not involve peers giving grades to others, their reflections and rating scales can provide insight to help the teacher make summative evaluations and provide ongoing feedback, as appropriate. Peers can use figure 4.13 (page 136) during peer assessment. Peers can modify it for external collaborators to provide feedback, such as if a team is collaborating with another school or with members of an outside organization for a longer period of time.

Use the following scale to reflect on your collaboration skills before, during, or after the collaborative task.

4—Consistently in ways that move the group forward

3—Often in ways that help the group

2—Sometimes, but needs reminders or gets the group off track at times; may take over the group so others don't have the opportunity to contribute

1—Needs work in order to productively contribute to the group (may feel shut down or uncomfortable contributing)

Learners on your team or external collaborators	Developing curiosity: Inquires and asks questions to clarify, connect, and generate ideas	Listening: Actively hears, paraphrases, and summa-rizes others' ideas to deeply understand alternative or competing perspectives	Contributing: Offers new, radical, and sometimes unpopular views	Following rules of engage-ment: Prompts other team members to perform their tasks	Understanding the problem: Shows knowl-edge of the components of the problem and the context in which it exists

1. What is working well in this collaboration?
2. What would make this collaboration more effective?
3. What are your needs to make this collaboration even better?

Figure 4.13: *Peer-assessment form for problem-solving and collaboration skills before, during, and after collaboration.*

Visit **go.SolutionTree.com/assessment** *for a free reproducible version of this figure.*

Tools for Fairly and Accurately Scoring Collaboration

Most issues with fairness and accuracy come into play when scoring collaboration for a summative grade. It is important that any summary of proficiency or mastery be individual and not an average of all group members. That said, there are times when isolating individual contributions can admittedly be challenging. While a shared grade could positively encourage collaboration, it is not necessarily an accurate reflection of the individual's collaborative skills. If the team generates a singular product, a small portion of the overall score might be shared among team members. Teachers should strive for individualized assessment but be open to using *some* team results to determine proficiency when collaboration itself is a separate reporting category.

However, when assessing collaboration skills, the teacher's observations, learners' reflections, and peer assessment can provide evidence of the level of mastery. Learner self-assessment and peer assessment of collaboration should only be reflections that contribute to the *teacher* assigning a summative mark based on the standard or learning criteria. Asking learners to assign points to their peers is neither fair nor accurate because of all the contextual factors beyond what the teacher sees or the learners perceive.

The following are considerations regarding the accuracy of a collaboration score.

- If there are factors out of the individual's control, how are they neutralized when determining the grade?

- What learning or standard is actually being assessed? Do the task and the process allow for ample opportunities for learners to demonstrate their level of achievement on the intended learning (standard or criteria)?

- What assumptions are made about what learners need to know? What experiences have they had for them to be able to successfully show their achievement?

- To what extent was there instruction on how to collaborate or use the collaboration method?

The following are considerations regarding the fairness of a collaboration score.

- Are there factors completely out of the control of the individual? Does the collaboration design account for those factors when the teacher assigns a grade to communicate achievement?

- Do learners receive feedback on clear criteria?

- Do learners get opportunities that require them to practice using feedback?

- How do individual personality characteristics influence collaboration scores? Are scores affected if the student is an introvert or extrovert?

Collaboration 1.0, 2.0, and 3.0 all have various assessment implications. Assess learners as individuals during the collaboration task (collaboration 1.0). Assess learners before, during, and after collaboration through observation, self-assessment, and peer assessment (collaboration 2.0). Self-assessment and peer assessment should inform the teacher's overall grade, but not be determining factors. Assess learners before, during, and after collaborative problem solving (collaboration 3.0). Again, observation, self-assessment, and peer assessment provide teachers insight into the collaborative assessment process. Table 4.2 is a summary of these recommendations.

Growing Collaboration

As teachers plan to ensure students grow in their ability to effectively collaborate, there are instructional moves that will lead to setting up the best conditions for collaboration. Many students have prior experience with "group work," and it is not always positive. As a result, it is helpful to engage students in dialogue about the differences between group work and true collaboration. As learners engage in this dialogue, they begin to co-construct criteria. This picture of quality collaboration will allow students to be able to self-assess and more deeply understand what it means to be an effective collaborator. Defining collaboration and noting how it's different than in the past can help students begin to learn what it means to collaborate.

To set up conditions for students to achieve the skills of collaboration, teachers work with students to co-construct qualities of effective collaboration. Together, learners and their teachers develop criteria and examples to understand more deeply what it takes to collaborate well. In addition, teachers set up routines and procedures to facilitate dialogue in ways that become familiar, so students gain practice in collaboration skills. Protocols and routines can help student collaborators tap into the expertise of each member and achieve a common goal. Collaborators may also identify roles in the process to ensure that they hear all voices, accomplish tasks, and achieve their goal. Finally, any student collaboration is best when the task is meaningful and authentic. Growing collaboration is a combination of redefining what it means to work, setting up the classroom conditions (routines and procedures), and ensuring learners are engaged in meaningful work.

Table 4.2: Collaboration Purpose, Criteria, and Assessment Implications

Purpose	Criteria	Assessment Implications
Collaboration 1.0 **To help students learn a concept**	Content standards Group behavior expectations	Assessment is individual. Administer after the collaboration to check all learners' individual progress on achieving the intended content standards.
Collaboration 2.0 **To develop collaboration skills**	Contributing to the team's work Interacting with teammates • Dealing with conflict • Listening • Seeking to understand another point of view • Considering the counterargument or perspective • Building on ideas of team members • Coming to a consensus or synthesizing ideas to generate an innovative, effective solution Keeping the team on track • Ensuring participation • Building on ideas • Expecting quality • Having relevant knowledge, skills, and abilities	Assessment is individual. Assessment is during the collaboration through a rubric or observation checklist. Self- and team reflections offer insight into what contributes to the effectiveness or ineffectiveness of the collaboration.

continued ➤

Purpose	Criteria	Assessment Implications
Collaboration 3.0 **To facilitate creative problem solving**	Comprehension of the problem Quality sources to research and understand the problem Clarity of potential solution Creativity: Solutions that put multiple ideas together in new ways to produce a viable solution	Assessment is individual and collective. Assessment is during the collaborative process, and each individual is assessed on his or her creative problem-solving and collaboration skills. Assessment is after the collaboration, and collective to assess the qualities of the product (smallest aspect of overall summative grade). Individuals reflect on both their collaboration skills and how and what they contributed to the end product. Grade is based on evidence from the reflection, end product, and trend data (observations over the course of the project).

Conclusion

There is no doubt that collaboration is critical to learners' success in the future. Whether the collaboration is with peers in the classroom, other people around the world, organizations relevant to the targeted studies, online, or in person, learners will require clear criteria and descriptions of what it means to collaborate. As with any of the critical competencies, there is significant overlap among competencies, and each context must clearly define the purpose and criteria of a task and the desired competencies to be mastered. It is through clarity that assessing collaboration will become natural, effective, and efficient.

Pause and Ponder

On your own or as part of a collaborative teacher team, consider the following reflective questions.

1. How is collaboration different today than in the past?

2. Which ideas in this chapter are most compelling? What might be one next step you take to help learners develop collaboration skills?

3. How might you begin engaging in collaborative thinking with your colleagues as you work to practice, implement, and ultimately provide models of meaningful collaboration?

4. Do the collaborative opportunities in your classroom most closely resemble collaboration 1.0, 2.0, or 3.0? Explain how they are similar and different.

5. Given your content area and grade level, what types of collaboration skills are most essential?

6. Given your content area and grade level, where are the natural places or times you might begin placing collaborative thinking opportunities?

7. Observation, self-assessment, and peer assessment are effective methods to use to gather evidence of learners' collaboration skills. Which of these do you currently use with learners? What tools do you currently use, and which tools do you need to design?

8. Which aspects of effective collaboration will be most seamless for your learners to develop? Which aspects will be more challenging for them to develop?

9. If you are facilitating learning for teachers in developing collaboration tools for learners, which of these ideas are most important? What strengths do your colleagues already possess, and what are their next steps to learn more about how to best facilitate this type of learning?

CHAPTER 5
CREATIVE THINKING

The future belongs to a very different kind of person with a very different kind of mind—creators and empathizers, pattern recognizers and meaning makers. These people . . . will now reap society's richest rewards and share its greatest joys.

—Daniel Pink

Few topics in assessment and instruction have generated more enthusiasm yet simultaneous concern than creative thinking. What is it? Who determines it? Can one measure it? *Should* one measure it? While the world outside school walls values and craves creativity, educators rarely teach it as a critical competency. The challenges behind teaching and assessing creativity are not exclusive to educators. According to creativity expert and Morgan Distinguished Professor in educational innovations at the University of North Carolina at Chapel Hill R. Keith Sawyer (2006):

> Psychologists began to study creativity in the 1950s, and right away, they had trouble defining it. In the 1950s and 1960s, psychologists searched for paper and pencil tests that could measure a person's creative potential. With a good test, they could simply have defined creativity as a high score on the test. However, this search was in vain. . . . In spite of several

decades of research, personality psychologists were not able to define a test to measure creativity, and the effort was abandoned by the 1970s. (p. 35)

Creativity, then, is virtually impossible to measure. Howard Gardner (2001) notes there is consensus in the field: "You could know every bit of neurocircuitry in somebody's head, and you still would not know whether or not that person was creative" (p. 130). If psychologists and researchers have had difficulty defining and measuring it, then it's no wonder educators struggle to teach and measure creativity. If left undefined at a systems level, the instruction for and evaluation of creativity are left to individual discretion, so it becomes shrouded in subjectivity.

But the challenge of teaching and assessing creativity cannot deter the effort. Creativity is a *critical* competency, and as such, educators must teach it. Creativity is the backbone of innovation, and humanity thrives on innovation; indeed, it is what improves the quality of living across all ages and continents. Sawyer (2006) states, "Innovation is the holy grail of today's modern corporation" (p. 297), arguably across all industries and disciplines. Put another way, authors Douglas Reeves and Brooks Reeves (2017) add, "Creativity is at the heart of the solutions to our most intractable challenges and is, therefore, essential for survival" (p. 1). If schools are to prepare students to be successful and thrive post-graduation, then they must help students identify and refine their own creative genius.

Fortunately, many experts believe educators should define and teach creative thinking (Drapeau, 2014; Reeves & Reeves, 2017; Robinson, 2011, 2013; Wagner, 2012). There are many different theories on how to teach creativity, and many K–12 educational systems have begun the rigorous work of developing shared understanding and agreements around teaching for creativity. Unfortunately, the issue, experts warn, is greater than simply providing working definitions and strategies for understanding and teaching creativity (Robinson, 2009, 2013; Sternberg & Spear-Swerling, 1996). The greater concern lies in educational policies (such as No Child Left Behind [NCLB], 2002, and other current state policies patterned after that law) that both publicly and financially reward or punish schools solely based on academic achievement in reading, writing, and mathematics literacies.

In his TED Talks and extensive writing on the topic of creativity, renowned expert in the development of creativity and innovation Ken Robinson asserts that education's dependence on an incomplete view of what makes someone smart and its overreliance on test scores grounded in right answers are all but killing creativity in school (Robinson, 2009, 2011, 2013; Robinson & Aronica, 2015). In 1996, less than twenty years after the onslaught of the accountability movement in education, Cornell University professor Robert J. Sternberg and Southern Connecticut State

University professor Louise Spear-Swerling (1996) say the "creative thinking of students" was being "undervalued," and that an overreliance on numerical data results in "an entrenched status quo that blocks creativity at all levels of the educational process" (p. 13). But little has changed, even with such an alarming forewarning from Sternberg and Spear-Swerling (1996).

It is time to change the paradigm. Creativity and innovation are paramount to a culture's basic survival and ultimate quality of life. More important, developing an awareness of one's natural talents, which is a separate but interdependent feature of refining one's creative skill, is crucial to each individual learner's long-term success and overall satisfaction. There is so much more to becoming a contributing member of society than being able to read, write, and calculate. Instead, "we need to make sure that all people have the chance to do what they should be doing, to discover the Element [a combination of personal passion and natural talent] in themselves and in their own way" (Robinson, 2009, p. xiii).

Defining Creativity

A standard dictionary definition might define *creativity* as a process or ability to surpass conventional thinking, patterns, rules, relationships, or practices to create a performance, product, solution, or idea that is original, imaginative, or progressive. Creativity is often recognized as innovation; as educational consultants and authors James Bellanca, Robin Fogarty, and Brian Pete (2012) state, "Innovation and creativity are inextricably linked. It has been said that innovation is imagination realized and that only when the creative thought is put into action does innovation occur" (p. 39).

Some experts suggest creativity is *not* universally defined. Sawyer (2006) states that creativity is "a culturally and historically specific idea that changes from one country to another, and from one century to another" (p. 36). Others note creativity can be defined generally, but there are so many key features and moving parts that it is nearly impossible to have an accurate, comprehensive glimpse into a true understanding of creativity (Paul & Kaufman, 2014; Runco, 2014; Sawyer, 2006). Still, there is general agreement among the experts of at least the following three significant features of creativity.

1. Creativity is an inventive and imaginative process that involves rigor and strategy (Gardner, 2001; Kaufman & Gregoire, 2015; Runco, 2014; Sawyer, 2006; Wagner, 2012). Contrary to popular opinion, it is not a free-for-all, messy mystique that only happens sometimes and for some people.

2. Creativity involves the generation of something unique or fresh in response to a situation or problem that requires addressing or solving. There is a newness that is purposeful, not random (Bellanca, 2015; Kaufman, 2013; Kaufman & Gregoire, 2015; Runco, 2007, 2014; Sawyer, 2006; Wagner, 2012).

3. Creativity necessitates the development of something that adds value; in other words, creative solutions or products add aesthetically pleasing or practical value, and they do not exist just for the sake of being different (Kaufman, 2013; Kaufman & Gregoire, 2015; Runco, 2014; Wagner, 2012).

In sum, "Creativity requires both novelty and usefulness" (Kaufman, 2013, p. 256). The value-added feature is key, though Sawyer (2006) notes that determining value can be for aesthetic appeal (for example, art or music) or equally be an ingenious solution (such as an invention to solve a significant scientific query). Either way, Sawyer (2006) writes, "Socioculturalists define creativity as a novel product that attains some level of social recognition" (p. 27). Without the recognition and appreciation of others, a product or solution might simply exist, but would not be deemed *creative*.

Laced throughout the agreed-on features of creativity are the widely accepted notions that creativity looks different from one discipline to the next, *everyone* is creative, and creativity is likely an everyday experience. Teachers can teach the process of thinking with creative intent as a critical competency learners can refine with rehearsal and adjustments from feedback.

When defining the human capacity to be creative, Sawyer (2006) notes there is the Big C version of creativity for those with raw talent, and the Little C version of creativity that everyone has:

> Scientists have used several different definitions of creativity, but they all fall somewhere between two camps. In one camp, only solutions to extremely difficult problems, or significant works of genius, are recognized as creative. This is sometimes called "Big C" creativity. The other camp, or "Little C" creativity, includes activities that people engage in every day. "Little C" creativity includes modifying a recipe when you don't have all of the ingredients called for; avoiding a traffic jam by finding a new way through side streets; or figuring out how to apologize to a friend for an unintended insult. (p. 27)

Little C creativity is a critical competency educators must teach and assess as it precedes Big C creativity.

Little C creativity often happens in seemingly insignificant but daily doses. Sawyer (2006) asserts everyone can be more creative in daily experiences, and condenses a growing body of research to help people understand what everyday creativity might look like:

1. Everyday creativity is collaborative;
2. Everyday creativity is improvised;
3. Everyday creativity can't be planned in advance, or carefully revised before execution;
4. Everyday creativity emerges unpredictably from a group of people;
5. Everyday creativity depends on shared cultural knowledge;
6. In everyday creativity, the process is the product (p. 296).

Given these guidelines, teachers can readily support the development of Little C creativity in their daily instruction and large and small assessment projects. It would, however, require an intentional effort to design for and then monitor Little C creative processes. Even though advanced planning can't manufacture everyday creativity, it's possible and even necessary to create instructionally provocative challenges for learners.

Considering Creativity Now and Going Forward

Teachers need to teach and assess creative thinking both for the future benefits of learners and the world they enter after graduation. Everyone has the capacity to be creative; as Robinson (2009) avows, "One myth is that only special people are creative. This is not true. Everyone is born with tremendous capacities for creativity. The trick is to develop these capacities. Creativity is very much like literacy" (p. 56). *Creative literacy* is as important as reading, writing, and mathematics literacies. All learners deserve to understand and develop their full creative potential.

Creativity, however, is often sacrificed for the benefit of traditional literacies (reading, writing, and mathematics) and conformity. Experts (Catmull, 2014; Csikszentmihalyi, 2007; Robinson, 2006, 2009, 2013; Robinson & Aronica, 2015) all lament that schools maintain a too narrow focus on what's essential. As Robinson (2009) writes:

> We place tremendous significance on standardized tests, we cut funding for what we consider "non-essential" programs, and then we wonder why our children seem unimaginative and uninspired. In these ways, our current education system systematically drains the creativity out of our children. (p. 16)

Likewise, psychologist Mihaly Csikszentmihalyi (2007) notes that educators could teach creative and critical thinking through the more traditional literacies, but most often do not.

Before educators can teach creativity, they must wrestle with and develop creative solutions for many challenges, including the following.

- Allowing for nonconformity
- Embracing productive failure
- Understanding the multifacets of creativity
- Removing bias
- Addressing value and plausibility
- Teaching the creative process

If not addressed, each individual challenge will ultimately undo an educator's best efforts to teach creativity.

Allowing for Nonconformity

Schools that wish to embrace teaching creativity will have to begin with an honest look at whether or not a system fundamentally predicated on conformity will be able to tolerate, much less nurture, nonconformist responses on behalf of learners. Conformity is necessary when asking learners to participate in a greater organization; for example, teaching learners the best way to proceed through hallways, seek the teacher's attention, submit work in a timely manner, and answer questions accurately—to name just a few areas in which educators crave conformity—helps to create a working system with clear, consistent expectations. There is a potential downside for learners, however, if conformity dominates the overarching expectations or spills into aspects of learning where flexible thinking is applicable and welcome. Creativity specialists and authors Scott Barry Kaufman and Carolyn Gregoire (2015) state:

> Children learn from an early age that a failure to conform can lead to disapproval from teachers and peers, which may motivate them to try to be like everyone else. . . . In schools, the workplace, and society in general, failure to conform can lead to social rejection. (p. 176)

While *creativity* is not synonymous with *nonconformity* (a refusal to comply with established customs, beliefs, behaviors, and so on), there *is* an element of breaking with the established norms in order to be inventive. Would an English teacher see a future e. e. cummings (who only used lowercase letters) as imaginative or uninformed or noncompliant? Would a fifth-grade teacher view the spontaneous comedic out-bursts of comedian Robin Williams as creative, or disruptive and disobedient? Would an art teacher see a future Picasso (who painted disjointed and abstract images) as inventive or uncultivated? Maybe today's teachers would view the learner as creative, given that those paths have already been paved—but what about altered paths for which there is no current experience or social acceptance? In one of the case studies from Robinson's (2009) book *The Element*, a high school art student poured his tainted paint brush water over the top of his art project, which the teacher had deemed finished prior to the dousing. Reportedly, she viewed his efforts as noncon-formist, not creative. His efforts to play with art were intentional, but the teacher did not appreciate his choice. Sadly, examples such as this are replicated far too often in classrooms today.

Creative thinking requires breaking with convention and seeing things through multiple lenses and in nontraditional ways, as Kaufman and Gregoire (2015) note:

> Defying the crowd takes courage, and there is no doubt that it's easier and more comfortable to follow popular opinion. . . . The most original contributions in any field are unlikely to result from efforts to please the crowd. (p. 167)

As teachers increasingly shift their thinking to understand that nonconformity can unleash creativity, they must prepare themselves to instruct, assess, and measure creative thinking.

Embracing Productive Failure

Productive failure is a necessary element in the creative process. Innovation often involves experimentation, and experiments are never perfect from the launch; rather, they improve over time after revisions because learning results from the failed attempts. Kaufman and Gregoire (2015) note that the output from even the most creative geniuses reveals far more false starts and failures than final great works, stat-ing, "While consistency may be the key to expertise, the secret to creative greatness appears to be doing things differently—even when that means failing" (p. 178). After all, before there can be a *breakthrough* moment, there has to be a block broken. Being stumped is a natural part of facing truly provocative challenges.

Can schools tolerate productive failure? In his 2006 TED Talk, Robinson high-lights the importance of mistake making and risk taking as part of the creative pro-cess, but points out that learners become "frightened of being wrong" in a system that rewards right answers. And if teachers score all aspects of a learner's work—from mis-take making during the practicing phases (homework, for example) to nonworking but innovative products that are *close* to answers but had to be turned in by a specific deadline—and those scores are ultimately included in the final grades, then it is not safe for students to learn from failure without penalty. If schools choose to teach creativity, educators will have to navigate the tumultuous waters of grading without punishing learner risk taking and potential failure.

Understanding the Multifacets of Creativity

Creativity will look different from one discipline to the next. People most often affiliate creativity with aesthetics, like an artistic painting, a magnificent concerto, or a captivating dance. Sawyer (2006) highlights the notion that the western hemisphere is biased toward the products and processes of fine arts, valuing appreciative value over functional value, but notes the sciences involve creativity as well. Sciences (chemistry, physics, technology, mathematics, business, and so on) comprise more than passive observation, methodical experimentation, and logical problem solving. Unlike the arts, Sawyer (2006) insists, creativity in the sciences doesn't involve "bursts of genius" as much as it involves "intensive social interaction" (pp. 269–270). Sawyer (2006) adds, "Top scientists realize that scientific creativity depends on conversations, and they do all that they can to create more collaborative connections" with both like-minded *and* "radically different" minded disciplines (p. 276). Creativity involves lateral (interdisciplinary) perspectives and skills and the emerging collective insights that result from blending them.

Removing Bias

It takes many reviewers, often over an extended period of time and within a given context, to determine whether or not something is truly creative. A single source should never determine the value of a work. According to Sawyer (2006):

> Science succeeds only because of the active involvement of a national network of critical review by journal editors, grant reviewers, and department chairs. The art world also requires that distinctions be made, that criteria be applied, and that selection and evaluation take place. (p. 22)

Many student inventors create products that can be used outside the school walls, but how is a teacher—without input from experts in the relevant industries—supposed to know if those products are, in fact, viable? Seeking outside perspectives isn't always feasible.

Still, evaluating creativity should never be left up to one person's individual preferences, even if that person is a teacher. In order to create a criterion-based and equitable approach to scoring the creative process, educators will want to develop shared knowledge of creative thinking as a process; common criteria and levels of proficiency to assess the process; and universally agreed-on tools to engage in the work. Tremendous harm can be done when a single teacher calls a learner (or a learner's work) uncreative based solely on his or her personal preference. Leaving the evaluation of creativity to one person's interpretation increases bias and ultimately inhibits creativity.

It's equally important to engage learners in self-assessing their own creative processes and products and seeking outside feedback to support their efforts. This too can remove the bias of a single-point evaluation. What's most important when teaching creativity is helping learners understand their own preferences and processes, and the best ways to continually hone their creative abilities.

Addressing Value and Plausibility

The value-added feature of creativity poses an almost insurmountable challenge for teachers when determining whether or not learners' work is creative. More often than not, discovering the *value* of something can only be through practical applications outside the classroom and after considerable time has passed, revealing either a broad appreciation or a sustainable application in a given industry.

Potential inaccuracies in prematurely scoring a product or solution as uncreative can severely inhibit a learner's willingness to continue refining his or her creative abilities. There are far too many examples of famous scientists, artists, musicians, entrepreneurs, and actors judged as uncreative during school but eventually recognized as wildly creative outside school. Robinson (2009) highlights story after story of modern creative geniuses who did not fare well in the traditional education system, concluding:

> Too many graduate or leave early, unsure of their real talents and unsure of what direction to take next. Too many feel that what they are good at isn't valued by schools. Too many think they aren't good at anything. (p. 36)

This underscores the importance of attending to how educators assess creativity so that learners are not unintentionally shut down in the learning process.

In addition, educators must consider age-appropriateness when determining value and plausibility as metrics for creativity. Experts note that creativity is based on a deep foundational knowledge (Sawyer, 2006) and the ability to *implement* the invention or solution, making it virtually impossible for very young children to produce solutions or products likely to have sustainability outside school. Instead, teachers would be wise to assess a learner's creative process or ability to think outside the box. Learners of all ages can engage in the creative process, document their efforts, note areas of strength and those needing improvement, and continually refine their creative thinking. Teachers can observe, nurture, and assess these aspects of creativity in a manner that encourages learners to continue developing their creative capacity.

Teaching the Creative Process

It's never fair to assess something not taught, so if they assess the creative process, teachers must provide explicit instruction. Hattie (2009) notes, "Creativity programs that include explicit instruction are most successful" (p. 159). Moreover, the best explicit instruction options include efforts to develop thinking strategies and, as a direct result, instruction in the creative process has a positive impact on overall learners' achievement (Hattie, 2009).

Fortunately, 2018 national, local, and provincial standards' levels—for example, Common Core State Standards; state standards; Next Generation Science Standards; College, Career, and Civic Life Framework for Social Studies State Standards; Career and Technical Education Standards; National Physical Education Standards; and so on—offer teachers a multitude of options to teach the creative process across disciplines and content within disciplines. The following general expectations appear in many different actual standards, and each expectation provides rich options for the creative process in schools.

- Create and activate a plan to modify the materials before you.

- Use the internet and technology-based tools to produce, publish, and update individual or shared writing products.

- Establish an engaging context and point of view that both captivate attention and orient the reader.

- Use visual displays such as drawings, media clips, photos, or interesting data displays as appropriate to enhance and clarify ideas, thoughts, and feelings.

- Create engaging audio or video recordings of stories or poems that enhance meaning through voice and nonverbals.

- Construct a function to model a linear relationship between two quantities.

- Employ many different tools and methods to create formal geometric constructions.

- Synthesize information from a range of sources (for example, texts, experiments, or simulations) into a coherent understanding of a process, phenomenon, or concept, resolving conflicting information when possible.

- Demonstrate the concepts, principles, strategies, and tactics related to movement and performance.

- Design a simple machine using only the materials before you.

- Design and conduct a scientific investigation for a known or yet-unexplained scientific phenomenon.

- Build a simple machine that magnifies or changes the direction of a force.

- Create an application for a phone or a program for a computer to address a current challenge you, your family, or your peers face.

- Design the model for a green home.

While these expectations might sound like advanced-level work, many of them are already happening in the elementary grades. Consider, for example, a kindergarten class in which learners work in teams to plan and alter a given set of items representing gas, liquid, and solid matter (like ice cream, root beer, and cookies), or a first- and second-grade classroom in which learners make simple machines (like levers, pulleys, and pinewood derby cars). Young inventors are winning science fairs and earning patents with concepts and products that industries outside schools embrace. For example, six-year-old Kelly Reinhart created a system for kids to easily transport their video games; eight-year-old Abbey Fleck created a hanging system for cooking bacon without excess fat surrounding it; and ten-year-old Richie Stachowski created an underwater talkie for communicating with someone while submerged, to name just a few examples (Dahl, 2013). With creativity, anything is possible, and opportunities for creativity abound within today's standards.

There are many different models regarding the type and number of phases in creative thinking, but in general, there is some basic agreement on a few of the key phases. Teaching creative thinking means exposing students to the five phases of the creative process: (1) preparation, (2) incubation, (3) illumination, (4) verification, and (5) implementation (modified from the works of Runco, 2007, 2014; Sawyer, 2006; and Wallas, 2014). For each phase, learners must receive direct instruction, follow-up feedback, and ongoing support. Learners need to understand each phase, what questions might be involved, and guidance into exploring and ultimately discovering their own personal strengths or preferences in each phase. Table 5.1 (pages 154–156) provides a framework for understanding the type of thinking learners will need to go through the instruction of the five phases of the creative process.

Table 5.1: Instructional Questions for Teaching the Creative Process

Phase Defined	Questions to Lead the Process	Questions to Guide Learners' Self-Discovery
Preparation: Identifying an area of curiosity or a problem for further investigation	• What are your passions? • What's interesting to you? • What are the small (or big) things you wish you could fix for yourself or your loved ones? • What natural phenomena need more study or explanation? • What message would you like to send to the world? • What legacy would you like to leave behind?	• What specific strategies did you use while preparing? • What was hard and easy to do? • What helped you the most? • What did you do to slow your own process? What stopped you from moving forward? • How could you improve your efforts in this phase? • What have you learned about yourself?
Incubation: Pondering ideas by exploring intuition, synthesizing concepts, imagining possibilities, and preliminarily constructing possible products, processes, or solutions	• What are you noticing? • What's interesting about that? • What would happen if . . .? • If there were no hurdles, what could you do? • What's a radically different way of looking at that? • How many possibilities can you consider? • How many different connections can you make? • What is your intuition telling you?	• What specific strategies did you use while pondering your ideas? • What tools or templates helped you? • When did you have your best thoughts? What was the time of day or the activities you were engaged in or the location or setting when you could think best? • Did daydreaming or playing help you at all? • Did you procrastinate at all? If you did, why? Did it help? • How could you improve your efforts in this phase? • What have you learned about yourself?

Phase Defined	Questions to Lead the Process	Questions to Guide Learners' Self-Discovery
Illumination: Developing realizations, insights, epiphanies, and inspiration	• What's captivating about that? • What do you see that others might not? • What did you learn that others might not know yet? • How might what you understand now make the world a better place for others? • What odd combinations just might work?	• What specific strategies did you use while becoming inspired or developing your insights? • Were you aware of a defining moment when you knew what you needed to do next? • If you didn't have a defining moment, how did you make decisions about the best ways to proceed? • What criteria were you using to determine your next steps? • How could you improve your efforts in this phase? • What have you learned about yourself?

Verification: Seeking feedback and validation during the formative phase for whether or not potential solutions are worth pursuing; self-assessing; and making personal decisions regarding final steps	• What are your criteria for quality?
	• Where would feedback be most helpful to you?
	  • On one criterion?
	  • On a single part of the project?
	  • On the whole thing?
	• Will others appreciate this work or idea?
	• Whom can you ask?
	  • Whom do you trust to help you?
	  • Who might know the most about this?
	• How can you get a range of perspectives so you're prepared for the final stage?
	• What will you do with feedback you don't like? How can you make sure you get some feedback that forces you to examine your work carefully?
		• What specific strategies did you use while verifying your ideas?
		• Did you get enough feedback?
		• Was the feedback you received helpful?
		• How are you responding to positive feedback? To negative feedback?
		• What are you doing with the feedback you don't appreciate? Is your thought process helpful in that moment?
		• Were you accurate in your self-assessment, or were you too hard or easy on yourself? How will you know?
		• Are you clear about your next steps?
		• How could you improve your efforts in this phase?
		• What have you learned about yourself?

continued →

Phase Defined	Questions to Lead the Process	Questions to Guide Learners' Self-Discovery
Implementation: Moving idea from concept to reality by producing the product, process, or solution to share with others	• Is it finished? • Is it working? Or is it pleasing? • Are you ready to share it? • Are others appreciating it? Using it? Understanding it? • How do you feel about it? • What makes you proud of it? • Even though you're done, what might you have done differently in hindsight? • What have you learned through this process? • What comes next? Where do you begin again?	• What specific strategies or actions did you employ while finishing? • What was hard and easy to do? • What (or who) helped you the most? • What did you do that slowed your own process? What stopped you from moving forward? • How could you improve your efforts in this phase? • What have you learned about yourself?

*Visit **go.SolutionTree.com/assessment** for a free reproducible version of this table.*

Done well, instruction in the creative process helps learners recognize, understand, and appreciate their unique style and assets when engaged in the creative process. Understanding their own unique creative process will help learners better navigate their world.

Assessing Creative Thinking

When assessing creativity, it's important to begin with the culminating task, or summative assessment, in mind. This task always informs the necessary content, skills, and instruction learners need to be successful. But, when the task involves the creative process, it's even more important to begin the design early in the unit planning phase, as there are always challenges.

First, when assessing creative thinking, avoid the following common errors.

- Failing to teach creativity first, but requiring it of the learners in the task

- Using creativity only as an indicator that separates the best from the rest (for example, educators settle the difference between a proficiency score of 3 and 4 by using the degree of creativity as the defining attribute)

- Excluding creativity as a specific feature in the assessment task design, but including it in the criteria or measurement tools to determine quality

- Allowing a biased view of creativity by using descriptors such as *unique* or *masterful* that have not been clearly defined, outlined in advance, or consistently applied across the staff

- Evaluating the product rather than the process of creative thinking

Planning the assessment task in advance can help teachers avoid these common pitfalls when working with creativity.

Second, assessment tasks will not provoke creative responses if the task itself is not compelling or provocative. Additionally, a classroom task or project teachers use to assess the creative process must be designed with attention to the broader context of the work. Teachers must address the following five design considerations for an assessment to readily lend itself to creative work on behalf of students.

1. A solid knowledge base
2. Ample time
3. Provocative challenges
4. Lateral thinking or sharing
5. Verification options

If teachers ignore these considerations when designing creative-thinking tasks, success will likely be haphazard and depend largely on the natural skills or talents of some learners.

A Solid Knowledge Base

In general, researchers find that true creativity happens *after* one learns the necessary knowledge and the mind wanders and plays with the ideas and processes (Paul & Kaufman, 2014; Sawyer, 2006). (In this case, skills are required as part of the knowledge base.) This does not mean learning wouldn't occur throughout the creative task, especially if the task itself is designed to elicit thinking. It does mean, however, that learners should not enter the task without the necessary knowledge and skills to successfully navigate the work at hand.

This implies that assessments requiring creativity happen after a learner masters the knowledge and skills. Such assessments are best positioned after several units of study so learners can integrate multiple skills or more information to accomplish the task. In this case, teachers would need to conduct preassessments in order to certify a level of readiness in both the required knowledge and skills so learners could be freed up to work creatively with the task at hand. In other words, assessments aimed at determining if the knowledge base is solid should *not* seek to assess creativity simultaneously.

The idea that learners require a solid knowledge foundation also highlights their need to be aware of developmental appropriateness. There is an increase in both depth of knowledge and complexity of skills proportional with student age and readiness. Young learners with limited domain knowledge and skills would likely struggle to produce something of added value or plausible to society at large.

Ample Time

Creativity takes time. Time for revision, time for daydreaming, time for additional research, time to work through frustrations, time to explore and revise insights, time for lateral sharing, time for productive failure, time for critical review and polishing, and time for implementation. Highly creative works are often completed and then revised—sometimes repeatedly—before achieving a truly innovative insight or solution. Assessments that require creativity must allow sufficient time for learners to engage fully in the process, especially if teachers are assessing the *process*.

The early phases of the creative process—preparation, incubation, and illumination—require considerable time *and* a relaxed state of mind. Intense focus allows learners to accomplish something, but it doesn't free up the mental space required for random thoughts to percolate. Sawyer (2006) notes that such work rests just below the level of intentional focus. During the early incubation phases, Sawyer (2006) says, "Mental elements combine and insight occurs when certain combinations emerge into consciousness" (pp. 61–62). The subconscious brain is a big part of the creative process. It is free to wander, play, or daydream when someone is engaged in a more relaxed mode like when listening to music, going on a walk, or engaging in daily chores like gardening, making a meal, or taking a shower (Sawyer, 2006).

When people are in a relaxed state, their attention is freed up so they can focus inward. At that point, their stream of consciousness can begin to make interesting connections and consider remote possibilities. According to scientists, the brain is highly active during passive rest or when a person is looking inward (Kaufman, 2013). This activity is different from what people require for reasoning or executive function. When people are in a relaxed space, insights can occur. It's necessary for teachers to create this required time and space for learners to experience relaxed thinking and much-desired epiphanies.

Being creative at a moment's notice, on the other hand, is difficult. Demanding an insight can, ironically, prohibit insight from occurring; learners often need time and space to be creative. Therefore, it would be thoughtful for teachers to share the final creative task with learners in advance of instruction, giving them the rationale for their efforts, the big picture of what they are trying to accomplish in the long run, and the awareness of what to master during the instructional phases. This way, learners can be successful doing a task that might be weeks ahead of their current situation.

Provocative Challenges

Dull or meaningless challenges most often lead to dull and meaningless responses. In order to inspire creativity, teachers must first offer a provocative challenge. Too often, teachers give learners questions, prompts, or tasks which already have concrete answers. The purpose of such work involves getting learners to understand *what is*, but it completely removes the joy of discovering *what could be*. Alarming research highlights the need for re-engaging students: "Almost 50% of high school dropouts leave because school is not interesting for them, and nearly 70% say they are not motivated to work hard" (Bridgeland, DiIulio, & Morison, 2006, as cited in Newmann et al., 2016, p. 20). Uninspiring work leads to unimaginative and disengaged learners. Learners need more engaging experiences not only to keep them in school but also to inspire and excite them while in school.

Newmann et al.'s (2016) criteria for the Authentic Intellectual Work framework offer insight into what it takes to create a provocative challenge:

> When students have opportunities to construct knowledge rather than only reproduce what they have been given, to understand topics in depth instead of only superficially, to express themselves by explaining their ideas, and to study topics that have some significance beyond the classroom, they are more likely to care about and be interested in learning and willing to devote the serious effort that learning requires. (p. 20)

All three of their criteria for the framework—construction of knowledge, disciplined inquiry, and value beyond school (see chapter 1, page 15)—provide the foundation for meaningful tasks. Creativity cannot occur in a structure that demands single responses predicated on "right" answers. Instead, creativity requires larger tasks designed for multifaceted authentic challenges with multiple plausible solutions; solutions which experts in the field may not widely recognize.

Authentic experiences include genuine challenges or, in some cases, structured constraints. Challenges and constraints can enhance creativity because parameters naturally force individuals to think outside the box. Challenges often show up in open-ended, unsolved complex problems in the form of questions, such as "In what ways can we revitalize our school community?" One must consider the broader financial, geographical, political, social, and aesthetic realities of the community as well as local policies, procedures, schedules, and available resources, to answer this question.

Surprisingly, highly creative tasks often impose structured constraints. In the arts, for example, learners strive to produce work that meets predetermined criteria or requirements natural to the medium. Each of the following creative task examples holds a host of constraints.

- Write different types of poetry (haiku, sonnet, limerick).
- Write a dystopian short story.
- Perform a solo during a jazz performance.
- Compose and perform a rap.
- Create an expressionist painting.
- Build a mandala.
- Write and perform a poetry slam.
- Improvise a scene.
- Design an architectural blueprint.
- Design and conduct a scientific investigation.

Each of the previous examples involves guidelines, structures, or algorithms that form the constraints. People are most creative when faced with given constraints or structured challenges (Sawyer, 2006). Structure offers challenge, and challenge can motivate and inspire learners to find perfect options. Sawyer (2006) suggests that constraints and challenges within a body of knowledge are like the language of the domain, stating, "It's impossible to communicate without sharing a language. In the same way, it's impossible to create anything without the shared conventions of the domain" (p. 137). Creators always need working parameters.

If teachers require creativity, then the assessments must offer provocative challenges—authentic situations that are multifaceted, filled with credible constraints, and worthy of answering in service of a greater cause—one that leads to original thinking and even passion for the pursuit of the task.

Lateral Thinking or Sharing

Lateral means "on the side" and usually references equivalency. Because creativity often involves blending concepts—whether those concepts are of a similar platform within a discipline or of diverse platforms from different but related disciplines—lateral thinking is involved. Sometimes lateral work comes from a single creator (lateral thinking) or from across a group of individuals who share their individual expertise (lateral sharing). Creative individuals are masterful at lateral thinking. Kaufman and Gregoire (2015) state:

> Creative people are hubs of diverse interests, influences, behaviors, qualities, and ideas—and through their work, they find a way to bring these many disparate elements together. This is one of the reasons why creativity feels so ineffable—it is so many different things at the same time! (p. xx)

Naturally creative people draw from their many diverse interests to make their own horizontal connections. In classrooms, however, teachers should provide instruction in the areas of synthesis and divergent thinking to facilitate deliberate efforts for making lateral connections. Breakthrough thinking often occurs when concepts begin to merge.

Because lateral sharing is significant to facilitate the ability of learners to notice new connections and reframe a concept otherwise easily overlooked, it would be helpful if classroom assessments for creativity involve opportunities for such sharing. The multiple perspectives of many contributors, often from different lenses or categories of understanding, support the process. This is why experts like scientists, program designers, architects, and musicians (to name a few) usually work in common areas like laboratories and studios (Sawyer, 2006). Classroom creativity can increase with the informal and formal sharing of ideas.

Verification Options

It's natural to seek feedback when creating something new. Creators of all ages are curious to know if their ideas will work or if others will appreciate their products, performances, or solutions. *Verification* is about making sure something will work, a problem is solved, or a performance or product is appreciated for its communicated themes or messages. Soliciting verification before launching a solution can help learners smooth out the kinks in advance.

People are more creative when they examine ideas with a critical eye for review and refinement (Catmull, 2014; Sawyer, 2006). As people share ideas laterally and then challenge each other's assumptions and designs, they generate far more creative alternatives than by accepting an idea on a brainstormed list and acting on it without critical review. Highly inventive companies recognized for their creative products often share stories of how they tap into *all* viewpoints in the organization to address hurdles and enhance the creative process (Catmull, 2014).

It's important to note that the learner is the one eliciting and owning the feedback and verification process. In other words, teachers are not the ones verifying whether or not a creative project will be workable or valued. Learners should be encouraged to gather multiple data points of feedback from multiple groups of people—like teachers, classmates, and even stakeholders outside the school, such as family members or neighbors. As learners age, they can reach out to experts in a field as well. Teachers should encourage learners to gather positive and growth-oriented feedback and then teach them how to navigate feedback they do not like. How do learners accept negative feedback to encourage growth, and at what point can or should they ignore it? In the end, the creator is always the final decision maker, but the creator must also explain or justify his or her decisions.

Teachers should also encourage learners to experiment with ideas in different ways, gathering additional points of feedback with each variation or finding. Teachers can support all of these kinds of processes by providing learners with tools to document their progress, record their feedback, and reveal the adjustments when attempting future efforts. It's also helpful for teachers to provide learners with protocols and quality criteria to exchange feedback with others so they understand how to send and receive feedback in ways that enhance the experience. Feedback that devastates—even when it comes from another learner or a stakeholder outside the school—can obliterate a teacher's best efforts to keep learners engaged in the creative process.

Measuring Creative Thinking

Any assessment task a teacher assigns requires some level of teacher evaluation or learner self-reflection in response to the work produced. When learners are involved in assessing creativity, the goal behind the self-assessment and reflection strategies is to build a sense of hope and efficacy for learners and direct their primary attention to understanding and improving the creative-thinking process. In the grand scheme, the idea is to allow learners to improve over time and help them recognize themselves as creatively capable individuals.

Teachers are always tasked with measuring performance. The goal of teacher evaluation is to ascertain the degree of proficiency each student achieves relative to the learning intentions. In the realm of creativity, however, the work is a little different because it would be easy to eradicate a learner's sense of hope or efficacy in the creative process with evaluation marks that judge the quality of the person or the final outcome the learner produces. As outlined earlier in this chapter, *value* and *plausibility* are criteria that may not be immediately visible and are often domain-specific to a work world that extends beyond a teacher's experience within the school walls. It's more prudent for the learner to evaluate his or her own final product.

When teachers assess creative tasks, they can assess the learner's engagement in the creative process. The teacher can assess the final product, performance, or solution using rubrics specific to the knowledge and skills involved in the content-specific task, but teachers would not want to score the degree of creativity the learner achieved. So, for example, if a teacher tasks a learner with writing a dystopian story, the learner's final scores could reflect all of the following.

- The level of proficiency the learner demonstrated with each stage of the creative process

- How well the learner navigated the skills of narrative writing, using the predetermined narrative writing rubric in which the criteria are clearly identified

- How well the learner understood the dystopian medium and adhered to the appropriate constraints, using the predetermined dystopian rubric or scale

- How well the learner performed relative to predetermined relevant rubrics relating to any other specific feature intended to assess a learner's level of proficiency on the given task (for example, a learner's understanding of the systems of a repressive society)

What teachers should *avoid* assessing is how creative the final product is. As awkward as that might feel in execution, the cost of scoring creativity is too grave and the potential for inaccuracies is too great to justify the effort. In some circumstances, however, it would be appropriate to invite learners to reflect on their own proficiency as creative thinkers; such reflection on their final products can be leveraged to encourage continued exploration and growth in creativity.

Tools for Learner Reflection

Oftentimes, learners think creativity is reserved for an elite few. They don't even realize they have creative potential. Likewise, beginning the process of trying to find the original ideas frustrates them. Creative thinking is slow and sometimes tedious work, and when under pressure it can be easy to see more of what's *impossible* than what's actually *possible*.

Figure 5.1 (page 164) shows a self-reflection template, which can help learners understand their preferred modes of creating.

Getting to Know the Creative in Me: A Self Survey

Check the box of the one that *best* describes you as a creative person. After you select it, give practical examples or evidence of why that description is true.

☐ I am an innovator. I take risks and create something very unique.

☐ I am a synthesizer. I blend lots of concepts together from lots of different fields to create something new.

☐ I am a reproducer or modifier. I improve on other people's ideas.

☐ I am a practicalizer. I make random or abstract ideas practical for everyone to see or use.

☐ I am a dreamer. I have lots of great ideas, but I don't know how to put them into practice or make them real.

I believe I am a _____ (fill in the title you selected) because the following examples help shape my thinking:

My **strengths** as a creative thinker:	My **opportunities to improve** as a creative thinker:

Figure 5.1: *Self-reflection template to identify a learner's preferred modes of creating.*

*Visit **go.SolutionTree.com/assessment** for a free reproducible version of this figure.*

Each of the labels (reproducer, innovator, and so on) offers a version of creativity, and it's important for learners to realize they are likely more than one in their everyday lives. Teachers need to modify these terms (with fewer prompts) for younger learners. Sample prompts for younger learners might include the following.

- I am a **fixer**. I make stuff better.

- I am a **creator**. I like to start new ideas.

- I am a **blender**. I like to put lots of different things together to make a new thing.

- I am a **dreamer**. I have lots of great ideas, but I don't know how to make them real.

Teachers can ask elementary learners the same follow-up reflection questions as secondary learners with, as always, age-appropriate language. No matter the questions, the goal is to have learners of all ages reflect on the ways they are naturally creative.

It's equally important to acknowledge that mental blocks—frustrating periods of time when the ideas aren't flowing or solutions are beyond the creator's grasp—naturally emerge during the creative process. When learners understand what is blocking them, they can do a better job of monitoring it and finding strategies to get past the blocks. Figure 5.2 (page 166) offers a reflection tool to help learners identify some of their own roadblocks in the creative-thinking process.

Figures 5.1 (page 164) and 5.2 help learners identify themselves as creative—or identify their potential to become creative through their own actions—by highlighting their strengths and barriers as they approach the idea of creativity.

Once learners immerse themselves in the work of creativity, it's important for them to remain attentive to their creative-thinking process. Learners can use figures 5.3 (page 167) and 5.4 (page 168) to help self-monitor their efforts on each step of their creative journey. Figure 5.3 offers a secondary example, and figure 5.4 provides an elementary option. In each example, it's helpful if learners offer thoughts about both their strengths and their opportunities to improve in each part of the creative process.

Sometimes it helps to offer a more focused opportunity to self-assess the creative process using a rubric with clear criteria and levels of proficiency. Figure 5.5 (pages 169–170) offers a rubric for self-assessing the creative process closely aligned with the one teachers use for the same purpose (see figure 5.7, pages 173–174). Teachers should change the language to support the work of younger learners assessing their creative process.

I Try to Be Creative, But . . .

Removing the Blocks That Hinder Me

If I knew I couldn't fail, I would create _____.

Even if I couldn't fail, what sometimes holds me back? _____

How do I sometimes stop my own creative process with my thoughts? Select from the following sentences what you have heard yourself say in the past. Then, try to create alternative messages that might open up your creative thinking.

Self-Talk About Me		
	What if people think I'm stupid?	If I want to be more creative, what messages must I say to myself instead?
	I'm not creative or innovative.	
	I'm better off if I play it safe.	
	I'm not that interesting.	
	I could never do that!	
Preferences to Be Practical		
	It's already working. Why fix it?	What's the worst that could happen if I were less practical? How could I block my practicality from inhibiting my creativity?
	I've never done it that way before.	
	I tried it before, and it didn't work.	
	Why reinvent the wheel?	
	There's no need to change.	
Preferences to Be Critical		
	Here's why that idea won't work.	How can I become more of a daydreamer and risk taker?
	Others won't appreciate that idea.	
	It's not possible because . . .	
	As I see it, there are many problems with this because . . .	

Figure 5.2: *Self-reflection tool to identify roadblocks to creative thinking.*

Visit **go.SolutionTree.com/assessment** *for a free reproducible version of this figure.*

My Strengths		My Opportunities to Improve
	Preparation I was truly curious about something that required further investigation.	
	Incubation I played with a lot of ideas, even from different areas of study. I blended ideas, imagined new possibilities, and constructed possibilities.	
	Illumination As I played with my ideas, I had new insights or aha moments sparked excitement. I was confident my ideas were original and would be exciting to others too.	
	Verification I tested my ideas to make sure they were plausible or pleasing to others. I gathered feedback because I wanted to know what wouldn't work as much as what would work. I listened to feedback when I thought it was relevant and made focused revisions as needed so I could produce an excellent product, performance, or solution.	
	Implementation I completed my task and brought my project to life. I successfully moved it from an idea to a reality.	

Figure 5.3: Single-point self-reflection form for analyzing the creative process.

*Visit **go.SolutionTree.com/assessment** for a free reproducible version of this figure.*

Things I Do Well		Things I Could Do Better
	Preparation I had a very interesting question, and I wanted to find the answer.	
	Incubation I found many different ways to answer my question.	
	Illumination I had a spark or found a new way of thinking about my question.	
	Evaluation I asked for feedback, and others thought my ideas would work.	
	Implementation I solved the problem or created something new with my idea.	

Figure 5.4: *An elementary single-point self-reflection form for the creative process.*

*Visit **go.SolutionTree.com/assessment** for a free reproducible version of this figure.*

Because learners are developing their creative capacity, it's most important for them to monitor their creative process so they continue to understand, explore, and refine it even after they graduate.

Of course, learners naturally want to self-evaluate the fruits of their labor by assessing their final product, performance, or solution. Figure 5.6 (page 171) offers a rubric for learners to assess their final projects; while originality would apply to both the sciences and the arts, the criterion of *effectiveness* works better with creativity in the sciences while the criteria of *affect* or *appeal* work best with creativity in the arts. The criteria for the final results are different than the criteria for the creative process.

	Initiating	Developing	Achieving	Advancing
Preparation Prepares by identifying an area of curiosity for further investigation	I used one of the teacher-created problems or themes.	I took one of the teacher-offered problems or themes, but I changed it so it was a little different and matched more closely to something I was interested in.	I picked an area of great curiosity for me because I wanted to explore that problem or theme to see if I could find a way to address it.	I picked an area of great curiosity for me. I have always been curious about my topic, and I'm already excited about a plan for many different places to go to deepen my knowledge on the subject. I really believe I can find a way to address it.
Incubation Incubates ideas by synthesizing, imagining, and constructing possibilities	I used the teacher-created materials and filled in all details when asked.	I gathered a lot of additional information, but I was unable to connect the very different ideas. Once I gathered everything, I was a little overwhelmed and had trouble figuring out my next step.	I gathered lots of relevant and accurate materials and information and organized things into categories so I could begin making meaningful connections. I used charts and graphs to show how ideas related. I made some interesting connections between very different ideas.	I gathered lots of relevant and accurate materials and information and organized things into categories so I could begin making meaningful connections. I used charts and graphs to show related ideas. I moved ideas around into different categories and played with multiple interesting connections between very different ideas. I have lots of new possibilities emerging at this point.

continued ▸

Figure 5.5: Self-assessment form for the creative process.

Illumination Illuminates ideas with insights or epiphanies	I found and used a theme or solution I liked from another source. I had ideas, but didn't really create them.	My ideas all seemed to fit together well so my conclusion was very logical and maybe even a little predictable.	I was passionate and committed in my pursuit. I tried lots of strategies and different ways of thinking about things. I let my imagination run wild, and I had lots of really interesting ideas start to emerge. I had an aha moment that was pretty exciting.	I was passionate and I let my imagination run wild, and I had lots of really interesting ideas start to emerge. I also considered the insights of others and played with trying to connect all of those ideas. I had a eureka moment, and am certain my idea is very original and will only continue to improve.
Verification Pursues input and feedback on efforts. Seeks to understand whether or not a potential solution is worth pursuing based on plausibility or appreciation from others	The teacher gave me feedback about my project, and I followed all of those recommendations to improve it.	I tried to get feedback from my teacher and my friends so I could determine if I had a workable project and followed their recommendations so I could make it better.	I tried to get lots of feedback, from my teacher, my peers, and even people outside school. I found people who liked and disliked my project and using all that information, I tried to make all the right improvements so I could make the best project imaginable. I kept trying until satisfied with my outcome.	I tried to get lots of feedback, from my teacher, my peers, and even people considered experts outside school. Once I made connections with those people, I returned a few different times to get their new perspective after each revision. I found people who liked and disliked my project and using all that information, I tried to make all the right improvements so I could make the best project imaginable. I am proud of the outcome.
Implementation Implements idea, moving it from a concept to a reality	I shared my project as a picture or model of what it could really be someday.	My project is not working or not polished quite yet.	My project is completed and perfected. I can display or use it successfully.	My project is completed but not perfected. I can display or use it successfully, but I have some ideas about improvements or next steps that I'd still like to try in the future.

*Visit **go.SolutionTree.com/assessment** for a free reproducible version of this figure.*

	Initiating	Developing	Achieving	Advancing
Originality	I had trouble finding something original.	I made some improvements to someone else's original work, or I had a very unique idea but I was unable to make it happen.	All (or significant parts) of my creation is unique. I found nothing else exactly like it.	My creation is so original that others expressed interest in using or having it for continual application outside school.
Effectiveness (Sciences)	My solution or invention is not working, and I'm not confident it ever will.	My solution or invention might work or solve the problem, but I would need more time to make more improvements.	My solution or invention works, and it solves the question I set out to solve.	Others will actually employ my solution or invention to solve the same kind of problem with a much broader audience over time.
Affect or Appeal (Arts)	My creation (product or performance) seemed to have little impact, and I'm not confident it ever would.	My creation (product or performance) did not elicit the response I was anticipating. I can see what I would need to do to improve it in the future.	My creation (product or performance) captured attention and elicited the appropriate responses. It was admired or appreciated.	My creation (product or performance) will be shared with a much broader audience over time.

Figure 5.6: *Self-assessment of creative thinking for a science or an art project.*

*Visit **go.SolutionTree.com/assessment** for a free reproducible version of this figure.*

Learners analyzing their own results should begin to understand the impact they are trying to have when they engage in creative thinking. Quality criteria help learners understand that creativity serves a purpose, and ultimately, learners should want their products to elicit an appropriate response or fill a specific application. While teachers will make final judgments regarding content or skill proficiency, it's important for learners to make the final judgment regarding their creativity. The responses learners receive will likely influence their analysis as they share their work.

Tools for Teacher Scoring

When assessing creative thinking, it's important to remember a well-known Elliott Eisner quote: "Not everything important is measurable and not everything measurable is important" (Robinson & Aronica, 2015, p. 171). Creative thinking is a robust process that demands teachers develop relationships and have both diagnostic and reflective conversations with learners. In an effort to support continued work on the creative process, teachers will benefit most by assessing the creative process, not the product. Determining a product is less than creative will ultimately hamper a learner's willingness to re-engage in the process. Worse, the learner will begin to see him- or herself as not creative.

It's fair to use the evidence learners create at each phase and engage them in reflective conversations about their experience at each phase. Learners can use notes from their formative phases, data from failed or successful experiments, feedback (video, audio, or written formats), key samples, or even entire work portfolios over time. Including such artifacts in a dialogue with learners allows teachers to use assessment *as* learning. Figure 5.7 (pages 173–174) offers a teacher rubric to score the creative process.

Sometimes the creative process happens in groups. In that case, teachers should include additional criteria to score collaborative creativity. If collaborative creativity is desired, then learners should experience instruction with samples of strong and weak work, as well as clear targets and quality criteria to inform their efforts in advance. Figure 5.8 (page 175) outlines a possible rubric teachers can use for assessing team creativity. Scores are for the team, so all members receive the same score.

In addition to scoring the creative process for individual learners and collaborative creativity for teams, teachers can score the finished products using the predetermined knowledge and skills learners demonstrate in the final task. Those scales and rubrics are content-specific, and learners should know them before the teacher assigns the culminating creative-thinking task.

	Initiating	Developing	Achieving	Advancing
Preparation Prepares by identifying an area of curiosity for further investigation	Accepts a teacher-provided area of curiosity or task	Redefines an area of curiosity or task with a personal contribution or clarifying attribute, providing some ownership to the work	Self-selects an area of curiosity for deeper investigation and clearly articulates the question and task	Self-selects an area of curiosity for deeper investigation and clearly articulates the question and task; provides an early indication of the direction for the pending investigation and highlights related areas of study and possible interconnections among concepts
Incubation Incubates ideas by synthesizing, imagining, and constructing possibilities	Uses information, ideas, or artifacts that are simplistic, isolated, or unrelated to answering the question	Uses selective but largely unexamined information, ideas, or artifacts in terms of accuracy, relevance, and completeness; has a plethora of options, but few strong leads for next steps	Gathers and organizes information, ideas, or artifacts and generates an array of ideas from a variety of areas; has evidence of draft linkages between diverse ideas and the topic; has arrows and charts to show emerging combinations for the formulating early ideas and categories; reveals plausible or interesting possibilities for consideration	Gathers and organizes information, ideas, or artifacts and generates an array of ideas from a variety of areas; has evidence of draft linkages between diverse ideas and the topic Offers early insights as ideas, and connections are moved around during the play stage Begins to provide multiple solutions

continued →

Figure 5.7: Creative process scoring rubric for teachers.

Illumination Illuminates ideas with insights or epiphanies	Provides a simplistic solution or idea attributed to an external source; shares little or no personal insight	Draws a logical and predictable idea or conclusion based on gathered and easily linked concepts	Exemplifies strong habits of divergent thinking, imagination, insight, and style; demonstrates passion and commitment to proceed with development	Develops an innovative, rare epiphany, reaching unique insights; demonstrates openness to new insights (for example, ideation is never done). Remains passionate about moving to implementation.
Verification Pursues input and feedback on efforts; seeks to understand whether or not potential solution is worth pursuing based on plausibility or appreciation from others	Relies on teacher feedback to discern viability of project; follows recommendations	Relies on teacher and peer feedback and uses provided self-assessment processes to discern viability of project; commits to improvement	Actively solicits feedback from peers, teachers, and individuals outside the classroom; purposefully seeks alternative perspectives to discern viability of project; engages in multiple revisions until satisfied	Actively solicits feedback from peers, teachers, experts in the field, and other individuals outside the classroom; purposefully seeks alternative perspectives to discern viability of project; continues gathering feedback as changes are made; engages in multiple revisions until proud of outcome
Implementation Implements idea, moving it from a concept to a reality	Primarily submits project in concept form	Submits project with the initial concepts moved to reality, but final version is unrefined	Submits project with the initial concepts moved into a highly functioning reality	Submits project with the initial concepts moved into a highly functioning reality and has already identified next steps for improvement or additional contributions

Visit go.SolutionTree.com/assessment for a free reproducible version of this figure.

Collaborative Creativity	Initiating	Developing	Achieving	Advancing
Teamwork	A team was formed, but individuals did their own work and submitted their individual parts. There was no blending of ideas or materials developed. There was no real discussion involving collaboration or learning, but parts of the task were completed.	The team functioned more like a group. All members participated, but they did not hold each other mutually accountable. Roles were assigned and rules were followed, but the workload was unbalanced and the team did not address the conflicts independently or in a healthy manner.	All members shared responsibility and held each other mutually accountable to accomplishing the task. The team was both healthy and productive, using rules, roles, and protocols to navigate emotions and resolve conflicts internally as they arose. Shared learning occurred.	Team processes and protocols were seamless. Members flowed in and out of key roles, capitalizing and blending on each other's strengths and challenges. Team maintained an organizational awareness and collaboratively engaged with other stakeholders or teams.
Lateral Sharing	All sharing was like-minded with little diversity in thinking across members of the group or change in status quo.	All members shared what they knew. The final concept reflected the beliefs and skills of a select few on the team.	All members contributed expertise, used resources to enhance expertise where they experienced gaps, and blended all their ideas in a manner that created new concepts.	Team strategically identified and accessed auxiliary members to support required domain knowledge and skills, integrating expertise into their emerging concepts.
Verification	Team relied on teacher feedback and defaulted to completing the task without desiring to improve it.	Team gathered some feedback, mostly internal, and focused on things they liked to hear. Improvements aligned with positive feedback.	The team gathered meaningful, constructive feedback from internal and external sources, tested its own procedures and hypotheses, and revised accordingly.	Team intentionally sought ways their creation would not work through feedback and experimentation and successfully resolved any hurdles.

Figure 5.8: *Collaborative creativity-scoring rubric for teachers.*

Visit **go.SolutionTree.com/assessment** *for a free reproducible version of this figure.*

Growing Creative Thinking

There is no doubt that creative thinking requires direct instruction and nurturing along the way. In order to teach creative thinking, educators will need to focus instruction on the processes and steps involved. Likewise, it is important to engage learners in monitoring their own thinking during the process, their personal preferences for how best to engage in each stage, and their self-assessment of their progress along the way.

There is also the need for educators to alter their own understanding of creative thinking if they are to support students in more fully developing it. It's important to understand, for example, that all disciplines provide space for creative thinking, though it doesn't look the same from one discipline to the next, and that all learners have the capacity to think creatively. Educators who wish to teach and even inspire creative thinking must themselves be creative as they generate tasks that provide multiple options or platforms and offer the space for many different right answers. To nurture creative thinking, educators will want to avoid judging how creative a student's response is and instead focus on how well the student navigated the phases of creative thinking.

Conclusion

The challenges of teaching and assessing creativity are many, but one of the biggest challenges involves arriving at a shared understanding and collective approach to handling creativity in classrooms. Creativity will remain a mysterious talent for the elite few unless educators can begin to understand it, define the process of it, and ultimately teach it. Such work is necessary before anyone can *require* creativity from learners. Before a teacher can assess a concept, it must be taught; before it can be taught, it must be understood. And, because it is a shared value, it is imperative for educators to develop a shared understanding and collective processes for teaching and assessing creativity.

Pause and Ponder

On your own or as part of a collaborative teacher team, consider the following reflective questions.

1. In what ways will the work of designing for and teaching creative thinking require you or your team to be creative? What have you learned from this chapter that will support you in doing so?

2. How can you infuse more creativity into your classroom instruction and assessments? Where does it fit naturally?

3. How have you or could you take advantage of your current curricular standards to intentionally develop learners as creative thinkers? How could you thread it through multiple units of study so learners can improve over time?

4. How comfortable are you or your team in accepting nonconformity? How will you nurture it? How will you recognize the difference between nonconformity and misbehavior or disobedience?

5. What can schools do—especially when it comes to grading—to allow for *productive failure* during the learning process? How should teachers handle productive failure so learners can fail and then ultimately succeed (though maybe not with the just completed task)?

6. What can schools do to promote improved collaborative learning and peer feedback in the service of teaching creative thinking?

7. How can you or your team remove as much bias as possible when scoring creative thinking? How will you develop a shared understanding of the creative process in specific domains, the criteria for quality to use when assessing it, and the best processes or tools to use when doing so?

8. How have you or could you develop a learner-centered approach to developing creative thinkers? What practices, processes, and tools allow learners to self- and peer assess their creative thinking skills and dispositions?

CHAPTER 6
COMMUNICATION

*Take advantage of every opportunity to practice your
communication skills so that when important occasions arise,
you will have the gift, the style, the sharpness, the clarity,
and the emotions to affect other people.*

—Jim Rohn

Communication has always been, and will most likely always remain, a critical competency, no matter the era, region, or quantity and quality of supportive technology. *Communication* involves sending and receiving messages. Though it sounds simple enough, what is said, how it is said, and how it is received will always pose challenges because people can quickly muddy messages through contexts beyond the communicator's control. The message communicator cannot always understand and, therefore, control the recipients' past experiences, state of mind, or ultimate interpretation of the message. Likewise, unforeseen or unknown contexts can also challenge the communicator—like the politics behind a relatively simple message at a given moment in time.

Strong communicators anticipate all potential interpretations of messages and then select the most appropriate means to generate the most favorable response from recipients. Likewise, strong interpreters of messages know how to read between the lines, check for nuances or inferences, consider the context and the subtext, scrutinize credibility, and then examine potential pros and cons before simply accepting a message at face value. Though many people excel at communication, there really is nothing simple about it.

While technology can ease the challenges of communication, in many ways it only exacerbates them. In the 21st century, for example, the combination of ubiquitous instant access, burgeoning digital applications, and undefined etiquette for digital citizenship creates the perfect storm for modern communications. Challenges such as the following are more the norm than the exception.

- Curt emails are misunderstood among colleagues.

- Angry anonymous respondents make snap judgments and post uninvited and insensitive responses to an online article or blog post.

- Bullying occurs over text messages.

- Wedding pictures are shared on Instagram before the bride and groom have a chance to share them first.

- Private moments in open spaces (for example, a marriage proposal in an airport) are shared on Snapchat without requesting permission.

- Artistic or athletic performances captured through video and audio recordings are posted without consent.

- Death announcements are posted on Facebook before all of the family members are personally notified.

- Quotes are taken out of context or credited to the wrong source and then mass-tweeted around the world.

- FaceTime and vehicle audio calls are broadcast to a wider public audience without the knowledge or permission of unsuspecting callers.

Important stories are "scrubbed" to hide truths, and falsities are broadcast to disparage truths. These few examples are unfortunately fairly common experiences.

Now, however, the unmonitored Wild West of digital communications has moved from merely disturbing families and communities to disrupting entire nations. In 2016, the United States public took to social media for the presidential election and mayhem ensued; the explosion of opinions and unfettered information, the discovery of digital bots to sway outcomes, and the consequent outcries of "fake news" or rebuttals of "alternative facts" made it even more clear that communication skills cannot be left to chance. It is imperative that teachers help learners unravel the messages they are sending and receiving.

In their report *Preparing 21st Century Students for a Global Society: An Educator's Guide to the "Four Cs,"* the National Education Association (n.d.) states, "Students must be able to effectively analyze and process the overwhelming amount of communication in their lives today. Which information sources are accurate? Which ones are not? How can they be used or leveraged effectively?" (p. 13). In other words, there is so much more to communication as a critical competency than simply sending and receiving messages. Communication also involves a tremendous amount of critical thinking if learners are to communicate effectively and accurately.

Defining Communication

The definition of *literacy*—the ability to read, write, interpret, and use language appropriately—has been expanded to include variations like informational literacy, global literacy, digital literacy, and media literacy. However, at its core, literacy was and will always be about *communicating*. The most basic forms of communication involve reading or viewing, writing, speaking, and listening. When combined and exhibited thoughtfully, these literacies define what it means to be educated. Educators already understand that literacy matters greatly to both an individual's future opportunities and to society's well-being. Fisher, Frey, and Hattie (2016) frame the significance of literacy as such:

1. Literacy is among the major antidotes for poverty.
2. Literacy makes your life better.
3. Literate people have more choices in their work and personal lives, leading to greater freedom.
4. Literacy is great at teaching you how to think successively—that is, making meaning one step at a time to then build a story.
5. Literacy soon becomes the currency of other learning. (p. 3)

Specifically, communication, whether it is verbal or nonverbal, means imparting thoughts, feelings, ideas, messages, questions, concerns, and solutions. Effective communication means imparting those same things in a healthy and productive manner that is readily consumable by the target audiences.

With the update of state and national standards in 2010, expectations for all communication strands increased in rigor and specificity. Teachers can often find the following statements sprinkled throughout their communication standards.

- Communicate coherent instructions.
- View and analyze the effectiveness of multimedia-based information.

- Express thoughts clearly.

- Crisply articulate opinions.

- Analyze and frame effective arguments.

- Maintain a sustained conversation with diverse audiences over a period of time.

- Motivate others through powerful speech.

While these statements are most closely aligned with the Common Core standards (Common Core State Standards Initiative, n.d.), they also appear in other state or provincial standards. The list of expectations regarding a learner's ability to communicate has advanced beyond simple clarity and accuracy, likely in response to the growing demands of a digitally connected and globally expanding world.

Considering Communication Now and Going Forward

Haven't educators *always* taught communication skills? Beyond increasing the expectations to argue effectively, what makes today's standards so different? Traditionally, the instruction and assessment of reading and writing were the sole responsibility of English and language arts teachers. After the turn of the 21st century, people began to understand and widely accept that communication includes a cross-curricular set of competencies that require specific attention from *all* disciplines. For example, the way a mathematician writes is different than the way a historian, scientist, or novelist writes. The introduction of the Common Core standards in 2010 designates communication as everyone's responsibility and, further, requires a more robust set of expectations for each of the core skills (Common Core State Standards Initiative, n.d.).

In other words, every discipline—from the arts to the sciences—is now tasked with helping learners improve their communication skills in discipline-specific ways. As a result, new curricula and how-to books are emerging for topics like *how to read like a historian, how to write like a scientist*, and so on. This poses as a challenge, as many educators are untrained in the discipline of English language arts and do not feel comfortable teaching reading or scoring writing.

Even English language arts teachers are struggling to change the paradigm of how they routinely operate. The traditional practices of focusing more on fiction than nonfiction, of using passages within the realm of the readers' comfort zones, and of teaching reading, writing, speaking, and listening skills in isolation will not work with current standards (Common Core State Standards Initiative, n.d.). Questioning strategies for learners after they read a passage also changed as comprehension is now measured on multiple levels: literal, structural, inferential, and interpretive (Fisher, Frey, & Hattie, 2016).

Challenges abound with teaching modern communication skills—not the least of which includes educators themselves learning to operate in a different way with the required instruction and assessments, and even with the literacies themselves. After all, in order for teachers to model the updated communication expectations, they must be active practitioners of them.

A Fresh Look at What to Communicate

Learning has always involved layers—from surface knowledge to application of skills to deep integration of content and skills. According to Fisher et al. (2016), these layers of learning also apply to literacy:

> Literacy learning goes part and parcel with the goals of deepening learning. Students need to talk about and listen to the ideas of others, especially those ideas that challenge their own current thinking. Students consolidate their conceptual understanding by writing. (pp. 76–77)

The integration of literacy skills contextualizes learning in authentic ways and paves the way for deep understanding.

Sophisticated teachers know how to integrate literacy pathways: they first use reading or viewing to introduce new information, then speaking and listening skills to make meaning regarding the new information, and, after multiple conversations to explore the many layers of any one message, they conclude by asking learners to produce the writing necessary to explain their thinking as a result of the new information. Internationally recognized education leader and author Heidi Hayes Jacobs (2014) suggests it is not enough to blend the literacies and call them 21st century teaching; she advocates for blending and aligning "these classical formats [informative, persuasive, and narrative] to new technologies, media, or methods of delivery" (p. 11).

As teachers prepare to teach the critical skill of communication to learners in a rapidly changing world, they must be cognizant of three major issues affecting the information that is communicated in modern times: (1) the type and quality of information, (2) the positive and negative aspects of argumentation in a technology-driven world, and (3) the need to embed communication within disciplinary thinking.

Information

Information is information—or is it? In an era of self-publishing, photoshopping, and opinion-based blogging, the vetting processes to ensure quality information have become somewhat moot. The rate of available information is exploding so quickly, people can hardly keep up with what's real and what's not. In response to the mushrooming chaos, a modern skill called *information literacy* has emerged. Information literacy is the ability to recognize when information is needed, locate relevant sources or sections within documents, evaluate the usefulness and accuracy of the information, and then use information effectively to address the specific need. Information literacy is as much about creating quality information as it is about eliminating the "noise" of excess, bias, or inaccurate information.

There seems to be a lot of noise. Montclair State University professor Alina Reznitskaya and The Ohio State University professor Ian A. G. Wilkinson (2017) state, "For its 2016 word of the year, Oxford Dictionaries selected *post-truth*, referring to the dangerous way in which many people have come to think about reality and the human capacity to know it" (p. 33). Sadly, if one were to get caught up in the realm of *post-truth*, *fake news*, or *alternative facts* bandied about in the media, it could quickly feel like all knowledge is biased and the search for truth is meaningless. More than ever before, learners need to understand what constitutes quality information, develop the skills to search for it, hone the skills to challenge it, and master the craft of providing it.

Argumentation

Arguments are discussions involving different points of view, and they happen all the time. The concept of argumentation isn't bad, though uncomfortable at times. Arguments are actually necessary. In their book *Crucial Confrontations*, authors Kerry Patterson, Joseph Grenny, Ron McMillan, and Al Switzler (2005) provide compelling evidence that when people don't challenge others, the consequences can be dire— even life-threatening. Likewise, arguments can lead to large-scale positive changes, such as generating freedoms for oppressed people or altering legislation to require seatbelts. Without arguments, nothing would really need to change, and people would be stuck blindly following someone else's will. Fortunately (and maybe unfortunately to some degree), argumentation is alive and well in the modern world of communication.

Social media has both invited and exacerbated the need for better argumentation skills. Stanford University professor emerita of English Andrea A. Lunsford and Department of Rhetoric and Writing at the University of Texas at Austin professor John J. Ruszkiewicz (2012) note that the digital age brings a daily dose of argumentation right to everyone's doorstep: "Anyone, anywhere, with access to a smart phone, can mount an argument that can circle the globe in seconds" (p. 5). Worse, the digital era allows anonymous immediate responses to unknown recipients, to the degree that knee-jerk reactions are cast without empathy.

Contrary to popular belief, argumentation isn't about winning versus losing. Some arguments are meant to inform or persuade. Some are meant to invite further involvement or exploration, and still others are framed for the sole purpose of finding common ground (Lunsford & Ruszkiewicz, 2012). The challenge in good argumentation lies in understanding the desired outcome and underlying complications, tracing the logic, evaluating the premise and its defining details, and ultimately making informed counterarguments or decisions.

Disciplinary Thinking

A huge shift in teaching communication involves embedding it in the context of disciplinary thinking. Authors Emily C. Rainey, Bridget L. Maher, David Coupland, Rod Franchi, and Elizabeth Birr Moje (2018) define disciplinary literacy practices as the "shared language and symbolic tools that members of academic disciplines (e.g., biology, philosophy, musical theater, architecture and design, psychology) use to construct knowledge alongside others" (p. 371). Rainey et al. (2018) note the nature of *what* teachers ask and *how* they explore it is different from one discipline to the next. Teachers will explore an intriguing science question using a specific framework for an investigation, and those processes will differ from the compelling historical question that drives the historian into primary documents (Rainey et al., 2018). In other words, every discipline maintains its own unique ways of asking and answering questions, so educators must teach how *real* mathematicians, musicians, or journalists read and write in the appropriate discipline.

The shift in how modern teachers must view and explore information, argumentation, and disciplinary thinking must run as constant threads through the assessment practices for each of the communication literacies.

A Fresh Look at How to Communicate

In keeping with the times, modern communication standards require learners to update their skill sets. Reading, viewing, and listening are all *consumption skills*, whereas speaking and writing are *production skills*. Each skill, whether it's consumption (input) or production (output), requires a great deal of analyzing, evaluating, and synthesizing as learners deconstruct and reconstruct information and arguments in the appropriate disciplines. In the new paradigm for literacy as outlined in standards such as the Common Core and other state standards, these skills must be interconnected in an intentionally sequenced flow like the following.

1. Learners begin by consuming information (reading, viewing, listening).

2. Learners then move to processing information (listening and speaking) collaboratively.

3. Learners next produce their own thoughts in writing or developing other discipline-specific products.

Reading and Viewing

In a burgeoning multimedia world, the skill of *viewing* is as important as *reading*. Both skills require learners to interpret and make meaning about what they are consuming. The content, whether on screen or in text, must increase in complexity for learners to be career- and college-ready (National Governors Association Center for Best Practices & Council of Chief State School Officers [NGA & CCSSO], n.d.). While the research suggests that the K–12 reading texts have reduced complexity over the last several years, it also "indicates that the demands that college, careers, and citizenship place on readers have either held steady or increased over roughly the last fifty years" (NGA & CCSSO, n.d., p. 2). As a result, teachers must increase the complexity of texts they expose to learners.

Increasing the complexity of texts involves exposing learners to primary documents in the designated discipline. Primary documents can be filled with discipline-rich language, symbols, and context-specific nuances. An increase in complexity, then, requires the use of processing strategies that empower learners to make sense of the text. Fisher et al. (2016) note:

> As texts become more complex, central ideas and key details are often scattered among several sentences, rather than definitely stated in a single sentence. Guided annotation of text, including underlining, circling, and making margin notes, can improve student understanding of new knowledge, and build the capacity of students to better engage in study skills. (p. 58)

Educators must teach learners *how* to read and view text in order for them to consume information effectively.

Learners no longer read or view to comprehend surface information; instead, they must search for subtext and elicit additional information that can come from how a text is structured or the author's intention. Many books help teachers guide learners through close reading strategies (Fisher & Frey, 2015c, 2015d; Fisher, Frey, & Lapp, 2012a, 2012b) because the work is foreign to the traditional classroom and complex in nature. Fisher et al. (2016) advocate using focusing questions that address the literal, structural, inferential, and interpretive levels of a text. There's always more to reading and viewing than what meets the eye!

Listening

Teachers always expect listening but rarely teach it. If learners are to engage in conversations in which they question validity or trace logic, they must concentrate, understand, and respond; they cannot do so if they are not actively listening. *Active listening*—a system of strategies to help listeners remain attentive—requires learners engage in a structured, intentional state of focus while doing a myriad of different tasks: attending, inquiring, acknowledging, inviting, and paraphrasing. Active listening can be mentally challenging and somewhat exhausting.

Even the most socially adept learners will cringe at the idea of accepting a peer's criticism, challenging a teacher's argument, or inviting feedback for their ideas. Additionally, the irregular practice of paraphrasing can be clunky and uncomfortable at best. Educators must teach, rehearse, and refine such skills until they are so seamless, they are nearly invisible. When listeners are masterful at their craft, conversations are productive and likely even dynamic, and the transitions enable an inconspicuous rich flow. It helps when learners view videos of strong and weak examples of listening and then identify the characteristics of the conversation as well as the strategies. Developing criteria for quality listening experiences can help learners monitor and improve their own listening abilities.

In a world where people can disagree so intensely (and frequently), it's critical to engage and keep learners open-minded as they listen. According to University of Wisconsin–Madison dean and Karen A. Falk Distinguished Chair of Education Diana Hess (Richardson, 2017):

> In a time that is so hyperpartisan and hyperpolarized, we want to model for students the importance of being willing to change one's mind. It's hard for someone to take a public position on something and then change their mind. (p. 18)

Toward that end, it's helpful when teachers invite learners to prepare for conversations by reading in advance, but not framing their opinions before entering the conversation. It's equally helpful to teach the process of listening through structured experiences and protocols. Giving learners protocols that help them practice listening puts structures in place that help them focus their attention and seek to understand. As English teacher Daniel Sussman (2017) adds, "Focusing on listening creates a conversational space that more students will be willing to enter" (p. 51).

Speaking

Speaking is the bridge between reading and writing. When learners are speaking about complex text, they engage in making meaning. "Purposeful discussion of complex texts during the surface consolidation phase is an excellent way to provide access to readings" (Fisher et al., 2016, p. 67). Learners are expected to reference their background preparation from the reading *while* engaged in discussion; they are to make meaning, draw conclusions, challenge assumptions, probe arguments, and ask pertinent questions on the spot. Certainly some preparation is involved, but with speaking—unlike writing—the experience is live and reactions immediate.

People talk to make meaning. When using speaking to employ a bridge activity in various structured formats (like Socratic seminar or debate), learners are better equipped to produce meaningful thoughts, back their arguments with evidence, and even motivate others through powerful speech. Extended opportunities to speak and listen create opportunities for learners to summarize information in repeated and different ways until they come to own the information.

Writing

Even writing is different with the new standards. The traditional genres of narrative, opinion, information, or argumentation still exist, but there is far more emphasis on connecting the writing to texts and using evidence from the text to back assertions—even when those assertions are opinions. Narrative writing shifted from solely creating fictional stories to telling true stories in pointed and meaningful ways—as one would when filing an insurance claim, describing a work experience for a manager, or creating a marketing brand for a company. The life stories and powerful voices of learners can create the bridge to insight for teachers (Gallagher & Kittle, 2018).

A big challenge is getting learners to write regularly (often and lots) in discipline-specific ways. Since cross-curricular writing might have the greatest impact on disciplinary thinking and college or career readiness than any other school improvement factor, the challenge seems well worth the effort (Schmoker, 2018). After all, "decades of research attest to writing's unrivaled ability to facilitate understanding and help people evaluate, reconstitute, and synthesize knowledge" (Schmoker, 2018, p. 22). With a renewed emphasis on writing, teachers and learners must study the format of complex, discipline-specific passages and then work to recreate them in appropriate ways. They must gather relevant information from multiple sources, challenge the credibility and accuracy of the sources, take meaningful notes, analyze, and then integrate information to back their concise arguments while avoiding plagiarism. In doing so, they must provide their own sound reasoning.

State, national, and provincial writing standards aim to help learners find their voice, power, thoughts, creativity, and agency as writers (Gallagher & Kittle, 2018; McKenney, 2018; Schmoker, 2018), forcing tremendous shifts in writing instruction. First, teachers must de-emphasize strict structures (like five-paragraph essays) because, as McKenney (2018) states, "Reducing writing to formulas may make it easier to teach and assess, but this method invariably leads to forced communication" (p. 34). Second, the evaluation of writing must focus more on the quality of ideas than on mechanics because "nothing kills a student writer's desire to write quite like a teacher's excessive emphasis on writing mechanics—spelling, grammar, and usage" (McKenney, 2018, p. 35). Third, writing must be more text based, as a common thread in all standards is to have students anchor their thinking and their arguments in concrete details, and more frequently in *every* discipline, as writing is a required skill in almost every professional field. Finally, teachers need to rely on more modeled, focused, whole-class instruction and feedback regarding "whole-class patterns of progress or need" on specific writing skills rather than relying on "onerous amounts of paper grading" (Schmoker, 2018, p. 26). The changes in teaching writing are significant for learner and teacher alike.

When teachers focus more on ideas and content and the structure of various types of writing, they not only free themselves from having to spend lengthy amounts of time engaged in in-depth grading practices, but they also free students from their inhibiting concerns of being grammatically incorrect so that they can instead find their voice, free their thoughts, and access their individual creativity. This is not to say grammar doesn't matter; it does. But when the heavy emphasis on the writing rules *leads* the writing exercise, as it so often does, teachers become daunted by the sheer notion of grading all of the writing that is produced, and learners freeze at their initial attempt to produce something meaningful. Initially, learners need to understand the form and function of the various types of discipline-specific writing. They need the space to think critically and produce creatively. Then, once the writing is produced, grammar can be used as a diagnostic tool to help learners improve the quality of their writing, especially when learning about revision on the pieces that will be made "publish ready."

Assessing Communication

Proof of whether or not schools have fully implemented a new set of standards is always revealed through both the assignments teachers generate to measure the standards, and the subsequent work learners produce in response. The shifts outlined in the communication standards have been so significant that it appears educators are struggling to implement the right changes. In a study conducted five years after the implementation of the Common Core standards, vice president of K–12 policy and practice at the Education Trust Sonja Brookins Santelises and former director of literacy, teacher coach, and curriculum writer Joan Dabrowski (2015) used a protocol to review a significant sample size of middle school assignments and found:

1. Only approximately 5 percent of the assignments met the criteria for quality (appropriate levels of rigor, relevance, student choice, and so on)

2. Only 38 percent of the assessments were on grade level

3. Though 55 percent of the assignments were connected to a text, only 16 percent required students to cite evidence from the text in support of their own claim or position

4. About 85 percent of the assignments engaged students in recall and basic skills, while only 4 percent of the assignments challenged students' thinking by requiring inferences, critiques, or structural analysis

5. Only 2 percent of the assignments met both indicators for assessment engagement: relevance and choice

Communication is something educators have always assessed, but in future classrooms the assessments must clearly hit a higher standard. In addition to engaging learners in connecting the pathway of reading and speaking to listening and writing (and doing so in a discipline-specific manner), teachers must address the following factors when assessing communication.

- Avoiding the desire to over-scaffold

- Providing prompts and questioning

- Tackling complex disciplinary issues

- Employing modern mediums

These tremendous and uncomfortable paradigm shifts still need to take place for the new communication expectations to come to fruition in classrooms.

Over-Scaffolding

Of course, educators must build in or *scaffold* supports to help learners develop skills. And the younger the learner, the more scaffolding required. Young learners who don't read yet must have stories read to them. They can still, however, engage in the work of answering questions that help them dig below the surface of a text read to them.

There are many common scaffolding strategies educators use when teaching communication skills, most often in the area of writing, including the following.

- Using visual tools to create the writing plan

- Creating paragraphs with a topic sentence, three supporting details, and a closing sentence

- Following a five-paragraph essay structure with an introduction, three supporting paragraphs, and a conclusion

- Giving five-minute speeches with a compelling introduction, three supporting details, and a powerful conclusion

- Chunking reading with the protocol: pause, ask questions, pause, review

Scaffolds are helpful because they offer a procedure or a tool to help the learner understand the process; they are especially necessary for younger students who are in the early stages of understanding the work. But as a whole, scaffolding often *does the thinking* for learners. Over-scaffolding is the equivalent of underempowering.

Teachers need to gradually remove scaffolds and, in their absence, learners need to *develop* their own scaffolds. For example, if the teacher asks learners to frame a legal argument, they might first explore the structure of a legal argument as a whole class. From that model, they could then find additional legal arguments to dissect in teams as they try to uncover the structure in each, and then compare the various structures in an attempt to discern which structures work best and for what reasons. After all of that, teachers can then ask learners to create their own legal argument and even diagram the structure of their argument to include with their written rationale of why they deem a particular structure the most appropriate. While this certainly takes more time, it's far more engaging than asking learners to fill in boxes and then find ways to weave the content of those boxes together in a written piece. The learner-generated scaffold also allows for deeper learning, and students have a better opportunity to comprehend and master the content in profound ways.

Learners aren't afraid of hard work; they are tired of meaningless work. Filling in boxes or following rote patterns can feel like just jumping through hoops. Such work is both uninteresting and underempowering; as Fisher et al. (2016) conclude, "Students appreciate challenge. They expect to work hard to achieve success in school and life. When tasks become too easy, students get bored. Similarly, when tasks become too difficult, students get frustrated" (p. 21). There is a time and a place for scaffolding early on the learning journey for students of all ages, but final communication products should never be based on activities that did not require learners' deep thinking, ownership, and pride.

A separate but linked concern with over-scaffolding involves prohibiting learner access to things like Wiki pages. In such cases, adults are making decisions about what's relevant and what's not, so learners don't have to think on their own. A better approach would involve teaching learners how to interpret and navigate less-credible sites and even determine when they have stumbled upon one.

Prompts and Questioning

Powerful classroom discussions and writing tasks require thoughtful prompts and questions. Deep thinking doesn't just happen—at least, not for teachers who stand before a classroom full of learners and try to generate meaningful questions on the spot, and certainly not for learners as they strive to answer on the spot. As Diana Hess (Richardson, 2017) explains:

> The first thing is to make sure discussions are planned and prepared for, not spontaneous. . . . Spontaneous discussions are almost always low quality, and they're low quality because most students will not know enough to be prepared to participate. So the participation among students is uneven and unequal and the quality of those discussions is not rigorous and interesting. (p. 17)

The use of modern, integrated standards demands advanced orchestration.

Additionally, the framing of a question determines the outcome of the responses. Fisher et al. (2016) state:

> Teacher questioning frames these whole class and small group discussions. The questions asked can limit thinking, as is the case when teachers ask narrow questions with only one response. On the other hand, teachers can invite further speculation by changing the nature of the question to prompt more discussion. (p. 86)

Moreover, Hess (Richardson, 2017) advises educators to consider the issues with their questions and then choose the appropriate frame for the conversation:

> Empirical questions are those that can be answered through systematic inquiry requiring observation or experimentation—such as weather climate change is occurring. Policy issues are what we should do as a matter of policy—they are broader than empirical questions. For example, what we should do to stem the problems caused by climate change is the policy issue. (pp. 16–17)

Learners' deep thinking is born out of teachers' provocative questions.

Disciplinary Thinking

While non–English language arts teachers might be uncomfortable with teaching and assessing communication skills, they do know their content areas and can readily support disciplinary thinking. The challenge with disciplinary thinking involves not only looking back on the available content information but also looking forward to what could be, or even generating new content knowledge.

There are complex, ethical issues in all disciplines, and opening them up for discussion in the classroom can feel risky. For example, "What constitutes democratic social studies education? Broadly speaking, it is said to include deliberative instructional practice that focuses on controversial issues, explores political themes, and aims to close gaps in students' civic literacy" (Gibbs, 2017, p. 21). The topics are no less controversial and the processes no less risky in science:

> Argumentation is particularly relevant in science education since a goal of scientific inquiry is the generation and justification of knowledge claims, beliefs and actions taken to understand nature. Commitments to theory, methods, and aims are the outcome of critical evaluation and debates among communities of scientists. (Jiménez-Aleixandre, Rodríguez, & Duschl, 2000, p. 758)

The most exciting conversations are interdisciplinary. They are also the most authentic. According to education experts David C. Owens, Troy D. Sadler, and Dana L. Zeidler (2017), "When teachers employ a socioscientific issues (or SSI) approach to classroom instruction, they engage students in developing and evaluating arguments about challenging problems of public importance" (p. 46). Conversations such as these become compelling! It is a rich experience for learners to function as adults in an authentic field of study.

Modern Mediums

Teachers must modernize communication assessments to meet modern standards. Assistant superintendent for curriculum, instruction, and professional development Jeanne Tribuzzi and educational consultant and instructional coach Michael L. Fisher (2014) state:

> Modern literacy is about the evolution from traditional reading, writing, listening, and speaking to using multiple types of print and digital media, online communication, and collaborative structures to enable depth in learning and knowledge for the sake of sharing ideas and communicating in a global society. (p. 28)

In other words, the *producing* phase can offer many more choices than just writing a paper. For example, learners can still frame their thoughts and back them with text evidence through blogs posts, podcasts, YouTube videos, debates, newspaper articles, and infographics, to name just a few.

The following criteria can help teachers determine if a potential task or product would fit the bill as a modern assessment medium. Ask, "Is the proposed activity . . .":

- Real world?
- Relevant to the discipline?
- Interesting?
- Logical?
- Clearly defined?
- Inviting to the student?
- Supported with rubrics for quality?

Other important questions include, Is the medium selected (for example, designing a webpage or making a movie), authentic, or contrived? Does the concluding task include the full sequence of input (reading and viewing), processing (speaking and listening), and producing? Will teachers ask learners to engage in discipline-specific inquiry and problem solving? Will learners have ample time to engage in discipline-specific inquiry and problem solving?

Finally, are there criteria in place so teachers can score the final student work on its merits for deep learning and not on the glitzy moving parts? Of course, it would be unfair to assign learners to create something for which they have no knowledge, skills, or previous experience, so another consideration involves learner readiness.

There are many concerns with employing modern assessment designs, and a significant one has to do with finding the heart of what the teacher is supposed to assess in the student product or performance and scoring *that* over the beauty of the final result. As Jacobs (2014) states, "It is easy for contemporary teachers to be swept up in the tidal wave of new technologies, and we run the risk of employing these new tools and literacies in a piecemeal, halfhearted manner" (pp. 6–7). It's also important to ensure that learners of all backgrounds have access to the necessary tools and skills to produce such products.

Access to technology in classrooms is almost ubiquitous. While some schools might be unable to afford the relevant technologies, learners at all ages often carry them in their pockets. That changes things.

According to Jacobs (2014):

> If we step back and look at the contemporary classroom as cultural anthro-
> pologists, it is obvious that the exposure to multiple media formats has
> shifted learning to visual modalities, audio soundtracks, and animated imag-
> ery. Communication between individuals and groups is immediate, ranging
> from FaceTime on cell phones worldwide to Twitter feeds. (p. 6)

It's time for assessments to engage students to match their engaging ways of communicating.

Measuring Communication

To measure communication is to measure thinking: "Humans can only provide evidence of cognitive and affective learning through four observable actions: (1) what they say, (2) write, (3) make, or (4) do" (Heritage, 2013, p. 183). *Thinking* demonstrates depth of learning, but thinking is not obvious without an outward demonstration. Fortunately, there are many common rubrics and scales for measuring speaking, listening, reading, and writing skills.

Speaking

Figure 6.1 (pages 196–198) offers a general communication rubric teachers can use to grade conversations (or speeches) in groups of any size or for any purpose.

It is best to use the communication rubric in figure 6.1 in a structured conversation like a Socratic seminar, a debate, or a forum where teachers task learners with incorporating text into their discussions and developing supportive resources to enhance their messages. Figure 6.2 (page 199) offers a simplified communication rubric geared toward elementary use in the primary grades.

Notice that eye contact is left off the communication rubrics in figures 6.1 and 6.2. This is important because incorporating eye contact would generate cultural bias in the assessment tools as some cultures find it disrespectful to make eye contact during conversations. Eye contact could, however, be included in a rubric for giving a speech, as it is a universal expectation during a formal presentation. A simple addition of eye contact could turn the communication rubric in figure 6.1 into a speech rubric as well. Figure 6.3 (page 200) provides an example of the possible criteria for quality eye contact.

Aspect	Initiating	Developing	Achieving	Advancing
Focus	The focus of the message is stated but not supported, *or* the ideas are loosely coupled without a key focus.	The focus of the message is stated and key points are used to clarify the focus, but the key points are either insufficient in number or weak in strengthening the core message.	The message is purposeful and focused. All supporting details serve to further enhance the core message.	The message is purposeful and focused. All supporting details, gestures, and paralanguage (pitch, tone, rate) are engaged to further illuminate and punctuate the core message.
Discipline-Specific Message	The message addresses a related issue in the discipline but does not follow the discipline's protocols for organization, content, presentation, formatting, and stylistic choices, *or the* discipline's protocols are followed but the message is not essential to the discipline.	The message addresses an important issue in the discipline, but the message is developed using only some of the discipline's protocols for organization, content, presentation, formatting, and stylistic choices, *or all* the protocols are followed, but the quality and accuracy of the application are low.	The message addresses essential issues in the discipline, and the message is executed using the discipline's protocols for organization, content, presentation, formatting, and stylistic choices.	The message addresses a core concern in the discipline and offers a fresh or innovative stance worthy of consideration or further exploration by the discipline. The message is executed adhering to the discipline's protocols for organization, content, presentation, formatting, and stylistic choices.

Language	Noticeable errors (grammar, inaccurate use of industry terms, or choppy transitions) interrupt communication. The language impedes a natural cadence.	The language use offers minimal errors in grammar, industry terms, or transitions. The cadence has a choppiness that interrupts the message but does not interfere with the reader's understanding.	The language use is error free. It follows grammar rules, uses industry terms accurately, and employs academic transitions to support a logical sequence and natural cadence.	The language use is error free in all aspects. The cadence is enhanced as the messenger overtly plays with language in a manner that further enhances the message (rhyming, using metaphors, organizing around acronyms, creating new terms, and so on).
Text-Reference Enhancements	The messenger demonstrates limited industry knowledge by using few (or no) direct quotes and paraphrases, or references may dominate the message. Sources used might be suspect within the industry. References are included but not accurately cited.	The messenger demonstrates a beginning understanding of industry knowledge by paraphrasing or referencing relevant sources in the industry. References support but do not dominate the message. All references are cited, but there may be errors in the citations.	The messenger skillfully demonstrates industry knowledge by including direct quotes and paraphrases from relevant and credible sources within the industry. References support but do not dominate the message. All references are accurately cited.	The messenger skillfully demonstrates industry knowledge by synthesizing and analyzing direct quotes and paraphrases from relevant and credible sources within the industry. References are linked in an insightful manner that supports but does not dominate the message. All references are accurately cited.

Figure 6.1: Communication-scoring rubric.

continued ►

Digital and Hard-Copy Enhancements (for example, back channel chat applications, videos, podcasts, audio-recorded interviews, charts, graphs, models, illustrations, photos, drawings, and so on) *Digital and hard-copy enhancements only apply if some form of print results from the speaking and listening task(s).	Resources are employed but may not be directly supportive or may hijack the message. Resources may be inappropriate or do little to add interest or clarification for the audience. The application is intrusive, redirecting attention from the message to focus on the use of the enhancement.	Some of the supporting resources enhance the message, but more or better resources may offer further clarification or generate more interest. Resources are appropriate, but the integration may be clunky enough to distract the audience for brief periods of time.	Supporting resources are used to enhance but not hijack the message. Resources are appropriate and integrated seamlessly to improve communication, adding interest or clarification to support audience understanding.	Supporting and appropriate resources are used professionally, and mediums are integrated in powerful or innovative ways that amplify interest and deepen understanding, or both.
Audience	The messenger delivers to but barely interacts with the audience. The messenger may be aware of audience member needs and interest, but is not aware of or responsive to audience cues. As a result, this communication barrier marginalizes the audience's learning.	The messenger interacts with the audience in a manner that demonstrates a partial awareness of audience member needs and interests but is only somewhat aware of or responsive to audience feedback or nonverbal cues. The audience learns something interesting or new, but it does not advance the audience members' knowledge, skills, or perceptions about the industry.	The messenger interacts with the audience in a manner that (1) demonstrates awareness of audience member needs and interests, (2) is responsive to audience feedback or nonverbal cues, and (3) moves the audience's knowledge, skills, or perceptions forward within the industry. The messenger disperses attention equally across all audience members.	The messenger is highly engaged and interactive, inviting audience members to incorporate their needs and interests into the conversation and then adapting accordingly to audience feedback and cues in order to ensure the audience's knowledge, skills, or perceptions advance within the industry or even advance the industry.

Source: Adapted from Lake Washington Institute of Technology, n.d.

Visit go.SolutionTree.com/assessment for a free reproducible version of this figure.

Aspect	Initiating	Developing	Achieving	Advancing
Engaging in Formal Discussions or Informal Conversations	**Listening:** Has to be invited to listen repeatedly and needs to be reminded of what was said **Comprehending:** Struggles to grasp the speaker's or the group's main ideas; new information might overwhelm or distract from engaging further in the conversation **Contributing:** Must be prompted to ask or answer questions or add new ideas or opinions so the contributions are forced and not used to check personal understanding **Interacting:** Does not respond well to feedback or input by all speakers; may need to be advised repeatedly to change behavior (interrupting, proximity, volume, rate, gestures, and so on) so everyone can be comfortable or have equal sharing time	**Listening:** Pays attention to what others are saying sometimes and demonstrates some listening behaviors (like nodding) but is impatient to add and cuts others off as a result **Comprehending:** Understands most of the speaker's or group's main ideas; may require repeats or clarifications of new information as it is shared **Contributing:** Asks and answers questions naturally but contributions may seek to understand or add to the conversation; adds new ideas or opinions that support the conversation **Interacting:** Responds well to most feedback or input (especially by the teacher, but not as much by peers); changes behavior when reminded but generally is not self-aware and might dominate the discussion	**Listening:** Pays attention to what others are saying and demonstrates listening behaviors (waiting turns, nodding, adding to what was said before, and so on) **Comprehending:** Understands the speaker's or the group's main ideas and can address new information as it is shared **Contributing:** Asks questions to check personal understanding; answers questions during a discussion; adds new ideas or opinions that support the conversation **Interacting:** Responds positively to feedback or input by all speakers and changes behavior (proximity, volume, rate, gestures, and so on) as needed so everyone is comfortable; invites others to participate	**Listening:** Pays attention to what others are saying and sometimes identifies the feelings or subtext behind a message based on how it is said; remains attentive **Comprehending:** Understands the speaker's or the group's main ideas and can link ideas from one speaker or source to the next; makes new connections to emerging information and shares understanding with others **Contributing:** Asks questions to check personal understanding; answers questions to improve the speaker or group's understanding; links the ideas of others or adds thoughtful ideas or opinions that enhance the conversation **Interacting:** Responds positively and even seeks feedback or input from all speakers or groups; does not require prompts to change behavior; naturally seeks to engage everyone

Source: Adapted from Catalina Foothills School District, 2016.

Figure 6.2: Communication-scoring rubric for elementary grades.

Visit go.SolutionTree.com/assessment for a free reproducible version of this figure.

Aspect	Initiating	Developing	Achieving	Advancing
Eye Contact	Is dependent on notes and reads most of the presentation, rarely looking up to acknowledge audience; may use furtive, brief glances aimed at the center of the audience in the immediate vicinity	Has a balance between referencing notes and making eye contact with the audience; makes direct eye contact with some individuals, focusing attention on known individuals or those within the immediate vicinity; duration may be too brief, making the connection unrecognizable or too long, and therefore uncomfortable	Seldom references notes and never turns back to the audience to read slides; makes direct eye contact with individuals, sweeping the depth and breadth of the entire audience equitably; holds attention for appropriate lengths of time to demonstrate the connection comfortably	Does not require notes or references notes in ways that are imperceptible; uses eye contact as a means to understand how the audience is receiving the information; captivates attention of the entire audience by directly and randomly connecting with audience members through eye contact–based interactions and acknowledgments

Figure 6.3: Eye-contact rubric to add to other communication rubrics for speeches.

Visit go.SolutionTree.com/assessment for a free reproducible version of this figure.

Of course, making eye contact does not guarantee the audience is listening. True eye contact involves looking *and* listening so the connection is about understanding and building relationships.

Listening

Active listening is not often taught at any grade level in schools. However, educators must provide direct instruction, rehearsal, and feedback if learners are to improve their active-listening skills. Sometimes in casual conversation, other rubrics (such as listening rubrics) might be more appropriate. According to communications experts Sherod Miller and Phyllis A. Miller (1994), listening skills are observable too: people demonstrate active listening when they attend, acknowledge, invite, summarize, and ask questions. When listeners are engaged in these skills, they recycle them as needed to generate clarity or advance the conversation. Figure 6.4 (page 202) offers an active-listening tool learners can use when engaging in five active-listening processes.

Practicing the types of listening responses will take time and rehearsal. Teachers could use the protocol in figure 6.4 to guide direct instruction and teach specific skills. Eventually, teachers could encourage students to write in their own favorite sentence leads as a replacement to the initial proposed options. Teachers could also use it to help learners observe or document behaviors through modeling in a fish-bowl-type setting. Ultimately, it is best for learners to use it to support self-reflection during their practice experiences. Learners will likely be uncomfortable using this rubric at first. But with much practice, they should find their own voice and sentence leads.

Reading

Communication standards require much integration of text evidence. When learners *can't* use text evidence well, the issue might involve reading. Teachers can only assess comprehension through some type of response from learners, so a measurement tool must be based on evidence learners produce during or after the actual reading. Teachers can help learners monitor reading specifically by using a rubric or scale that highlights the important features required in the standards. The reading response scale in figure 6.5 (page 203) can give both teachers and learners alike more clarity on *what* to look for or accomplish while reading.

Directions: When engaged in communication, try some of the following active-listening prompts. After the conversation is over, reflect on your strengths and growth areas. How can you get even better at active listening?

Listening Skill	Sentence Leads	My Strengths	My Growth Areas
Attending I observe the actions and unspoken emotions in the speaker.	• It seems like you might be sad. • Are you tense right now? • I noticed that made you smile.		
Inquiring I ask meaningful or interesting questions that keep the conversation going.	• Were you excited, scared, or sad when that happened? • What did you think of that? • Will you continue? • Why is that important to you?		
Acknowledging I take notice of, recognize, or confirm something the speaker said.	• I understand. • I agree. • I can see your point. • I'll add another idea to your point.		
Inviting I encourage the speaker to say more.	• I'd love to hear more about it. • I'm curious about that. Can you say more? • Can you explain that in another way? • Would you please expand on that idea for me?		
Paraphrasing I restate what the speaker said in different words so the speaker knows I heard the message correctly.	• If I understand correctly, you're saying that . . . • When you said . . . I thought you meant . . . . • So, if . . . is true, then I wonder if . . . . • Would this thought support what you just said?		

Figure 6.4: Active-listening tool.

Visit go.SolutionTree.com/assessment for a free reproducible version of this figure.

Readers navigate complex, discipline-specific texts for the purposes of understanding the important explicit and implicit information, interpreting meaning, drawing conclusions, solving problems, or creating new information.

	Reading Features
4	**Comprehension:** Demonstrates an in-depth interpretation of the text by isolating relevant implicit and explicit information, isolating challenges, gaps, or conflicts within the text, analyzing the author's purpose and text structure, and acknowledging different interpretations and offering concise supporting evidence **Interpretation:** Elicits concise information from the text to interpret significant concepts; to make solid, defensible judgments about the reasoning and main ideas related to the text; to challenge the ideas, implied bias, or distortions with clear rationale or arguments; and to develop in-depth inferences and personal insights as a result of the text **Annotation:** References readily available text annotations that include short notes, paraphrased ideas, key questions, important terms, and significant quotes **Integration:** Makes elaborate and valid text-to-self, text-to-text, and text-to-world connections independently using relevant and accurate text references
3	**Comprehension:** Demonstrates an accurate interpretation of the text by isolating relevant implicit and explicit information and summarizing in his or her own words, acknowledging different interpretations and offering supportive evidence **Interpretation:** Elicits information from the text to interpret significant concepts; to make solid, defensible judgments about the reasoning and main ideas related to the text; and to develop valid inferences and personal insights as a result of the text **Annotation:** References readily available text annotations that include short notes, paraphrased ideas, key questions, important terms, and significant quotes **Integration:** Makes valid text-to-self, text-to-text, and text-to-world connections, independently using relevant and accurate text references
2	**Comprehension:** Demonstrates partial understanding of the text by isolating relevant explicit information and summarizing in his or her own words; may be some early understanding of implicit information **Interpretation:** Uses key information from the text to determine quality of the messaging; may form some defensible judgements or valid inferences about the text **Annotation:** References some short notes, key questions, important terms, and significant quotes but may draw on the features that are not always the most relevant or significant **Integration:** Makes some text-to-self, text-to-text, and text-to-world connections, but may require prompting or cues to see connections
1	**Comprehension:** Struggles to understand the explicit information within the text **Annotation:** Identifies difficult words and offers more questions than answers regarding important ideas in the text

*Note: Interpretation and integration are virtually impossible if comprehension is missing.

Figure 6.5: *Reading response scale.*

*Visit **go.SolutionTree.com/assessment** for a free reproducible version of this figure.*

Of course, *what* learners are reading is also of concern. Because the quality of available print or digital material has become suspect in an online world that creates as much disinformation as it does information, aspiring powerful communicators must become critical of the sources and motivations behind the information they gather and share. Figure 6.6 offers a guide teachers can use to help learners determine the reliability of their sources.

Name or URL of source: _____ Today's date: _____

Authority:

Who is the author or agency behind the media?

What information could you find about the authority of the author or agency?

Do they have credibility in the field?

Purpose:

What is the source trying to accomplish?

_____ Inform   _____ Persuade   _____ Entertain

Accuracy:

How do you know what is shared is true? Could you validate it with alternative sources?

Are there any counterarguments to the message from other sources? Was the message ever discredited previously?

Are there any citations to show that the author or agency validated their own information?

Relevancy:

How current is the source? What is the date of publication, or what is the most recent update if it's a website?

How thorough or comprehensive is the information?

In your estimation, is this source credible? Why or why not? Back your assertion with evidence.

Figure 6.6: *Reliability of online sources tool.*

*Visit **go.SolutionTree.com/assessment** for a free reproducible version of this figure.*

Because arguing from evidence and addressing counterclaims is so important, helping learners ensure they have reliable sources is vital to their success. Given the insurmountable amount of available information in the age of acceleration, educators will have to teach learners how to validate their sources of information.

Writing

Writing is key to communicating and thinking. As Schmoker (2018) notes, cross-curricular writing is key to learner disciplinary thinking and college- or career-readiness. But too often, time becomes a barrier when it comes to employing more writing in the classroom. Not only does it take a long time for learners to produce writing, it also takes substantial time for teachers to score it. In fact, the impending magnitude of scoring mounds of writing often prevents teachers from even assigning writing. But learners must write *regularly* (often and prolifically) in discipline-specific ways if they are to improve their writing abilities *and* refine their own understanding of and reasoning abilities in discipline-specific ways.

Schmoker (2018) advocates for teachers to score writing by focusing on larger skills and concepts without getting lost in the specifics. Figure 6.7 offers a writing scale teachers can use to score writing across curricular areas. The scale focuses on the key aspects of writing and allows teachers to assign a single score to a piece of writing that *generally* aligns within the descriptors.

4	**Precise focus:** Provides an insightful, precise focus (thesis, claim, or controlling idea) that demonstrates an in-depth understanding of the topic or text; focus accurately represents the discipline from a unique perspective supported clearly and consistently throughout the writing **Development:** Creates clear and extended relationships among claims, reasons, evidence, and counterclaims, and provides logical reasoning backed with sufficient and relevant data, evidence, or examples from the text (as well as additional texts as relevant) to support the claim thoroughly and clearly **Language and style:** Demonstrates an expansive command of precise academic and discipline-specific vocabulary; piece mirrors the tone and style of the discipline **Fluency:** Creates a flow with a natural and unobtrusive cadence, bringing the message to the forefront and freeing the reader to only focus on the unique ideas present
3	**Precise focus:** States clear, precise focus (thesis, claim, or controlling idea) that demonstrates understanding of the topic or text, accurately represents the discipline, and maintains the focus clearly and consistently throughout the writing **Development:** Clarifies most relationships among claims, reasons, evidence, and counterclaims, and provides logical reasoning backed with sufficient and relevant data, evidence, or examples from the text (as relevant) to support the claim thoroughly and clearly **Language and style:** Uses grade-appropriate academic and discipline-specific vocabulary and maintains a consistent, proper tone and style for the field of expertise **Fluency:** Connects ideas using syntactic variety (varied sentence structures with smooth transitional words and phrases), generating a natural cadence that enhances reader comprehension and interest; minor errors do not interrupt message flow

Figure 6.7: Cross-curricular writing scale.

continued ➡

2	**Precise focus:** States a focus (thesis, claim, or controlling idea), but the statement is not precise or the follow-up support tends to shift through a variety of details linked to the text or topic **Development:** Notes some of the important relationships among claims, reasons, and evidence but is weak in addressing counterclaims; offers some reasoning but uses little relevant data, evidence, or examples from the text (as relevant) to support the claim **Language and style:** Uses many academic and discipline-specific terms, but the effort is choppy; some discipline-specific terms are lacking clarity (for example, dropped in sentences at inappropriate times or in inaccurate ways); tone does not align with the type of writing required within the discipline **Fluency:** Uses complete sentences with limited variance in structures (for example, favors simple and compound sentences); limited use of varied transitional words and phrases causes a staccato or stutter to the reading effort, but the message is still clear
1	**Precise focus:** Provides a content-related idea but there is no formal focus (thesis, claim, or controlling idea), and the writing is not tightly or accurately linked to the related topic or text **Development:** Few attempts are made to make connections between claims, reasons, or evidence; details are shared to support the message but reasoning is missing **Language and style:** Employs basic vocabulary, seldom referencing the necessary grade-appropriate academic and discipline-specific vocabulary; vocabulary interrupts the tone **Fluency:** Develops some complete sentences but still has some fragments; offers very few transition words or relies heavily on the same transition words; message is blurred as readers struggle to interpret the sentences

*Visit **go.SolutionTree.com/assessment** for a free reproducible version of this figure.*

Using a scale such as this, teachers can effectively provide more modeled, focused, whole-class feedback.

Sometimes it's helpful when learners have a scale for a single criterion or medium to monitor their own progress. Figure 6.8 provides a scale with a tracking tool and some reflection questions to help learners monitor their own ability to argue from evidence. Learners can use this scale for written or oral arguments.

Critical competencies like arguing from evidence require rehearsal and refinement over time and across multiple disciplines and even mediums. Creating tracking scales for such skills can support learners in monitoring and eventually mastering their own core competencies. It's helpful, then, when schools create such tools for learners to use across multiple curricular areas so they understand the skills from a more global perspective and can refine their ability through ongoing opportunities and within disciplines.

Self-Assessment Form for Argumentation

	Initiating	Developing	Achieving	Advancing
Argumentation The learner skillfully uses accurate, sufficient evidence and sound reasoning to convince the audience that his or her stated claim is the only appropriate option.	I require templates and prompts to help me develop my argument.	I can independently make a claim and use some evidence to support my assertion. I need more evidence or stronger reasoning to strengthen my claim.	I make a bold claim, and then I use strong and sufficient evidence to prove my claim. My reasoning is logical and convincing.	When I support my claim, I also include the counter-arguments within my own strong argument to further solidify that my claim is the only appropriate response.

Note: Each level builds on the previous descriptor, so level 4 includes level 3, and so on.

Advancing			
Achieving			
Developing		▉	
Initiating	▉		▉
Assessment Name	Assessment 1	Assessment 2	Assessment 3
Date	October 8	October 10	October 15

Enter your data and color in the bar graph to show your data.

What are your strengths?

Your opportunities for growth?

Your next steps?

Figure 6.8: Self-assessment form for argumentation.

Visit *go.SolutionTree.com/assessment* for a free reproducible version of this figure.

Growing Communication

Because communication is already complex, and because there are ever-changing ways to communicate in a digital age, it is vital that educators of all disciplines help learners refine their communication skills. In order to help students develop quality communication skills with modern standards, teachers must provide instruction for the following techniques in reading, speaking and listening, and writing.

- Making claims that are backed by evidence but that are individually owned (for example, the learner is not regurgitating what someone else said)

- Arguing from evidence

- Analyzing quality and sufficiency of arguments from self and others

- Analyzing structural components, author's purpose, and validity of sources and arguments

- Motivating others through powerful words

Technology isn't necessarily required (though it is most beneficial) when helping students learn to interact in powerful and convincing ways. Arming students to think critically, construct arguments based in solid evidence, and motivate others through powerful speech requires so much more than teaching the basics of how to read, listen, speak, or write. In a globally shrinking world where interaction is paramount to every citizen's success, communication skills will likely dictate how far a student can advance his or her station in life.

Conclusion

Modern national and state communication standards require a paradigm shift likely to cause discomfort for teachers and learners alike. Simply sending and receiving accurate messages will no longer suffice. Fortunately, the challenges to rethink how educators teach and assess communication can lead to exciting new opportunities as students learn to inspire others through powerful speech, provoke thinking through effective argumentation, or crisply articulate sound opinions. Moreover, the new standards open possibilities for learners (and teachers) to explore digital mediums and make meaningful connections on a global scale. Communication will forever be key on the pathway to success. As Plato once said, "Wise men speak because they have something to say; Fools because they have to say something."

Pause and Ponder

On your own or as part of a collaborative teacher team, consider the following reflective questions.

1. In what ways have you or your team altered your assessments to align with the paradigm shift in reading, speaking, listening, and writing? What's worked for you so far? What would you like to improve or change?

2. How comfortable are you or your teammates in teaching the communication literacies in ways that are authentic to the discipline?

3. How often and through what modalities do you allow students to engage in technology-based solutions or options for communicating?

4. How frequently do the adults in your school engage in the modern literacies as a staff (for example, reading complex texts, analyzing them, discussing them, arguing from evidence, and creating products to address your learning)?

5. How comfortable are you in teaching argumentation or facilitating it in your classroom? What would it take for you to be more comfortable? How will you help learners become comfortable?

6. How modern or dynamic would your learners consider your assessments to be? In what ways might you involve learners so they can help design the assessments they might love to do?

CHAPTER 7
DIGITAL CITIZENSHIP

In a world where students can instantly digitally interact with others across the globe, it is imperative that they understand what it means to be a good citizen with that global community.

—J. Michael Blocher

Before the phrase *google it* became part of our workflow, how did people find answers to their pressing questions? Using libraries, encyclopedias, and phone calls was more common, and it took a bit more time to research, review, and discover. Today, when people—especially learners who have not lived in a world without the internet at their fingertips—don't know how to do something, they frequently turn to YouTube or other online resources to instantly figure it out. Schools are increasingly embracing the changing world and incorporating digital technology use in their classroom assessments. For example, an English department in the Midwest relentlessly pursues engaging ideas, thinking carefully about their learners' interests and the rapidly changing society. This team grappled with ways to make the traditional informational speech—typically a two-week grueling exercise requiring all learners to give and listen to each other give an eight-minute lecture—more relevant to learners. Their answer was to ask learners to develop a how-to video—similar to what learners frequently consume on YouTube—on a topic of their choice. Learners then watched two or three of their peers' videos and provided feedback to each other. This English team also collaborated with the visual arts team, which provided consultation on the criteria to use to assess the how-to videos. This is one example of incredible teachers attending to this new digital environment and transforming their assessment and instruction to meet these new demands. They asked learners to communicate with each other in a digital environment—a critical skill to being global digital citizens.

Many educators lament the day smartphones were invented, as they have potential to cause learners significant distraction and may make learners appear at first glance to be disrespectful, unmotivated, or unfocused. There are certainly dangers of too much screen time, and schools and families are wise to pay close attention to the damaging effects of excessive social media use and cyberbullying. Learners may also have a preoccupation with taking selfies, and exploring the root cause of this and its potential harm is also something for teachers (and parents) to be aware of. Modern learners are more stressed and depressed than those of previous generations, partly due to the access learners have to their peers' online postings (Bennett, 2014). They feel left out, left behind, or maybe even depressed because of how they perceive their friends are experiencing life.

Additionally, adults—educators and parents alike—may be frustrated as learners avoid school work or other responsibilities because they are always on their smartphones. These and many more complaints can indicate a generation of learners more isolated and disconnected than ever before. However, Gloria Ladson-Billings, a renowned researcher and scholar on culturally relevant pedagogy, provides another perspective (American Stories Continuum, 2010). On August 20, 2010, Mark Larson interviewed her and posed this question: "When you look at the state of education today, what worries you the most?" Ladson-Billings said:

> I guess I'm most concerned about our inability to see the sheer brilliance of this generation. This is [*sic*] the smartest, most creative, most innovative kids the world has ever seen, and we don't recognize it. What they do with technology, what they do with the English language, the way in which they envision things. It blows me away. It absolutely blows me away. They are pushing against the boundaries of knowledge in ways that I don't think my generation did. My generation was out there in the streets, but we were trying to get at what is. "Let me in that school. Let me have that job." This generation is, "Let me show you a job I'm making. Let me show you a form of music and dance and self-presentation that's never been seen before. Watch this." I'm afraid we're missing all of that because we want to push them back into a very conservative constrained

vision of what it means to be learning, what it means to be creative, what it means to be artistic. (American Stories Continuum, 2010)

Ladson-Billings encapsulates the potential of global digital citizenship. Inherently, learners are creating through technology, connecting new ideas to create dramatically radical solutions and new innovations. Today, this younger generation doesn't want what others have, they want to create their own—their own jobs and their own pathways, and what they create and design using a phone or simple application is beyond the imagination.

At first glance, this engagement in technology can appear to be an obsession with things other than what some perceive learners need. National Board Certified teacher William M. Ferriter (2014) shares an infographic titled "What Do You Want Kids to Do With Technology?" and lists right and wrong answers, making the point that learners should use technology to "raise awareness, start conversations, find answers (to *their* questions), join partners, change minds, make a difference, take action, and drive change" (Ferriter, 2014). The end goal is not to "make Prezis, start blogs, create Wordles, design flipcharts, produce videos, post to Edmodo, use whiteboard, [or] develop apps" purely for the sake of getting technology into learners' hands in an attempt to engage them. While technology can itself be engaging, it serves a greater purpose when the task is tied to something meaningful like contributing to a local or global issue, producing for an audience outside of the teacher or classroom, or investigating something that matters to students.

To elaborate, Ferriter (2014) interviews his middle school students, who had embarked on a Twitter storm to inform the world about the dangers of sugar. While they used digital tools to engage in this project, when asked about what they were most proud of and excited about, it wasn't the digital tools themselves.

> Notice that my [Ferriter's] kids rarely mention the digital tools that make their #sugarkills mission successful. They aren't saying, "We are just so happy to be blogging because blogging is cool!" or "The most motivating part of our #sugarkills project is using computers in the classroom." Instead, they are driven by the notion that their work actually matters. "How many 12-year-old students can say that they are changing people's lives around the world?" they write. "The fact that we can is amazing! We're definitely most proud of that." (Ferriter, 2014)

Being a global digital citizen requires educators to capitalize on the potential of technology and provide learners opportunities to use it in ways that connect unique individuals and groups of people, build on individual and organizational strengths, solve authentic problems in context, and seek to understand new and varied perspectives.

Defining Digital Citizenship

Citizenship used to be one- or two-dimensional; learners lived and contributed to their local and school communities. These communities also influenced learners. Now, with unprecedented access to world communities, it is possible, probable, and inevitable that learners will interact with people worldwide. Citizenship has moved from this one- or two-dimensional experience to three- or even four-dimensional opportunities, where learners are not only able to learn about other parts of the world but also actually interact and collaborate with people worldwide. According to Common Sense Education (n.d.b), "Being a good digital citizen is more than knowing your way around the web. It's about connecting and collaborating in ways you didn't even know were possible." Digital citizenship is an integral part of the world, and there are opportunities and responsibility to teach learners how to live productively and successfully in that world.

The heart of being a digital citizen is being able to use this unprecedented access to the world in productive, innovative ways. Each of the other critical competencies comes into play in digital citizenship. While digital citizenship is a critical competency worthy of exploration in its own right, there are often natural and essential moments of interdependency with the other critical competencies. All of the competencies can add depth to being a global digital citizen.

Technology is the great connector in the changing world, and so the role it plays in learning provides context for being a digital citizen. While it is important to teach some stand-alone elements of being a digital citizen, developing as a global digital citizen in productive ways requires learners to integrate their digital skills to use technology in ways that contribute to the community.

For learners to acquire digital skills, they must do the following.

- **Create and track a digital footprint:** Common Sense Education (n.d.a) describes the importance of understanding one's digital footprint: "Students learn to protect their own privacy and respect others' privacy. Our digital world is permanent, and with each post, students are building a digital footprint. By encouraging students to self-reflect before they self-reveal, they will consider how what they share online can impact themselves and others. Awareness about one's own digital footprint can also help to support digital literacy."

- **Use digital content with creative credit and copyright:** Common Sense Education (n.d.a) recommends "students learn about their rights to their own copyrighted work; identify how they can use copyrighted work without permission through public domain and fair use; and understand that piracy and plagiarism are forms of copyright infringement that are unethical and unlawful."

- **Research in authentic and credible ways, including checking sources' credibility, bias, and influence:** Ensuring the credibility of a source is essential for learners to understand as they have unprecedented access to information. As learners research and explore this vast amount of information, knowing the critical questions to ask of the source will encourage more thoughtful and credible arguments and more informed and engaged citizens. Jennifer Snelling's (2018) blog post, "Top 10 Sites to Help Students Check Their Facts," provides useful resources to help learners achieve this skill.

- **Understand how to be safe and protect their privacy online:** Again, Common Sense Education (n.d.a) provides a series of lessons to help students understand how to do this in ways that are age-appropriate and empowering.

Teachers teach and assess digital skills over time, so learners achieve a clear sense of not only what it means to be a digital citizen but also how to live and learn in this fast-paced electronic world. Part of being a digital citizen is using digital skills for the following purposes.

- To productively collaborate with many different and varied individuals and groups of people

- To generate creative solutions to local and global issues

- To create new information, new solutions, and new and unique innovations

- To communicate ethically, effectively, and productively to inform others about meaningful topics

- To connect people to ideas, resources, and support

- To communicate with not only their peers but also experts, researchers, and authors in their specialized field to learn more

- To personalize learning in a flexible way so students are able to pursue their individual areas of interest (versus being directed to learn more about a specific topic assigned by the teacher) to learn more, to become more socially aware, or to seek additional resources to learn essential skills

- To generate dialogue and keep conversations going about critical and authentic issues

Technology changes both the source of knowledge and the ways learners engage with knowledge.

While remembering still has a finite place in learning, the overemphasis on memorization is no longer relevant; technology allows access to knowledge in an instant. Learners can use technology to create products and solutions to persisting local and global problems, and to facilitate a process of communication, creative problem solving, or critical thinking. Learners may, for example, start a Twitter survey and follow up with a Twitter campaign to inform the local and global community about the dangers of texting and driving. Technology propels engagement to the next level. Engagement comes from intriguing and relevant topics, but also by reaching an authentic audience beyond the classroom walls. It is about providing learners choice, allowing for different pacing, providing relevant challenge, getting unprecedented feedback, fostering access to experts all over the globe, and helping learners become active participants in critical issues at local, national, and global levels.

Considering Digital Citizenship Now and Going Forward

The International Society for Technology in Education (ISTE, n.d.) identifies standards for teachers and learners. These standards are the foundation from which learners begin to track their progress on becoming productive and contributing global digital citizens. Several of the standards (available online at www.iste.org/standards /for-students) related to global digital citizenship are summarized as follows.

- Students actively choose and utilize technology to demonstrate a level of proficiency in achieving the intended learning. To further achieve this learning, students access technology to seek feedback and explore new ways of growing in achieving skills deemed essential to be successful in their future endeavors.

- Students learn to use technology in safe, legal, and ethical ways. Students monitor and track their digital footprints, applying their understanding of how to use and not use information they find online or information they post online. Learners explore and practice using others' content in legal and ethical ways.

- Students use technology to contribute knowledge and new ideas. Not only do learners consume content, they also learn how to research, use credible sources, build on ideas, put new and unrelated ideas together to create solutions, and contribute to a field of study or an industry.

- Students learn to be critical consumers of online content, evaluating sources of information and contributing credible ideas with integrity in digital learning environments.

- Learners collaborate and communicate online in a positive, safe, and ethical manner. In this global collaboration, students deepen their understanding of multiple perspectives; work on teams that cross classrooms, districts, and countries; and develop new solutions to current local and global issues.

These skills capture what it means to be a contributing and productive global citizen in an age where technology provides limitless possibilities for collaborating, communicating, connecting, and contributing. Each description guides teachers to further define the skills they wish to develop in their students, which leads to improved planning of how to best assess and measure digital citizenship.

An initial attempt at digital citizenship may involve having learners use a technology application to do something previously done on paper; for example, learners might write an essay as a blog or complete an online quiz. Doing the same activities and assessments using technology offers initial elements of engagement, but the novelty wears off fast. Educators must begin to conceptualize how to use technology for purposes beyond just the technology itself. This challenges educators to look for true innovation in which technology allows learners to be globally connected to experiences and people that they previously would have just read about.

Technology transforms not only what learners are doing but also who they are doing it with. Being a global digital citizen means educators must move from isolated classrooms and schools to connecting with schools, classrooms, businesses, and organizations beyond the school walls. This prepares learners to be productive members of a global society and engages them in meaningful work.

When educators make the shift to connecting their students with a world outside the classroom, they will consider four assessment and instruction design shifts: (1) change in audience (for learners' work), (2) change in research (how and with whom), (3) change in purpose (for student work), and (4) change in students' online social etiquette, communication, and behavior. Each of these changes will inform the teacher's instructional and assessment practices.

Change in Audience

In the past, the audience observing learners' work or interactions was most often the teacher and other learners. In a digital world, the audience for learners' innovative solutions, insights about issues, or questions can be those in the topic's field. The audience can be the authors of the books learners are reading, the politicians who generate the legislation, the mathematicians and engineers working on the project, or various individuals in the healthcare industry. These experts shed light on medical, social, political, and economic dilemmas. The access to people and places is unending. This shifting audience has great potential to increase learners' engagement.

With these new audiences, learners have the possibility of authentic application. Educators have always pushed learners to develop higher-level thinking skills, and while many of these skills are not new per se, their form and function are dramatically different in a digitally driven world. In her book, *Hacking Digital Learning Strategies: 10 Ways to Launch EdTech Missions in Your Classroom*, Shelly Sanchez Terrell (2017), an award-winning tech presenter in the field of education, provides clear ways educators can move from their old way of thinking (where learners solely argued through essays written to the teacher) to online arguments (that open up the debate to an audience outside the classroom and to other individuals or groups with a stake in the debated topic). Argument is a critical skill learners need to develop for any future success, but all too often online debating becomes more personal. Terrell (as cited in Barnes, 2017) states:

> We need to transform the digital debating mindset and help students see debate as a vehicle to strengthen their intellect and character. The way schools teach debate doesn't align with how our learners conduct arguments in real life. Traditionally, we teach students to debate by writing argumentative or persuasive essays. While this is important, our digital learners need to engage in online debates. They need the opportunity to draft shorter arguments to share with the public, as well as practice in responding intelligently to those with opposing views. Our students may regularly debate or argue on social media, yet schools rarely afford them the opportunity to acquire respectful debate skills as part of the curriculum.

It is essential to understand online communication; it's far more concise than text, uses images and visuals to communicate, and is interactive and intuitive. Whether communicating online with experts in the field or classmates down the hall, the type of communication must be, Terrell (2017) emphasizes, about the issues and not personal attacks. The audience a learner communicates with and to has changed, which alters *how* learners communicate. When that audience is authentic, the relevance and engagement for learners exceed what the traditional classroom offers.

Change in Research

The most dramatic change in how learners research is their access to information and the speed with which they can find information. Research used to be exclusively accessible in libraries, where learners spent countless hours searching for the sources that best matched their intended purposes. Today, many of these same resources are available online. In a Pew Research Center study of more than two thousand AP and National Writing Project (NWP) middle and high school teachers, 77 percent report that the internet has a "mostly positive" impact on students' ability to research (Purcell et al., 2012, p. 3). The study also says:

> At the same time, 76% of teachers surveyed "strongly agree" with the assertion that internet search engines have conditioned students to expect to be able to find information quickly and easily. Large majorities also agree with the assertion that the amount of information available online today is overwhelming to most students (83%) and that today's digital technologies discourage students from using a wide range of sources when conducting research (71%). Fewer teachers, but still a majority of this sample (60%), agree with the assertion that today's technologies make it harder for students to find credible sources of information. (Purcell et al., 2012, p. 3)

While there is much more access to sources, determining their credibility and using evidence from a variety of sources are skills students need to slow down and learn.

Change in Purpose

The amount of information available can be overwhelming, and so *purpose* matters. The purpose is beyond just knowing to *know* since there is so much information available. Rather, the focus must turn to knowing how to evaluate, synthesize, and apply the content found online. For example, the purpose of asking learners to debate and research might be to help them research a water quality issue their city is dealing with and develop solutions to address these problems, rather than simply debate for the sake of learning about water quality. A debate that focuses on a local or global issue can be purposeful and targeted so students deeply explore the water quality issue and contribute potential solutions rather than keeping their insights locked within the classroom walls. In another example, students may research an animal of their choice. The initial purpose may be for students to individually learn to research and learn facts about their animal; however, with a move to global citizenship, teachers may ask students to research their animal, consider how it benefits the local habitat and what dangers there might be to its existence, and share that information with another school or classroom. In one case, the purpose shifted from the focus being on debate to also generating solutions to a critical issue. In the second case, the purpose shifted from learning about an animal to also sharing that information with another group of students.

Change in Social Etiquette, Communication, and Behavior

As global citizens, students also learn how to communicate in a digital environment in respectful and productive ways. Anonymity makes it easy to forget that digital communication is still between people. Students may feel bolder online than they might be face-to-face, but they need to learn how to be bold and respectful versus confrontational and flippant. Comments that are personal and cutting have no place in any communication, and especially online. Teachers must explicitly teach the type of discourse needed online, as it influences people's perceptions of the value of any given exchange of ideas and solutions. As teachers consider what to teach students, they may consider sharing phrases to guide communication:

- How do I communicate disagreement?
  - "I see it in a different way."
  - "This source provides a counterargument or the other side of the issue."
- How do I address bullying or name calling?
  - "That sounds more like a personal attack. It makes me uncomfortable. I would rather focus on asking what that person's reasoning is versus calling him or her a name."
- How do I address and question the credibility of a source or when someone is posing an opinion without specific evidence?
  - "Where have you seen or heard about that? I would like to dig in a little more."
  - "Have you looked at the opposing argument?"
  - "What might the other side say?"
  - "Where was the source? Any chance the source holds some sort of bias or stake in the issue?"

Learners must be able to monitor their own digital footprint. While there are significant benefits to being able to connect with people all over the world, there is also significant risk. Learners must be able to engage with others online in a safe way, understanding what and what not to share. In an age in which oversharing can lead to bullying, exposure to inappropriate content, or access to dangerous situations, teachers must provide learners with the skills and tools they need to process these things effectively.

Assessing Digital Citizenship

In 2006, Ruben R. Puentedura developed the SAMR (substitution, augmentation, modification, and redefinition) model, which provides a framework for thinking through the types of assessments and learning activities students engage in, and the extent to which technology enhances learning (Digital Learning Team, n.d.). In the first two stages of the model, *substitution* and *augmentation*, assessments and activities involve technology, but could be completed without it. These first two stages are considered *enhancements* since they essentially represent a more efficient (and possibly more effective) way for learners and teachers to do what they currently do. For example, learners could tweet their responses to their teacher instead of writing them on index cards; this allows teachers to more readily respond to learners or learners to respond to each other. However, this dialogue could occur on paper or face-to-face without the *enhancement* of Twitter.

As technology integration becomes more sophisticated, it moves into what Puentedura calls *transformation* (Digital Learning Team, n.d.). The third and fourth stages in transformation are called *modification* and *redefinition*. For example, learners may collaborate with a local business to develop a new video game to market to teenagers or design videos to help a community understand the benefits of a new playground (both modifications). Learners could also, for example, create tech-based solutions that allow people a more efficient way to monitor their water usage levels (redefinition). Figure 7.1 (page 222) describes the four stages and provides examples to further illustrate what each stage looks like (Digital Learning Team, n.d.).

No matter which stage teachers use to design a technology-rich task, it is essential to first determine which of the critical competencies and standards they will assess. This is the foundation for making a task relevant and viable, or meaningful and doable, given the resources and time frame.

ISTE's digital citizenship standards (described previously on pages 216–217 and available online at www.iste.org/standards/for-students) are recursive. Any time learners are online, there is an opportunity for teacher or peer observation. Learners can also self-assess their progress in achieving these standards, or global digital citizenship skills. Teachers can check if learners recognize effective digital citizenship by assessing the basic safety guidelines through a paper-and-pencil method or online tool.

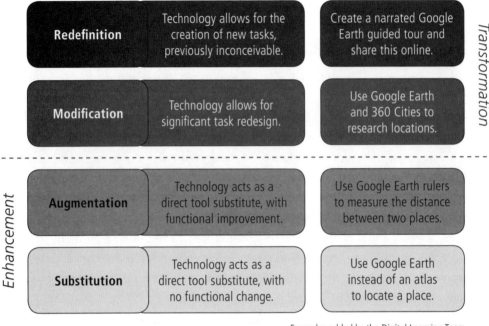

Source: Adapted from Digital Learning Team, n.d.

Figure 7.1: The SAMR model.

For example, having learners analyze a set of scenarios and name the best move to make in that situation might be an effective way to assess the extent to which learners understand the ways of a digital world. Figure 7.2 provides some ideas for such discussions and tasks.

At a deeper, application level, a teacher may ask learners to reflect on their own interactions and digital footprint, and those of their collaborators. This type of self- and peer assessment is a window into how students are making sense of this digital world. Teachers may also observe the ways learners are interacting and engaging in the digital world. Observations, accompanied by lists of criteria or observable characteristics, are valid methods of assessment for these types of application skills. These are excellent ways to assess the extent to which students know the ways of a global digital citizen and if they can apply them while engaging in meaningful tasks.

Directions: For each scenario, in the middle column describe how a positive contributing member of the digital world would respond. In the third column, describe the dangers if the actions are not stopped.

Scenario	Response	Dangers If Not Addressed
Third graders are working on an essay. While they are peer editing, a student copies and pastes a picture of a male body part into his friend's essay. This male body part is not part of the essay.		
The seventh-grade girls' basketball team is celebrating their victory. The girls start Snapchatting different moments from the game. Then, one girl makes a comment about how another team member did not help at all. She also says this team member almost lost the game for them.		
A high school student posts a picture of a teacher with a superimposed head of a monster. A comment references the class and how much the student hates the teacher.		
A group of students started a Facebook group to help them study for their calculus class. After a bullying incident in the larger school community, a student not in the calculus Facebook group was suspended. Some students in the calculus class were incredibly angry with the school administration and started posting their frustration in the calculus Facebook group.		
While preparing a YouTube video for his informative speech, a fifth grader copied and pasted images after searching general terms on Google. The YouTube video will be posted for other students in the school to view.		
While writing about China, a third grader found a great article and copied and pasted a few paragraphs into her Word document. She changed a few words and the title.		

Figure 7.2: *Digital citizenship scenarios.*

Visit go.SolutionTree.com/assessment for a free reproducible version of this figure.

It is essential students learn to monitor their postings and consider a set of criteria before responding impulsively. The well-known THINK acronym is useful in helping learners consider how to manage their online presence (Colan, 2014):

T—Is it true?

H—Is it harmful?

I—Is it illegal?

N—Is it necessary?

K—Is it kind?

Providing students feedback and experiences to practice how to effectively and responsibly communicate in digital spaces requires intention and persistence. While initial efforts may seem daunting, the benefits to students and the larger society are powerful. Beyond students being able to explain what it means to be productive in their online communication, practice in applying appropriate digital communication skills is the key to students achieving them. More thoughtful and positive interactions online lead to healthier communities and innovative solutions.

There are many helpful tools and organizations to guide teachers in creating engaging and meaningful tasks to cultivate digital citizenship. The following list (also accessible online at **go.SolutionTree.com/assessment**) is not intended to be exhaustive, as there are always new or improved applications, but it provides a starting point for educators just beginning their journey of assessing digital citizenship.

- **Pear Deck (https://peardeck.com):** Both free and paid versions of this application allow teachers to share slideshows with learners, make them interactive, and collect evidence for learning goals.

- **Google Hangouts (https://hangouts.google.com):** This video conferencing tool allows students to connect with other classrooms, peers, or experts in the field to dialogue and share ideas.

- **Google Docs (https://google.com/docs/about):** This application allows users to create a Word document, collaborate with others, and more. Learners and teachers can provide comments and offer feedback synchronously.

- **Google Forms (https://google.com/forms/about):** This survey tool is useful for generating assessments or collecting information as learners collect entries in a spreadsheet and then display the data as graphs. This tool is useful to generate all types of items for discussion or to collect evidence of understanding.

- **Google Expeditions (https://edu.google.com/expeditions /#about):** This is a virtual reality teaching tool in which learners immerse themselves in and explore the world through virtual- and augmented-reality tours. These experiences, or tours, provide many opportunities for students to dialogue about places they have not been, learn about faraway locations, and explore critical issues facing different places in the world as if they were there. These experiences provide evidence and experience for students to use when being assessed on the critical competencies.

- **Goobric (Rubrics on Google; goo.gl/jAfH4y):** When assessing critical competencies and digital citizenship, a rubric is most often the best tool to signal levels of quality or proficiency. Goobric allows teachers to use online rubrics that provide feedback and target scoring within an electronic document such as Google Sheets.

- **OrangeSlice extension (Google Docs; https://goo.gl/YSqdty):** This tool provides another way to add rubrics to a Google document and can easily transform into a teacher's gradebook.

- **Google Calendar (https://goo.gl/9qNceB):** Google Calendar is an electronic way to collaborate with others and share due dates, reading schedules, and collaborative project due dates.

- **Screencastify (www.screencastify.com):** Screencastify is an extension in the Chrome browser that allows students to record videos along with visuals. This is an excellent tool for instruction and assessment.

- **Google Earth (https://google.com/earth):** Google Earth is a tool used to guide students in exploring various locations around the world. This tool allows students to calculate distances between locations, produce interactive videos to explain various geographic concepts and issues, hear stories, and experience some locations in 3-D.

- **Book Creator (https://bookcreator.com):** This website works well with an iPad to allow learners to draw, create voiceovers, take pictures, and more.

- **Explain Everything (https://explaineverything.com):** This interactive whiteboard platform allows collaboration, works with the iPad, and is great for students of all ages.

- **Assistments (www.aboutus.assistments.org):** This tool for teachers and learners promotes uncovering misconceptions, providing feedback, and tracking progress over time.

- **Agile Mind (www.agilemind.com/our-approach):** This program helps teachers develop more cognitively demanding tasks for secondary students (Cook, Seeley, & Chaput, 2011).

- **Strategic Reader (https://pearson.com/us/higher-education /products-services-teaching/learning-engagement-tools/strategic -reader.html):** This tool for middle-school readers allows for a personalized, responsive workflow. Teachers can gather evidence during instruction and then use interventions as needed with accurate assessment information (Cohen, Hall, Vue, & Ganley, 2011).

- **Padlet (https://padlet.com):** This application allows learners to post on a common wall to share questions, ideas, and resources in an interactive and synchronous manner.

- **Augmented Reality**: Teachers can use or create a live or computerized view into an actual geographic location, science concept, or other experience. Students will feel like they are immersed in the concept as they explore what they are learning in this authentic context.

- **Twitter (https://twitter.com):** This platform helps users connect, get data, and share work happening in class.

Organizations like ISTE and Common Sense Education provide excellent resources and up-to-date information regarding technology tools, use, and design. It is important to determine the purpose of the task before choosing the tool, as the novelty of any application will wear off. Instead, it is a meaningful purpose that will create a sustainable practice and help learners develop into productive, contributing, and ethical digital citizens.

There are various ways to propel learners into the digital world as global citizens; the key is to ensure a clear purpose and meaningful task. These will help learners develop critical competencies. *Curation* offers one example of how technology provides a new way for learners to engage in content, generate new ideas, and contribute to a global conversation. Just as a museum curator pulls together a series of artifacts to display and inform, learners can collaborate to create a curation of a topic or an issue. Through the process of collaboration, teachers observe learners as digital citizens and collaborators, and help them develop unique resources such as a website, podcast, or other digital tool to share their curation. Learners can share this set of artifacts with other peers, other classes around the globe, or even experts in the field (Gonzalez, 2017). Assessing digital citizenship has endless possibilities.

Measuring Digital Citizenship

As with many of the other critical competencies, rubrics, checklists, and self-assessment tools are effective both in providing learner feedback on levels of proficiency and when guiding learners in monitoring their progress on becoming digital citizens. In any given assessment, it is important to clearly outline the learning expectations. The following learning targets provide an example of the kind of descriptions that specify what teachers and learners measure in digital citizenship.

- I can develop a digital identity and reputation. This means I know the strategies to use to develop an identity and how to apply them in my context.

- I can manage my digital identity and reputation. This means I'm aware of the permanence of my actions in the digital world. If I make a mistake, I know how to fix it.

- I engage in positive, safe, legal, and ethical behaviors when using technology. This includes my social interactions online or when using networked devices, like the school's iPad.

- I demonstrate respect for the rights and obligations of using and sharing intellectual property.

- I copy and paste images or texts with proper permission.

- I properly cite and give credit to the creator when I share intellectual property. This includes images, text, videos, and other multimedia.

- I can manage my personal data and maintain digital privacy and security.

- I can identify data-collection technology used to track my navigation online. This means I can describe what the tracking technology does and how to ensure my safety.

As teams of teachers define digital citizenship and write learning targets to share with students, these descriptions become the foundation for the types of assessments used to monitor progress and ensure students master these essential concepts.

Checklists

Checklists are effective when they provide concrete lists of binary skills students need to develop. Being a digital citizen is certainly a competency that is ubiquitous online, and the previous set of learning targets (see page 227) can guide learners toward understanding all the components of digital citizenship. Figure 7.3 provides a template for teachers to use as they observe learners applying these skills. Observation is a valid method of assessment, especially when teachers and learners co-construct what each learning target might look like by describing how these skills play in out in various tasks and situations. The checklist in figure 7.3 is for teachers and learners to use when measuring digital citizenship.

Self-Assessment Tools

If learners are to act with integrity independently and productively in the absence of adults, they must self-manage and monitor, or *self-regulate*. Learners can use figure 7.4 (pages 230–232) to assess their thinking about each learning target before, during (check 1 and 2), and after a project or unit on digital citizenship. The part 1 score is a confidence indicator; learners consider how confident they are about this particular skill. The part 2 score is a knowledge and application measurement that indicates the level of implementation a learner has with that particular skill. For younger learners, teachers may use visuals to show examples of what each learning target looks like. In addition, younger learners may only focus on one or two areas.

Rubrics

Rubrics are descriptions of quality that help learners and teachers see the pathway to more sophisticated achievement. The first step in designing an effective rubric is writing learning goals and finding criteria to focus the rubric. Figure 7.5 (page 233) is a single-point digital citizenship rubric that provides a list of criteria to guide teachers' rubric development.

Use the following scale to reflect on students' digital citizenship skills.

4—Consistently **3**—Often **2**—Sometimes, but needs reminders **1**—Rarely

Learner's name	Develops a digital identity	Manages his or her digital footprint to ensure respectful and responsible practices	Employs positive, safe, legal, and ethical behavior when using technology	Ethically cites and gives credit when sharing other people's ideas	Identifies and uses data collection techniques to track data responsibly and effectively

Figure 7.3: Tracking form for learners' digital citizenship.

Visit go.SolutionTree.com/assessment for a free reproducible version of this figure.

Name: _____   Date: _____

Part 1. Rate your confidence and application level for each learning target.

Confidence level: Indicate how confident you are about the quality of your response.

- Unsure what this means
- Mostly know what it means, but have questions
- Confident I can do this
- Confident I could teach others this

Scoring: Check your work and indicate which criteria you feel are present in your response.

1—Know it   4—Apply it consistently
2—Recognize it   5—Advocate for it
3—Apply it

Learning Targets	Confidence level				Scoring			
	Pre	Check #1	Check #2	Post	Pre	Check #1	Check #2	Post
I can develop a digital identity and reputation. I know the strategies I use to develop an identity and how to apply them in my context.								
I can manage my digital identity and reputation. I'm aware of the permanence of my actions in the digital world. If I make a mistake, I know how to fix it.								
I engage in positive, safe, legal, and ethical behavior when using technology. This includes my social interactions online or when using networked devices, like the school's iPad.								

I demonstrate respect for the rights and obligations of using and sharing intellectual property. I copy and paste images or texts with proper permission, and I properly cite and give credit to the creator when I share intellectual property. This includes images, text, videos, and other multimedia.		
I can manage my personal data and maintain digital privacy and security. I regularly update passwords and check security settings.		
I can identify data-collection technology used to track my navigation online. I can describe what the tracking technology does and how to ensure my safety.		

continued →

Figure 7.4: *Learner reflection on digital citizenship learning targets.*

Part 2. Reflect on your experiences with global digital citizenship.

Timing	What is working well?	What questions persist?	What is not working well and is something you want to work on in the next few weeks?
Pre			
Check 1			
Check 2			
Post			

1. Describe examples of strong global digital citizenship you have observed in your interactions with peers in class and online:

2. Describe examples of global digital citizenship that need to improve based on your observations and interactions with peers in class and online:

3. Have you encountered any personal safety issues? If so, how did you handle them?

*Visit **go.SolutionTree.com/assessment** for a free reproducible version of this figure.*

Specific Aspects in Need of Strengthening	Advancing	Specific Aspects of Strength
	I can cultivate a digital identity and reputation. I know the strategies to use to develop an identity and how to apply them in my context.	
	I can manage my digital identity and reputation. I'm aware of the permanence of my actions in the digital world. If I make a mistake, I know how to fix it.	
	I engage in positive, safe, legal, and ethical behavior when using technology. This includes my social interactions online or when using networked devices, like the school's iPad.	
	I demonstrate respect for the rights and obligations of using and sharing intellectual property. • I copy and paste images or texts with proper permission. • I properly cite and give credit to the creator when I share intellectual property. This includes images, text, video, and other multimedia.	
	I can manage my personal data and maintain digital privacy and security.	
	I can identify data-collection technology used to track my navigation online. This means I can describe what the tracking technology does and how to ensure my safety.	

Figure 7.5: Single-point digital citizenship rubric.

*Visit **go.SolutionTree.com/assessment** for a free reproducible version of this figure.*

Growing Digital Citizenship

Being a digital citizen is not just for learners. Adults should model being responsible digital citizens because students are always watching. Educators promote digital citizenship by what they ask learners to do. As technology advances, it will be important to consider the following tips when both measuring what it means to be a digital citizen as well as implementing tasks that are more global. As learners become global digital citizens, they will develop other critical competencies such as creative problem solving, critical thinking, online collaboration, and effective communication. Consider the following tips when helping all learners achieve and become global digital citizens.

- Pick one or two tools and learn to use them well.

- During your first time through, teach learners with something fun and engaging—and consider limiting the amount of academic content. Teach the process and how to navigate the program. The next time, use it with content so there are not so many variables for learners.

- Experiment in a topic or class where you feel confident.

- Acknowledge that you don't have to be an expert. Let the learners explore different technologies. Make mistakes and solve them in front of learners.

- Problem solve in front of learners so they begin to see how to persist, try different things, and stick with tasks. However, know when to move on and when to keep problem solving.

- Realize there is a good amount of upfront work to make the instruction of digital citizenship engaging and meaningful. Remember it is incredibly worth it in the end, and it gets easier as you keep trying.

- Be aware that technology allows you to manage learners at varying levels of understanding with clear expectations, directions, and workflow (time for feedback and revision).

- Provide time and resources to learn, experiment, and deeply implement quality technology practices in assessment.

Being a productive and contributing digital citizen is essential to students' future success. They are living and working in a digital world, and teachers can facilitate and ensure success through targeting specific and manageable steps when assessing these skills.

Conclusion

Citizenship has transformed from simply integrating with one's school and local communities to a digital and global experience where one has opportunities to not only learn about other parts of the world but also actually interact and collaborate with people worldwide. As Common Sense Education (n.d.b) states, "Being a good digital citizen is more than knowing your way around the web. It's about connecting and collaborating in ways you didn't even know were possible." Digital citizenship is an integral part of the world, and there are opportunities and responsibility to teach learners how to live productively and successfully in that world.

Pause and Ponder

On your own or as part of a collaborative teacher team, consider the following reflective questions.

1. What quote or passage encapsulates your biggest takeaway from this chapter? What immediate action (large or small) will you take as a result of this takeaway? Explain both to your team.

2. What is a global digital citizen? What are the key elements to becoming a productive global digital citizen? How does the description in this chapter affirm, differ from, or extend your understanding of global digital citizenship?

3. Do you currently help learners develop as digital citizens? If so, how?

4. What might be the best ways to assess digital citizenship given the age of the learners you teach?

5. How does or could global digital citizenship seamlessly connect to the other critical competencies?

6. Which local and global issues might be relevant to your context? How could learners develop a local or global digital presence in order to contribute to these local or global issues?

7. Are there local businesses or global organizations that might be natural partners for your learners?

CHAPTER 8
SOCIAL COMPETENCE

There is growing evidence from international longitudinal studies that clearly suggests noncognitive factors play a critical role in one's success as a citizen.

—Yong Zhao

While there is no dispute that academic achievement still matters, the focus on noncognitive skills is gaining importance. According to renowned educator and speaker Yong Zhao (2016), "Noncognitive factors such as personality traits, motivation, interpersonal skills, and intrapersonal skills have been found to correlate significantly with educational attainment, workplace productivity, and life earnings" (p. 4). Social competence—noncognitive skills that include what some refer to as *soft skills, social and emotional learning, or global literacy* to name a few—now occupies a parallel space in terms of what important outcomes learners are supposed to achieve. The intent is to create parallel goals of excellence between cognitive skills and social and emotional well-being to help learners in *all* aspects of their future, not just those related to academics.

Proficiency with social competence is essential to the success of learners in their present and future lives. Lucinda Fickel (2015), associate director of policy at the University of Chicago's Urban Education Institute, writes, "What we all know is that these skills, traits, attributes, mindsets and behaviors are profoundly important for children's success in school and in life." Social competence is lifelong, since these social characteristics are fully transferable across all aspects of life. Being *respectful* or *responsible* toward oneself and others, for example, can habituate to the point where, regardless of situation or circumstance, it becomes the default response—this is who the person is. Learning to be responsible in school has the potential to transfer to being a responsible adult at work, at home, with family, or with friends.

Defining Social Competence

Social competencies include any behavioral attribute, characteristic, emotional disposition, or action that allows learners to socially adapt so as to align more seamlessly with the most immediate conditions. Intentionally broad, this definition allows for a more finite, contextually sensitive definition to emerge. Social competencies are contextually dependent since countries, states or provinces, cities, and even communities can have unique social norms. Many U.S. states, Canadian provinces, and countries around the world actively engage in defining such competencies for their schools.

Like so many of the critical competencies, social competence is not so much a *new* priority as it is a *renewed* priority. As the pendulum swings to more of the clinical side of assessment and instruction, educators throughout the world note an important gap. The skills some might deem *soft* (such as demonstrating empathy, making ethical decisions, and maintaining positive relationships, to name a few) are actually the hardest—but most worthy—things to teach. Educators recognize the critical role social competence plays in an interconnected world. Jurisdictions quite literally around the world are now articulating a clear position on the importance of social competence and its authentic place in preparing learners for success in the present and future.

In its position statements, the Partnership for 21st Century Learning (P21, n.d.) lays out a set of 21st century themes that go beyond the four critical competencies (critical thinking, creativity, collaboration, and communication) most often associated with its work. Figure 8.1 outlines these essential themes for the success of all individuals in the 21st century.

In many ways each of these themes is a social competency schools and districts can contextualize for their own purposes. The embedded social competence is obvious in the statements surrounding the themes of global awareness, civic literacy, health literacy, and environmental literacy. And, schools and districts can quite seamlessly embed financial, economic, business, and entrepreneurial literacy within the broader context of social competence. For example, *knowing how to make appropriate personal economic choices* not only has financial ramifications but also is directly related to

Global Awareness	• Using 21st century skills to understand and address global issues • Learning from and working collaboratively with individuals representing diverse cultures, religions, and lifestyles in a spirit of mutual respect and open dialogue in personal, work, and community contexts • Understanding other nations and cultures, including the use of non-English languages
Financial, Economic, Business, and Entrepreneurial Literacy	• Knowing how to make appropriate personal economic choices • Understanding the role of the economy in society • Using entrepreneurial skills to enhance workplace productivity and career options
Civic Literacy	• Participating effectively in civic life through knowing how to stay informed and understanding governmental processes • Exercising the rights and obligations of citizenship at local, state, national, and global levels • Understanding the local and global implications of civic decisions
Health Literacy	• Obtaining, interpreting, and understanding basic health information and services and using such information and services in ways that enhance health • Understanding preventive physical and mental health measures, including proper diet, nutrition, exercise, risk avoidance, and stress reduction • Using available information to make appropriate health-related decisions • Establishing and monitoring personal and family health goals • Understanding national and international public health and safety issues
Environmental Literacy	• Demonstrating knowledge and understanding of the environment and the circumstances and conditions affecting it, particularly as it relates to air, climate, land, food, energy, water, and ecosystems • Demonstrating knowledge and understanding of society's impact on the natural world (for example, population growth, population development, resource consumption rate, and so on) • Investigating and analyzing environmental issues, and making accurate conclusions about effective solutions • Taking individual and collective action toward addressing environmental challenges (for example, participating in global actions or designing solutions that inspire action on environmental issues)

Source: Partnership for 21st Century Learning, n.d.

Figure 8.1: Essential 21st century themes.

personal wellness; and, *understanding the role of the economy in society* can easily be infused into discussions about social justice. The point is, these themes can serve as a foundation through which schools and districts develop social competencies in their learners.

Likewise, as part of its new curriculum, the Ministry of Education in British Columbia (Government of British Columbia, 2016) identifies three social competencies to go along with the other critical competencies now emphasized throughout the province. The following list illustrates these social competencies and the big ideas. This an example of how a jurisdiction creates a more thorough definition of what it means to be *socially competent.*

1. Positive personal and cultural identity:

    * Relationships and cultural contexts—Students understand that their relationships and cultural contexts help to shape who they are. ("Culture" is meant in its broadest sense, including identifiers such as ethnicity, nationality, language, ability, sex or gender, age, geographic region, sexuality, and religion.) Students define themselves in terms of their relationship to others and their relationship to the world (people and places) around them.

    * Personal values and choices—Students define what they value. They understand how what they value has been influenced by their life experiences. They identify ways in which what they value helps to shape their choices in all contexts of their lives.

    * Personal strengths and abilities—Students acknowledge their strengths and abilities, and explicitly consider these as assets that can help them in all aspects of their lives. Students understand that they are unique and a part of larger communities. They explain how they are using their strengths and abilities in their families, their relationships, and their communities.

2. Personal awareness and responsibility:

    * Self-determination—Students who are personally aware and responsible have a sense of personal efficacy and a growing confidence in a variety of situations. They value themselves, their ideas, and their accomplishments. They are able to express their needs and seek help when they

need it, to find purpose and motivation and act on it, and to advocate for themselves.

- Well-being—Students who are personally aware and responsible recognize how their decisions and actions affect their mental, physical, emotional, social, cognitive, and spiritual wellness, and take increasing responsibility for caring for themselves. They keep themselves healthy and physically active, manage stress, and express a sense of personal well-being. They make choices that contribute to their safety in their communities, including online interactions. They recognize the importance of happiness, and have strategies in place that help them find peace in challenging situations.

- Self-regulation—Students who are personally aware and responsible take responsibility for their own choices and actions. They set goals, monitor progress, and understand and regulate their emotions. They are aware that learning involves patience and time. They are able to persevere in difficult situations and to understand how their actions affect themselves and others.

3. Social responsibility:

- Valuing diversity—Students value diversity, defend human rights, advocate for others, and act with a sense of ethics in interactions, including online.

- Solving problems in a peaceful way—Students identify and develop an appreciation of different perspectives on issues; they generate, use, and evaluate strategies to resolve problems.

- Building relationships—Students develop and maintain diverse, positive peer and intergenerational relationships in a variety of contexts.

- Contributing to community and caring for the environment—Students develop awareness and take responsibility for their social, physical, and natural environments by working independently and collaboratively for the benefit of others, communities, and the environment.

These personal and social competencies represent a balanced approach to developing learners' critical competencies since they are three of the six competencies; the others are *critical thinking, creative thinking,* and *communication,* which includes collaboration. According to the Ontario Ministry of Education (2016):

> The redesign of the curriculum maintains a focus on sound foundations of literacy and numeracy while supporting the development of citizens who are competent thinkers and communicators, and who are personally and socially competent in all areas of their lives. (p. 1)

It is critical for teachers to avoid viewing social competence as a separate silo of instructional outcomes. Noncognitive skills are embedded within so many of the other critical competencies that educators can naturally develop and assess them alongside critical competencies and content proficiency; teachers don't need to create yet another stand-alone assessment for noncognitive skills.

Developing personally and socially competent learners allows teachers to focus on developing *thinkers with a conscience* who consider the residual effect of their actions to both themselves and the world around them. Dividing social competence into inter- and intrapersonal social competencies is a helpful distinction as schools and districts begin to explore what is contextually relevant for their learners.

Interpersonal Social Competence

Interpersonal competencies are related to the interaction or communication between people. As learners age, their experience, sophistication, and scope of interpersonal competencies expand.

Interpersonal social competence for elementary learners will likely focus on their most immediate interactions. Schools can begin developing learners as respectful, empathetic, caring, and cooperative individuals at the earliest ages. As well, educators can teach learners the importance of nonverbal communication through *paralanguage* (such as pitch, speed, and volume) and *body language* (such as facial expressions, gestures, and body positioning) so they understand the ways people interact with one another. Teachers can develop this understanding in learners at a very young age. As learners develop, teachers can begin to nurture an awareness of how learners' interpersonal social competence impacts not only those in their immediacy but also those around the periphery. Learners will begin to understand how respectful behavior not only consists of a positive interaction with a singular person or group but also actually contributes in a larger context to create a respectful community.

As a learner's perspective on the world expands, so will his or her ability to develop more community and global social competencies. Obviously, an individual learner's firsthand experience will influence the degree to which he or she can comprehend the ramifications of personal choices and actions. Those who, for example, have the good fortune to travel to different countries are more likely to understand the diversity of the world and how their actions potentially add something to (or detract from) the community's level of cultural awareness and appreciation. But all learners, regardless of their traveling experience, have the potential to develop into considerate citizens who display curiosity about and show respect for other cultures and groups, if teachers instruct them in such behaviors. Again, much of this ability is contextually relevant and nuanced, but as the breadth and depth of understanding expand, learners can, with some sophistication, begin to fully appreciate what it means to exercise civic rights and responsibilities, develop an authentic level of global awareness, or understand fully how their actions impact the environment. Learners can, for example, understand that political discourse fosters critical thinking and collaboration. It is a collective social competence for a society to not only engage in discussion to understand the issues but also to discover how that engagement contributes to the collective good.

As learners engage in a more global society, it becomes more critical for them to understand the nuances of different cultures. In Japan, for example, pointing is a less-than-favorable nonverbal action; bowing is customary. For older, sophisticated, more globally focused learners, fully understanding the unique customs and etiquette of various countries allows them to socially adapt more seamlessly in any relevant situation or context. While it is true that the majority of learners may not travel to other countries, the possibility of interacting with people from other countries is increasingly likely in the age of global digital citizenship, making the understanding of cultural nuances much more important.

Intrapersonal Social Competence

Intrapersonal social competence, on the other hand, is more about how one acts within or toward oneself. A learner who has strong intrapersonal skills maintains an awareness of his or her own thoughts and feelings, and manages emotions carefully when communicating with others, making decisions, or navigating responses. Intrapersonal skills are critical to help learners maintain an appropriate attitude or initiate a responsible reaction due to their own positive internal dialogue.

It is important for teachers to highlight, develop, and reinforce these intrapersonal competencies in learners to ensure they develop a level of awareness about how they act toward themselves and others. Again, the range from the simple to the most sophisticated is a sliding scale that expands as learners develop, but the characteristics or habits they develop are essentially universal.

Initially, some intrapersonal competencies are habits of the mind that essentially allow learners to discover who they are. Being reflective, self-aware, and self-respectful is a desirable, habitual way of thinking; acting with integrity while unsupervised is a sure sign of intrapersonal social competence. Teachers can purposefully develop learners' abilities to be self-regulatory about their self-messaging, learning, and behavior. As they increase in sophistication, learners realize how they think inwardly will shape how they see and interpret events around them. As well, learners' intrapersonal competence serves as a building block for how they develop their ethical minds (Gardner, 2010) when facing social or moral dilemmas where more than one course of action is possible and a difficult decision is at hand. The intrapersonal competencies are not a prescription for *what* learners are to think, but more a road map for *how* to think as they shape their own perspectives on themselves and the world around them.

Considering Social Competence Now and Going Forward

With the emerging development of social and emotional standards, educators are now purposefully bringing a clearer articulation of what dispositional habits and attributes are essential for learners. As such, social competence must now become a forethought as teachers, schools, and districts think through the implications for instruction and assessment.

What was once a seemingly hidden curriculum is now a front-end construct teachers must actively seek to develop in each and every learner. This construct creates a balance between the learning and the learner—there are both academic and behavioral competencies in the educational experience. Table 8.1 highlights the International Baccalaureate Organization's (2013) IB learner profile. According to the IB, "The aim of all IB programmes is to develop internationally minded people who, recognizing their common humanity and shared guardianship of the planet, help create a better and more peaceful world."

Clearly the IB learner profile articulates a more holistic view of the educational experience—social competence is an embedded part of the overall expectations of learners; and being caring, open-minded, and principled sits alongside being a thinker, inquirer, and communicator. The IB Organization (2013) adds, "The IB learner profile represents 10 attributes valued by IB World Schools. We believe these attributes, and others like them, can help individuals and groups become responsible members of local, national and global communities." Social competency expectations are laws (standards) or curriculum expectations, so educators' approach must be positive, proactive, and instructionally focused.

Table 8.1: IB Learner Profile

IB Learner Attribute	Student-Centered Explanation
Inquirers	We nurture our curiosity, developing skills for inquiry and research. We know how to learn independently and with others. We learn with enthusiasm and sustain our love of learning throughout life.
Knowledgeable	We develop and use conceptual understanding, exploring knowledge across a range of disciplines. We engage with issues and ideas that have local and global significance.
Thinkers	We use critical and creative thinking skills to analyze and take responsible action on complex problems. We exercise initiative in making reasoned, ethical decisions.
Communicators	We express ourselves confidently and creatively in more than one language and in many ways. We collaborate effectively, listening carefully to the perspectives of other individuals and groups.
Principled	We act with integrity and honesty, with a strong sense of fairness and justice, and with respect for the dignity and rights of people everywhere. We take responsibility for our actions and their consequences.
Open-Minded	We critically appreciate our own cultures and personal histories, as well as the values and traditions of others. We seek and evaluate a range of points of view, and we are willing to grow from the experience.
Caring	We show empathy, compassion, and respect. We have a commitment to service, and we act to make a positive difference in the lives of others and in the world around us.
Risk-Takers	We approach uncertainty with forethought and determination; we work independently and cooperatively to explore new ideas and innovative strategies. We are resourceful and resilient in the face of challenges and change.
Balanced	We understand the importance of balancing different aspects of our lives—intellectual, physical, and emotional—to achieve well-being for ourselves and others. We recognize our interdependence with other people and with the world in which we live.
Reflective	We thoughtfully consider the world and our own ideas and experience. We work to understand our strengths and weaknesses in order to support our learning and personal development.

Source: International Baccalaureate Organization, 2013.

This proactive approach is gaining sponsorship at the highest levels. All fifty U.S. states have a set of standards for social and emotional learning; they are similar, but not exact, in expectations. While such standards were once reserved for elementary years, educators must now move toward developing the *whole* learner from elementary to high school.

The State of Washington Office of Superintendent of Public Instruction (2017) wholeheartedly endorses the P21 framework as part of its Career and Technical Education (CTE) program, which includes many aspects of social competence. (See www.k12.wa.us/CareerTechEd/TwentyFirstCenturySkills.aspx for more information.) Similarly, the Ontario Ministry of Education (2016), when defining 21st century learning, asserts that a focus on cognitive, interpersonal, and intrapersonal domains "encourages a more balanced approach to assisting students in developing the knowledge, skills, and characteristics that will lead them to become personally successful, economically productive, and actively engaged citizens" (p. 11). These examples of sponsorship make it clear at a systems level that a focus on social competence is not only important but also essential.

Intentional Assessment

Any jurisdiction claiming learners prepared for the 21st century must back up this proclamation with evidence. While the assessment of social competence is different than more traditional assessments, it is nonetheless important so teachers can identify the discrepancy between the learner's current status and desired status. Far too often, the so-called hidden curriculum of the past is paired with hidden assessment, especially when learners act in a less-than-favorable manner. Only when a student acted *inappropriately* (for example, submitted an assignment late) did the topic of *social competence* (in this case, responsibility) come up. Now, the focus is on being more proactive, rather than simply reacting to undesirable characteristics. As attention to teaching social competence increases, so too must the assessment of those social competencies. Moreover, many districts include their social and emotional standards on report cards, so teachers must also often grade social competencies.

The intentionality of assessment brings with it the need for educators to clearly express criteria. Figure 8.2, which shows the Approaches to Learning (AtL) of the American Community School (ACS) of Abu Dhabi in the United Arab Emirates, illustrates a more granular example of the criteria that measure this school's identified critical social competencies.

AtL Skill	Specific Performance Criteria
Collaboration: Collaborative skills that elevate the learning for oneself and for others	• Commits to and works productively toward the shared goals of the group • Takes an active role without dominating the group • Engages in give-and-take dialogue to build on learning and ideas of others • Encourages others to share ideas
Responsibility: Responsible skills that maximize learning opportunities	• Comes to class prepared to learn • Uses time constructively • Listens actively • Sustains focus on tasks • Follows rules and expectations • Takes responsibility for actions and consequences
Self-Directed Learning: Reflective skills that lead to greater self-efficacy	• Demonstrates self-awareness • Persists when facing a challenge • Approaches mistakes and challenges as opportunities to grow • Seeks and uses feedback • Reflects on past and present learning • Adjusts thinking to new contexts
Citizenship: Respectful skills that demonstrate open-mindedness and global awareness	• Shows respect • Demonstrates a consideration of multiple perspectives • Contributes to a positive learning environment and respects others' right to learn • Recognizes needs and actively responds

Source: © 2013 by the American Community School of Abu Dhabi. Used with permission.

Figure 8.2: ACS K–12 Approaches to Learning.

It is evident that the learning approaches in figure 8.2 constitute the kind of social competencies the school anticipates learners must have to thrive both in and out of the school context. Standards-based grading drives the separation of learner attributes and competencies at ACS, where the articulation of achievement and behavioral attributes is separate to ensure greater accuracy (Schimmer, 2016); however, this separation only makes the emphasis on *social competence* more seamless and possible. By identifying clear and specific success criteria, K–12 teachers establish successful alignment.

Productive Disruption

Some of the social competencies teachers are developing cut across what has been traditionally the "right" way to act in school. In the past, quiet compliance was the desired state, and those learners who violated that desired state were often seen as disruptive and noncompliant. However, the absence of antisocial behavior (passive compliance) is not evidence of prosocial behavior, which means teachers need to see overt demonstrations of the desirable social competencies rather than simply assuming the quiet, compliant learner is socially competent. This sounds simple, but teachers must prepare for the implications of some social competencies.

Being a risk-taker, for example, means teachers can anticipate a few failures initially since taking risks—especially early in a learning progression—constitutes uncharted territory for some learners. As such, teachers must ensure that not learning fast enough isn't held against learners in perpetuity. Other social competencies, such as personal wellness, global awareness, and social responsibility, create a kind of productive disruption to the norm as learners develop and practice their skills. This is not a license for learners to be obnoxious, rude, or disrespectful, but teachers should anticipate respectful challenges, requests for justification, or even pushback to what they assert. Proactively pursuing the desirable social competencies could feel a little disorderly at first, but as teachers become clear on what productive disruption looks like, learners will understand how to *disrupt* without *disrespect*.

Given this context (teachers instructing learners on social competencies to prepare them for a changing world), there are a number of considerations educators must take into account when preparing to assess these traits.

Assessing Social Competence

Assessing social competence is not necessarily easy, but it's still necessary to purposefully create opportunities for learners to demonstrate their social competence, either informally or formally. Like all critical competencies, teachers (or the learners themselves) can most effectively assess social competence in a natural context so authenticity is maintained. Equally, if not more important, educators require clear criteria for scoring social competence beyond the bias of personal preferences or opinions regarding a learner's response.

Contextual Application of Assessments

People are more or less socially competent in relation to a specific context, not necessarily at a general level (Aarkrog & Wahlgren, 2017). Like most critical competencies, the residual payoff for learners is when what teachers ask them to know, do, or understand reflects an authentic learning experience. Context matters, which means it is possible for learners to show socially competent actions and attitudes in one area (for example, social responsibility toward the environment) while having a limited level of social competence in another (for example, personal and cultural awareness). As well, social responsibility itself could present on a sliding scale; a learner could be very competent at valuing diversity through respectful and inclusive actions but be more challenged with examining complex social issues through multiple perspectives. Context will always matter, and while it may not be possible to replicate the depth and breadth of contexts people face day to day, it is most desirable when teachers contextualize social competence for greater accuracy in assessment. Assessing social competence is not about more *tests* where students answer hypothetical questions with generic responses, and it's not about memorizing the collection of social skills. The assessment of social competence is more about the *doing* rather than just the *knowing*. Of course, learners will have to know before they do, but ultimately the goal is to have learners become socially competent through their actions toward themselves, others, and the world around them.

Replicating an authentic context is not always easy. Some demonstrations of social competence such as citizenship are easier to replicate than others. Additionally, when learners are collaborating, the criteria for effective collaboration and social competence will align—and even overlap. Much of what learners do in collaboration with one another blends critical thinking, creative thinking, and social competence. Social competence should not be viewed as a separate silo; rather, it is simply another lens through which teachers can examine their learners' growth toward proficiency with all critical competencies as they assess learners with both formal and informal assessments.

Formal Assessment

A theme throughout this book is that purposeful assessment of any critical competency requires teachers to create opportunities for learners to show what they know, can do, and understand. Social competence is no different. Certainly, some teachers might find assessing social competence daunting, as their interpretation of what it means to be competent isn't always universal. Still, it is necessary to create formal opportunities and criteria so nothing is left to chance. Furthermore, teachers can mitigate the potential assessment grievance of *bias* if the entire staff works to clarify their standards, criteria, and expectations of proficiency levels; develop a shared understanding of what quality assessment prompts work with such skills; and continually examine learners' work for the purposes of calibrating their scoring regarding social competencies.

Once schools decide how to define social competence, they can take advantage of situations that are already in play. One of the ten IB (2013) learner profile attributes, for example, is to be *principled* ("to act with integrity and honesty, with a strong sense of fairness and justice, and with respect for the dignity and rights of people everywhere"). Teachers could ask learners to analyze ethical dilemmas, such as: "If it was guaranteed that you wouldn't get caught, would you cheat on a final exam?" "What is the difference between lying to your parents about your whereabouts versus lying to someone about his or her new haircut?" Learners could respond individually or collaboratively. If the latter, not only could teachers assess collaboration but also critical thinking (analyzing the ethics of the dilemma) and social competence (the most likely decision the learners would make).

Informal Assessment

Assessing social competence could theoretically occur any time throughout an entire school day using formal and informal constructs. A learner's school experience is an inherently social situation, so the informal assessment of social competence can happen in real time. Learners' personal and cultural awareness, empathy and compassion, and contribution to a positive environment (just to name a few) will become evident over time, especially if teachers clearly articulate the desirable characteristics of someone who is socially competent. Even when not formally arranged, teachers can assess social interactions and responses as learners simply go about the business of school.

The IB (2013) learner profile trait of being balanced, as an example, will manifest without the need for any formal assessments. In fact, sometimes informally assessing social competence is more advantageous. Teachers, as their relationships with learners develop, will see whether learners can balance the intellectual, physical, and emotional aspects of their lives. The informality of this assessment is an advantage since the level of balance or imbalance will be an authentic setting, with residual effects of the learners' choices at any given point. The key for teachers is to be aware of the characteristics defining social competence at all times, then to actively look for them. Admittedly, it might be easier for teachers to first administer more formal assessments, since being intentional with social competence would align with the common practices of intentionality around all other aspects of learning; however, the *social* part of social competence lends itself nicely to a real-time, informal approach that simply asks teachers to examine their learners' habits, actions, attributes, and characteristics through a social competency lens.

Measuring Social Competence

Since evidence of social competence will likely involve learners providing either thorough explanations of their thinking (constructed response) or some kind of demonstration (performance assessment), the tools should follow suit. Not dissimilar to the other critical competencies, teachers and learners can most seamlessly measure social competence using robust criteria in a rubric or scale. Some social competencies lend themselves to a progression of quality (rubric), while others to the consistency (frequency) with which learners act socially competent. Admittedly, the lines between quality and consistency can blur, but it is an important distinction to keep in mind when developing criteria.

Measuring Quality

Any measurement of social competence requires high-quality criteria if it is to be reliable, easily understood by learners and teachers alike, and consistently assessed from one teacher to another. As part of its support material, the Ministry of Education performance standards describe the professional judgments of a significant number of British Columbia educators about standards and expectations within reading, writing, numeracy, social responsibility, and healthy living (Government of British Columbia, 2016). Figure 8.3 (pages 252–253) shows the BC Performance Standards Quick Scale for Grades 8 to 10 Social Responsibility (Government of British Columbia, n.d.b)—an analytic rubric; however, the altered scale descriptors across the top now align with the language of other rubrics in this book.

There are a few points to consider when examining figure 8.3. First, notice how the predominant language illustrates a progression of *quality*. The progression of "Contributing to the Classroom and School Community" goes from *apathetic*, to *courteous*, to *friendly*, to *inclusive,* and each is described through specific descriptions. Without the descriptions, the progression would be unhelpful as, for example, *apathetic* would have no clear contextual reference. There are also some elements of frequency present (for example, *sometimes* and *usually* in the "Valuing Diversity and Defending Human Rights" row); however, the performance standard for social responsibility is clearly focused on *quality*.

Learners can use these performance standard descriptors to measure social responsibility for themselves and as tools to initiate general discussions about social responsibility in all instructional areas. For example, learners could assess characters in a novel, politicians, local leaders, or public personalities in the community against the social responsibility performance standards, allowing learners to interact with the criteria in an impersonal way. Teachers may choose to familiarize learners with the criteria in this way before using learners themselves as the subjects of assessment. As well, assessing *others* provides learners with some insights into how teachers apply the criteria. Making scoring inferences about fictional characters or politicians allows learners to experience (in a non-threatening way) what their teachers will do when assessing how socially responsible the learners themselves are.

Aspect	Initiating	Developing	Achieving	Advancing
Contributing to the Classroom and School Community	• Appears apathetic or unfriendly and may try to manipulate or dominate others • Avoids participating in class and group activities; shows little sense of responsibility	• Usually courteous and friendly • Participates in class and group activities, but takes little responsibility for the school or community	• Usually kind and friendly • Takes some responsibility for the school or community and contributes willingly to class and group activities	• Kind, friendly, and inclusive • Works actively to improve the school or community; often volunteers for extra responsibilities and shows leadership skills
Solving Problems in Peaceful Ways	• In conflict situations, often uses put-downs, insults, or sarcasm; has difficulty stating position clearly; may be illogical • Can describe simple, concrete problems or issues and generate some strategies; often ignores consequences	• In conflict situations, tries to manage anger appropriately, listens respectfully, states opinion clearly, and tries to be fair • Can describe problems or issues, generate some strategies, consider immediate consequences, and evaluate actions	• In conflict situations, usually manages anger appropriately, listens respectfully, presents logical arguments, and can paraphrase opposing views • Can clarify problems or issues, generate strategies, weigh consequences, and evaluate actions	• In conflict situations, shows empathy and a sense of ethics, presents soundly reasoned arguments, and considers divergent views • Can clarify problems or issues, generate and analyze strategies, create an effective plan, and use evidence to evaluate actions

Valuing Diversity and Defending Human Rights	• Sometimes disrespectful; may stereotype or avoid those perceived as different in some way	• Usually respectful; supports those who speak up or take action to support diversity and defend human rights	• Respectful and fair; increasingly willing to speak up or take action to support diversity and defend human rights	• Respectful and ethical; speaks out and takes action to support diversity and defend human rights, even when that may not be a popular stance
Exercising Democratic Rights and Responsibilities	• Tends to be egocentric and apathetic; displays little sense of community or responsibility for others	• Shows some sense of community-mindedness; may go along with others' organized positive actions, but without much commitment	• Shows a sense of responsibility and community-mindedness; increasingly interested in taking action to improve the world	• Shows a strong sense of community-mindedness and accountability; can describe and work toward an ideal future for the world

Source: Adapted from Government of British Columbia, n.d.b.

Figure 8.3: Grades 8–10 social responsibility quick scale.

Visit go.SolutionTree.com/assessment for a free reproducible version of this figure.

Figure 8.4 takes the BC Social Responsibility Performance Standards, Grades 4 to 5 (Government of British Columbia, n.d.a) and reformats them into a single-point rubric, so teachers can personalize feedback for each learner. The advantage of single-point rubrics is the level of specificity; the disadvantage is they are more labor-intensive, so teachers will have to balance effectiveness and efficiency when utilizing this tool. The criteria for social responsibility are almost the same for learners in kindergarten through twelfth grade, but clearly the sophistication of the expected performance levels should be developmentally appropriate and applicable.

Specific Aspects in Need of Strengthening	Advancing	Specific Aspects of Strength
	• Friendly and kind, and often seeks opportunities to help or include others • Voluntarily takes responsibility in classroom and group activities (effective)	
	• Considers others' views and uses some effective strategies for resolving minor conflicts; takes responsibility and shows good judgment about when to get adult help • Can explain an increasing variety of problems or issues and generate and evaluate strategies	
	• Fair and respectful; shows growing commitment to fair and just treatment for everyone	
	• Shows a strong sense of responsibility in the classroom and an emerging sense of idealism—wants to make the world a better place; beginning to notice opportunities for action	

Source: Adapted from Government of British Columbia, n.d.a.

Figure 8.4: *Social responsibility single-point rubric.*

*Visit **go.SolutionTree.com/assessment** for a free reproducible version of this figure.*

The simplicity of this rubric involves the singular statements about expected levels of social responsibility; the complexity comes with the robust descriptions of strengths and aspects in need of strengthening. Providing personalized feedback, while certainly desirable, is labor-intensive. Using the single-point rubric primarily for instruction and formative feedback will create a balance. Use the quick scale (see figure 8.3, pages 252–253) for self-assessment and possibly reporting. To be clear, each tool is useful for all these purposes; however, the balance between efficiency and effectiveness is always a reality that teachers must consider.

Once schools and districts define the depth and breadth of social competence, their assessment fundamentals will allow them to make proper decisions about the most desirable tools to use. Use either of the rubrics for constructed response (tangible demonstrations) and performance assessments (seen or heard).

Measuring Frequency

Using a frequency scale may be more appropriate during assessment, as the scalability of a social competence may be inapplicable. There are certain binary aspects of being socially competent (for example, responsibility), which lends them nicely to a frequency scale. Rather than looking for four versions of correctness within responsibility, teachers could instead determine the consistency with which a learner demonstrates responsible behavior.

Figure 8.5 (pages 256–257) reformats the ACS Approaches to Learning (see figure 8.2, page 247) to create a frequency scale teachers could use to measure their learners' overall consistency levels. Teachers could use this tool exclusively; alternatively, they could also use it as a self-assessment tool; learners assess their own consistency levels (using one color or symbol) and then the teacher uses a different color or symbol. Where there is overlap, teachers confirm the learners' self-assessed consistency levels but also their self-assessment skills (another aspect of social competence). Where there is a discrepancy, the teacher has the opportunity to engage in a conversation about why the learner over- or under-rated his or her consistency, leading to teachable moments.

Including the bottom portion of figure 8.5 provides space for teachers to identify three areas of strength, two areas in need of strengthening, and one area for stretch. This 3-2-1 approach provides teachers space for personalized feedback, balances the need to address both strengths and areas of challenge, and provides a self-imposed limit to the amount of feedback (and balances effectiveness and efficiency). Learners themselves could use this scale for self- and peer assessment internally or for reporting. Schools and districts must create tools that work best for them and that serve the widest possible audience. The greatest challenge with taking a frequency approach is

AtL Skill	Criteria	Rarely	Sometimes	Usually	Consistently
Collaboration Collaborative skills that elevate the learning for oneself and for others	• Commits to and works productively toward the shared goals of the group • Takes an active role without dominating the group • Engages in give-and-take dialogue to build on learning and ideas of others • Encourages others to share ideas				
Responsibility Responsible skills that maximize learning opportunities	• Comes to class prepared to learn • Uses time constructively • Listens actively • Sustains focus on tasks • Follows rules and expectations • Takes responsibility for actions and consequences				
Self-Directed Learning Reflective skills that lead to greater self-efficacy	• Demonstrates self-awareness • Persists when facing a challenge • Approaches mistakes and challenges as opportunities to grow • Seeks and uses feedback • Reflects on past and present learning • Adjusts thinking to new contexts				
Citizenship Respectful skills that demonstrate open-mindedness and global awareness	• Shows respect • Demonstrates a consideration of multiple perspectives • Contributes to a positive learning environment and respects others' right to learn • Recognizes needs and actively responds				

Three specific areas of strength:

1. _____

2. _____

3. _____

Two specific areas in need of strengthening:

1. _____

2. _____

One area to stretch yourself:

1. _____

Source: Adapted from © 2018 by the American Community School of Abu Dhabi. Used with permission.

Figure 8.5: *ACS K–12 Approaches to Learning frequency scale.*

*Visit **go.SolutionTree.com/assessment** for a free reproducible version of this figure.*

ensuring teachers understand and agree on what *consistently*, *usually*, *sometimes*, and *rarely* mean. The labels aren't as important as the interpretation; *mostly*, *often*, *occasionally*, and *seldom* work just as well. The key is for teachers to openly discuss—in collaborative teams or as a whole faculty—how they interpret those frequency levels, what they should look for, and even the type of corrective action they might take given an undesirable demonstration. These discussions should be revisited at regular intervals or whenever necessary (for example, with new staff members) so that clarity and consistency are maintained. Avoiding number-based assessment is as important as, for example, a student being responsible five times in a year is quite different than one who is responsible five times in a week.

Growing Social Competence

The biggest hurdle for teachers might be accepting they can teach social competence. Teachers often view academic and social missteps through different lenses; however, there is evidence that educators can teach, develop, and grow the social skills that lead to social competence in the same manner as academic knowledge, skills, and deeper understandings.

For example, researchers George Sugai and Timothy J. Lewis (1996) find that social competencies serve as the basis of social skills training programs. Educators are increasingly utilizing that same idea in schools as well. Authors and response to intervention (RTI) experts Austin Buffum, Mike Mattos, Chris Weber, and Tom Hierck (2015) and Weber (2018) write about the importance of teaching learners how to behave. These authors highlight the message that too often, social missteps are viewed as *won't dos* and typically result in some form of discipline; by contrast, academic missteps are often viewed as *can't dos* and typically result in further support (Buffum et al., 2015). Educators can teach social competence, but the process of instruction is incomplete without providing learners with *replacement* behaviors (Maag, 2005). This means eliminating deficits in social competence is not enough; teachers need to identify, teach, develop, and refine prosocial behaviors, attributes, and characteristics in learners.

Many schools are turning to a multitiered system of supports for addressing social concerns (Bradshaw, Pas, Debnam, & Johnson, 2015). This system is often in the form of a three-tiered framework (positive behavior interventions and supports [PBIS] or response to intervention [RTI]) creating a systemic, instructional approach to social skills development that aligns with the instructional process typically reserved for cognitive learning. Tier 1 is about a universal, general education and core curriculum for all learners, while Tier 2 is for a targeted, group-based intervention, and Tier 3 is individualized interventions for learners unresponsive to the previous two tiers (Albrecht, Mathur, Jones, & Alazemi, 2015; Buffum, Mattos, & Malone, 2018). While all learners receive Tier 1 instruction, it is predictable that some will need more support. In layman's terms, Tier 1 focuses on *prevention*, Tier 2 focuses on a *programmed* type of intervention, while Tier 3 is about *personalization*.

In essence, the three-tiered PBIS, RTI, or multi-tiered system of supports (MTSS) framework submits that one size never fits all, and the intensity of any intervention must match the intensity of the presenting challenge. If there is a deficit in a social skill or competence, the instructional approach has to match the intensity of the deficit, or the intervention will likely fall short of achieving the desired result—namely, reconciling the social deficit. Schools can safely predict executing universal, schoolwide approaches with high fidelity to social competence will positively impact roughly 80 percent of learners, with 20 percent needing additional support (via Tier 2 or Tier 3) interventions (Buffum, Mattos, & Malone, 2018; Hawken, Vincent, & Schumann, 2008). Teachers would be wise to predict that any schoolwide or classwide approach to intervention will result in some learners needing *more*. This is often more difficult for teachers to comprehend regarding social competence than it is for academic proficiency.

It is important to note that the higher-level qualities of social competence build (like advanced academic skills) on more granular, lower-level social traits first. According to University of Nebraska–Lincoln professor John Maag (2006), *social competence* is a general expression referring to the adequacy of social functioning, while *social skills* are the specific behaviors targeted for social skills training. Understanding this distinction is advantageous to teachers since the fundamental contract of *skills-to-competence* aligns with the distinction commonly made in academic instruction between curricular standards and more granular learning targets (Erkens et al., 2017). Teachers can use their assessment literacy and instructional prowess to create a learning progression of social skills development that leads to social competence in the same manner they scaffold learning toward proficiency with academic standards.

If teachers see social competencies as *standards*, then the collection of social skills that allows one to be socially competent is the *target*—the specific granular underpinnings that would, in combination, allow a person to function at a high level socially. Therefore, teachers could identify a collection of social competencies, then unpack them to reveal the collection of social skills necessary for social competence. Using the example in figure 8.3 (see pages 252–253), if *social responsibility* is a social competency, then *contributing to the classroom and school community, solving problems in peaceful ways, valuing diversity and defending human rights*, and *exercising democratic rights and responsibilities* are the social skills that, when combined, make someone socially responsible. To be *principled* (a competency from the IB learner profile, see table 8.1, page 245) one must be honest, act with integrity, be respectful, be fair, and so on. This characterizes a person as *principled* and increases the likelihood that he or she will function at a socially adequate level.

Practically, schools and districts would be wise to examine the relationship between social skills and social competence. Certainly, at each grade level, schools can identify the social skills to scaffold toward social competence in and outside the school environment. Districts have the opportunity to create a K–12 macroprogression; the emphasis is on *social skills* at the younger grade levels and *social competence* as learners mature. This is not to suggest both can't be done with all learners at all ages, but does suggest a particular point of emphasis. Admittedly, the lines of transition would be blurry in the middle grades as there is no definitive place where that kind of transition should occur. This is a local decision that requires a consideration of context and nuance. But from a big-picture perspective, it could be a way for districts to create a road map that purposefully creates a progression toward social competence.

Conclusion

While once a hidden curriculum, *social competence* is now rightly placed alongside other essential outcomes of the school experience. As the world gets smaller and more diverse, it is crucial that all people (not just learners) draw upon their social skills to be competent in a variety of social settings. Learning is a social experience that begins with oneself, so the cultivation of intrapersonal social skills lays a foundation for more socially competent interpersonal engagements. This purposeful focus makes it essential for schools to prioritize social and emotional learning to ensure the whole child is being attended to.

In the end, there are many benefits to incorporating social competence features into the curriculum. The critical-thinking competencies don't happen in a vacuum. Applying such robust skills and processes can only thrive in a broad and healthy social context. Social competence is imperative to both an individual learner's well-being and a school's overall culture of learning. If learners are to think critically, creatively, and collaboratively through engineered, engaging, and inquiry-based dialogues, then social competency is a must. If educators teach and model the respectful mind, the ethical mind, and collaborative processes, then creating a socially competent culture open to differences and intellectual risk taking is vital to success. The ultimate goal is to create a kinder, gentler, more democratic world in which civil discourse fosters intellectual risk taking and lifelong learning.

Pause and Ponder

On your own or as part of a collaborative teacher team, consider the following reflective questions.

1. What quote or passage encapsulates your biggest takeaway from this chapter? What immediate action (large or small) will you take as a result of this takeaway? Explain both to your team.

2. In what ways was your current view of social competence reaffirmed? In what ways was it challenged? Explain.

3. Is your school or district's approach to social competence more of a *hidden* or *overt* approach? Is there an appropriate balance between intra- and interpersonal skills?

4. Do your current assessment practices, processes, and systems for social competence suffice? Are they more formal or informal? What's working well? What needs more attention?

5. How have you or could you find the right balance between assessing quality versus frequency? Do you think the age of your learners makes this decision easier or more difficult?

6. How do you or could you blend existing structures and systems (for example, PBIS or RTI) to enhance the efficiency and effectiveness of developing social competence in your learners?

7. Does the learning progression of social skills (targets) to social competence (standards) align with your current academic learning practices? How could this approach enhance what you already do to develop social competencies?

REFERENCES & RESOURCES

Aarkrog, V., & Wahlgren, B. (2017). Developing schemas for assessing social competencies among unskilled young people. *International Journal for Research in Vocational Education and Training, 4*(1), 47–68.

Abdi, A. (2014). The effect of inquiry-based learning method on students' academic achievement in science course. *Universal Journal of Educational Research, 2*(1), 37–41.

Abrami, P. C., Bernard, R. M., Borokhovski, E., Waddington, D. I., Wade, C. A., & Persson, T. (2015). Strategies for teaching students to think critically: A meta-analysis. *Review of Educational Research, 85*(2), 275–314.

Achieve, Inc. (2007). *Closing the expectations gap 2007: An annual 50-state progress report on the alignment of high school policies with the demands of college and work.* Washington, DC: Author. Accessed at www.achieve.org/files/50-state-07-Final.pdf on July 30, 2018.

ACT, Inc. (2006). *Reading between the lines: What the ACT reveals about college readiness in reading.* Iowa City, IA: Author.

ACT, Inc. (2009). *The condition of college readiness 2009.* Iowa City, IA: Author.

Albrecht, S. F., Mathur, S. R., Jones, R. E., & Alazemi, S. (2015). A school-wide three-tiered program of social skills intervention: Results of a three-year cohort study. *Education and Treatment of Children, 38*(4), 565–586.

American Community School of Abu Dhabi. (2013). *ACS K–12 Approaches to Learning.* Abu Dhabi, United Arab Emerites.

American Community School of Abu Dhabi. (2018). *ACS K–12 Approaches to Learning frequency scale.* Abu Dhabi, United Arab Emerites.

American Stories Continuum. (2010). *Gloria Ladson-Billings: "I take the long view."* Accessed at http://americanstoriescontinuum.com/2014/06/gloria-ladson-billings on June 11, 2018.

Andrade, H. L. (2010). Students as the definitive source of formative assessment: Academic self-assessment and the self-regulation of learning. In H. L. Andrade & G. J. Cizek (Eds.), *Handbook of formative assessment* (pp. 90–105). New York: Routledge.

Azevedo, R. (2005). Computer environments as metacognitive tools for enhancing learning. *Educational Psychologist, 40*(4), 193–197.

Balch, D., Blanck, R., & Balch, D. H. (2016). Rubrics—Sharing the rules of the game. *Journal of Instructional Research, 5,* 19–49.

Barell, J. (2010). Problem-based learning: The foundation for 21st century skills. In J. Bellanca & R. Brandt (Eds.), *21st century skills: Rethinking how students learn* (pp. 175–199). Bloomington, IN: Solution Tree Press.

Barnes, M. (2017). *Your mission: Teach kids to debate, rather than to diss people on social media.* Accessed at www.hacklearning.org/debate on June 8, 2018.

Barrow, L. H. (2006). A brief history of inquiry: From Dewey to standards. *Journal of Science Teacher Education, 17*(3), 265–278.

Baxter, G. P., & Glaser, R. (1998). Investigating the cognitive complexity of science assessments. *Educational Measurement: Issues and Practice, 17*(3), 37–45.

Beatty, R., & Blair, D. (2015). Indigenous pedagogy for early mathematics: Algonquin looming in a grade 2 math classroom. *The International Journal of Holistic Early Learning and Development, 1*, 3–24.

Beers, S. Z. (2011). *Teaching 21st century skills: An ASCD action tool.* Alexandria, VA: Association for Supervision and Curriculum Development.

Bellanca, J. A. (2015). Advancing a new agenda. In J. A. Bellanca (Ed.), *Deeper learning: Beyond 21st century skills* (pp. 1–18). Bloomington, IN: Solution Tree Press.

Bellanca, J. A., Fogarty, R. J., & Pete, B. M. (2012). *How to teach thinking skills within the Common Core: 7 key student proficiencies of the new national standards.* Bloomington, IN: Solution Tree Press.

Bennett, M. (2014, May 12). Social media linked to student anxiety. *The Columbia Chronicle.* Accessed at www.columbiachronicle.com/health_and_tech/article_aa2daa9a-d7e4 –11e3–9286–001a4bcf6878.html on May 28, 2018.

Bennett, R. E. (2010). Cognitively based assessment of, for, and as learning (CBAL): A preliminary theory of action for summative and formative assessment. *Measurement: Interdisciplinary Research and Perspectives, 8*(2–3), 70–91.

Bennett, R. E., & Gitomer, D. H. (2009). Transforming K–12 assessment: Integrating accountability testing, formative assessment and professional support. In C. Wyatt-Smith & J. Cumming (Eds.), *Educational assessment in the 21st century: Connecting theory and practice* (pp. 43–61). New York: Springer.

Biesta, G. J. J., & Stams, G. J. J. M. (2001). Critical thinking and the question of critique: Some lessons from deconstruction. *Studies in Philosophy and Education, 20*(1), 57–74.

Blocher, J. M. (2016). Global digital citizenship. In L. R. Miller, D. Becker, & K. Becker (Eds.), *Technology for transformation: Perspectives of hope in the digital age* (pp. 215–228). Charlotte, NC: Information Age.

Boekaerts, M. (2006). Self-regulation and effort investment. In K. A. Renninger, I. E. Sigel, W. Damon, & R. M. Lerner (Eds.), *Handbook of child psychology, vol. 4: Child psychology in practice* (6th ed., pp. 345–377). New York: Wiley.

Bradshaw, C. P., Pas, E. T., Debnam, K. J., & Johnson, S. L. (2015). A focus on implementation of positive behavioral interventions and supports (PBIS) in high schools: Associations with bullying and other indicators of school disorder. *School Psychology Review, 44*(4), 480–498.

Bridgeland, J. M., DiIulio, J. J., Jr., & Morison, K. B. (2006). *The silent epidemic: Perspectives of high school dropouts.* Washington, DC: Civic Enterprises.

Brookhart, S. M. (2013a). Classroom assessment in the context of motivation theory and research. In J. H. McMillan (Ed.), *SAGE handbook of research on classroom assessment* (pp. 35–54). Thousand Oaks, CA: SAGE.

Brookhart, S. M. (2013b). *How to create and use rubrics for formative assessment and grading.* Alexandria, VA: Association for Supervision and Curriculum Development.

Brown, G. T. L., & Harris, L. R. (2013). Student self-assessment. In J. H. McMillan (Ed.), *SAGE handbook of research on classroom assessment* (pp. 367–394). Thousand Oaks, CA: SAGE.

Buck Institute for Education. (n.d.). *K–2 critical thinking rubric.* Accessed at www.bie.org /object/document/k_2_critical_thinking_rubric on June 11, 2018.

Buffum, A., Mattos, M., & Malone, J. (2018). *Taking action: A handbook for RTI at Work.* Bloomington, IN: Solution Tree Press.

Buffum, A., Mattos, M., & Weber, C. (2012). *Simplifying response to intervention: Four essential guiding principles.* Bloomington, IN: Solution Tree Press.

Buffum, A., Mattos, M., Weber, C., & Hierck, T. (2015). *Uniting academic and behavior interventions: Solving the skill or will dilemma.* Bloomington, IN: Solution Tree Press.

Casner-Lotto, J., & Barrington, L. (2006). *Are they really ready to work? Employers' perspectives on the basic knowledge and applied skills of new entrants to the 21st century U.S. workforce.* New York: Conference Board.

Catalina Foothills School District. (2016). *Communication rubric, grades K–2.* Accessed at https://cfsd16.org/application/files/2715/2989/2798/K-12_COMMUNICATION _2018.pdf on May 29, 2018.

Catmull, E. E. (2014). *Creativity, Inc.: Overcoming the unseen forces that stand in the way of true inspiration.* New York: Random House.

Chappuis, J. (2015). *Seven strategies of assessment FOR learning* (2nd ed.). Boston: Pearson.

Cipollone, P. (2014). Foreword. In R. D. Crick, C. Stringher, & K. Ren (Eds.), *Learning to learn: International perspectives from theory and practice* (pp. xiv–xv). Abingdon, England: Routledge.

Cleary, M. N. (2017). Top 10 reasons students plagiarize and what teachers can do about it (with apologies to David Letterman). *Phi Delta Kappan, 99*(4), 66–71.

Cohen, N., Hall, T. E., Vue, G., & Ganley, P. (2011). Becoming strategic readers: Three cases using formative assessment, UDL, and technology to support struggling middle school readers. In P. E. Noyce & D. T. Hickey (Eds.), *New frontiers in formative assessment* (pp. 129–140). Cambridge, MA: Harvard Education Press.

Colan, L. (2014, March 26). *T.H.I.N.K. before you speak.* Accessed at www.inc.com/lee-colan /think-before-you-speak.html on October 7, 2018.

Common Core State Standards Initiative. (n.d.). *Read the standards.* Accessed at www .corestandards.org/read-the-standards on June 11, 2018.

Common Sense Education. (n.d.a). *Creative credit & copyright.* Accessed at https://common sense.org/education/digital-citizenship/creative-credit-and-copyright on June 8, 2018.

Common Sense Education. (n.d.b). *Digital citizenship.* Accessed at https://commonsense .org/education/digital-citizenship on January 3, 2018.

Cook, K., Seele, C., & Chaput, L. (2011). Customizing and capture: Online assessment tools for secondary mathematics. In P. E. Noyce & D. T. Hickey (Eds.), *New frontiers in formative assessment* (pp. 69–85). Cambridge, MA: Harvard Education Press.

Crick, R. D., Ren, K., & Stringher, C. (2014). Introduction. In R. D. Crick, C. Stringher, & K. Ren (Eds.), *Learning to learn: International perspectives from theory and practice* (pp. 1–6). Abingdon, England: Routledge.

Csikszentmihalyi, M. (2007). *Creativity: Flow and the psychology of discovery and invention.* New York: HarperCollins.

Cunningham, G. (2010, September 22). *We all do better when we all do better* [Blog post]. Accessed at www.startribune.com/we-all-do-better-when-we-all-do-better/103588254 on June 8, 2018.

Dahl, W. (2013, July 10). *10 great inventions dreamt up by children.* Accessed at www.great businessschools.org/10-great-inventions-dreamt-up-by-children/ on October 6, 2018.

Darling-Hammond, L., Ancess, J., & Falk, B. (1995). *Authentic assessment in action: Studies of school and students at work.* New York: Teachers College Press.

Darling-Hammond, L., Barron, B., Pearson, P. D., Schoenfeld, A. H., Stage, E. K., Zimmerman, T. D., et al. (2008). *Powerful learning: What we know about teaching for understanding.* San Francisco: Jossey-Bass.

Depka, E. (2017). *Raising the rigor: Effective questioning strategies and techniques for the classroom.* Bloomington, IN: Solution Tree Press.

Diamanduros, T., & Downs, E. (2011). Creating a safe school environment: How to prevent cyberbullying at your school. *Library Media Connection, 30*(2), 36–38.

Digital Learning Team. (n.d.). *The SAMR model—Enhancing technology integration.* Accessed at https://digitallearningteam.org/2012/06/07/the-samr-model-enhancing-technology -integration on June 11, 2018.

Doubet, K. J., & Hockett, J. A. (2017). Classroom discourse as civil discourse. *Educational Leadership, 75*(3), 56–60.

Drapeau, P. (2014). *Sparking student creativity: Practical ways to promote innovative thinking and problem solving.* Alexandria, VA: Association for Supervision and Curriculum Development.

Dweck, C. S. (1999). *Self-theories: Their role in motivation, personality, and development.* Philadelphia, PA: Psychology Press.

Dweck, C. S. (2006). *Mindset: The new psychology of success.* New York: Random House.

Dweck, C. S. (2007). The perils and promises of praise. *Educational Leadership, 65*(2), 34–39.

Ennis, R. H. (1989). Critical thinking and subject specificity: Clarification and needed research. *Educational Researcher, 18*(3), 4–10.

Ennis, R. H. (2011). Critical thinking: Reflection and perspective part I. *Inquiry: Critical Thinking Across the Disciplines, 26*(1), 4–18.

Erickson, J. (2012, May 2). Ecosystem effects of biodiversity loss could rival impacts of climate change, pollution. *Michigan News.* Accessed at http://ns.umich.edu/new/multimedia /slideshows/20366-ecosystem-effects-of-biodiversity-loss-could-rival-impacts-of-climate -change-pollution on January 22, 2017.

Erkens, C. (2016). *Collaborative common assessments: Teamwork. Instruction. Results.* Bloomington, IN: Solution Tree Press.

Erkens, C., Schimmer, T., & Vagle, N. D. (2017). *Essential assessment: Six tenets for bringing hope, efficacy, and achievement to the classroom.* Bloomington, IN: Solution Tree Press.

Erkens, C., Schimmer, T., & Vagle, N. D. (2018). *Instructional agility: Responding to assessment with real-time decisions.* Bloomington, IN: Solution Tree Press.

Every Student Succeeds Act of 2015, Pub. L. No. 114-95, 20 U.S.C. §1177 (2015).

Facione, P. A. (1990). *Critical thinking: A statement of expert consensus for purposes of educational assessment and instruction—Research findings and recommendations.* Newark, DE: American Philosophical Association.

Facione, P. A., & Facione N. C. (2011). *The holistic critical thinking scoring rubric - HCTSR: A tool for developing and evaluating critical thinking.* Accessed at www.insightassessment .com/About-Us/Measured-Reasons/pdf-file/Holistic-Critical-Thinking-Scoring-Rubric -in-English-PDF/(language)/eng-US on November 9, 2018.

Feldman, J. (2018). The end of points. *Educational Leadership, 75*(5), 36–40.

Ferriter, W. M. (2014, November 11). *Are there WRONG ways to use technology?* [Blog post]. Accessed at www.solutiontree.com/blog/wrong-ways-to-use-technology on June 8, 2018.

Fickel, L. (2015, May 1). What's in a terrible name? *U.S. News & World Report.* Accessed at www.usnews.com/opinion/knowledge-bank/2015/05/01/non-cognitive-skills-are -important-but-have-a-terrible-name on June 8, 2018.

Fiore, S. M., Graesser, A., Greiff, S., Griffin, P., Gong, B., Kyllonen, P., et al. (2017). *Collaborative problem solving: Considerations for the National Assessment of Educational Progress.* Washington, DC: National Center for Education Statistics.

Fisher, D., & Frey, N. (2015a). Selecting texts and tasks for content area reading and learning. *The Reading Teacher, 68*(7), 524–529.

Fisher, D., & Frey, N. (2015b). Teacher modeling using complex informational texts. *The Reading Teacher, 69*(1), 63–69.

Fisher, D., & Frey, N. (2015c). *Text-dependent questions, grades 6–12: Pathways to close and critical reading.* Thousand Oaks, CA: Corwin Press.

Fisher, D., & Frey, N. (2015d). *Text-dependent questions, grades K–5: Pathways to close and critical reading.* Thousand Oaks, CA: Corwin Press.

Fisher, D., Frey, N., & Hattie, J. (2016). *Visible learning for literacy, grades K–12: Implementing the practices that work best to accelerate student learning.* Thousand Oaks, CA: Corwin Press.

Fisher, D., Frey, N., & Lapp, D. (2012a). *Teaching students to read like detectives: Comprehending, analyzing, and discussing text.* Bloomington, IN: Solution Tree Press.

Fisher, D., Frey, N., & Lapp, D. (2012b). *Text complexity: Raising rigor in reading.* Newark, DE: International Reading Association.

Friedman, T. L. (2016). *Thank you for being late: An optimist's guide to thriving in the age of accelerations.* New York: Farrar, Straus, and Giroux.

Friesen, S., & Scott, D. (2013). *Inquiry-based learning: A review of the research literature.* Accessed at www.galileo.org/focus-on-inquiry-lit-review.pdf on June 8, 2018.

Frey, N., & Fisher, D. (2013). *Rigorous reading: 5 access points for comprehending complex texts.* Thousand Oaks, CA: Corwin Literacy.

Frey, N., Fisher, D., & Everlove, S. (2009). *Productive group work: How to engage students, build teamwork, and promote understanding.* Alexandria, VA: Association for Supervision and Curriculum Development.

Frey, N., Fisher, D., & Hattie, J. (2018). Developing "assessment capable" learners. *Educational Leadership, 75*(5), 46–51.

Fullan, M. (2015). Breakthrough learning. In J. Bellanca (Ed.), *Deeper learning: Beyond 21st century skills* (pp. 275–284). Bloomington, IN: Solution Tree Press.

Galileo Educational Network. (2008). *Guide to assessing critical thinking.* Accessed at www.galileo.org/tips/rubrics/ct_rubric.pdf on September 27, 2018.

Gallagher, K., & Kittle, P. (2018). Giving students the right kind of writing practice. *Educational Leadership, 75*(7), 14–20.

Gardner, H. (2001). Creators: Multiple intelligences. In K. H. Pfenninger & V. R. Shubik (Eds.), *The origins of creativity* (pp. 117–143). New York: Oxford University Press.

Gardner, H. (2007). *Five minds for the future.* Boston: Harvard Business School Press.

Gardner, H. (2010). Five minds for the future. In J. Bellanca & R. Brandt (Eds.), *21st century skills: Rethinking how students learn* (pp. 9–31). Bloomington, IN: Solution Tree Press.

Gaut, B. (2014). Educating for creativity. In E. S. Paul & S. B. Kaufman (Eds.), *The philosophy of creativity: New essays* (pp. 265–287). New York: Oxford University Press.

Gibbs, B. (2017). The complicated pursuit of democratic teaching. *Phi Delta Kappan, 99*(4), 21–25.

Goleman, D., & Boyatzis, R. (2013). Social intelligence and the biology of leadership. In *HBR's 10 must reads on collaboration* (pp. 15–30). Boston: Harvard Business Review Press.

Gonzalez, J. (2017). To boost higher-order thinking, try curation. *Cult of Pedagogy.* Accessed at www.cultofpedagogy.com/curation on February 22, 2018.

Goodwin, A. P., & Perkins, J. (2015). Word detectives: Morphological instruction that supports academic language. *The Reading Teacher, 68*(7), 510–523.

Government of British Columbia. (n.d.a). *BC performance standards: Social responsibility—Grades 4 to 5.* Accessed at www2.gov.bc.ca/assets/gov/education/administration/kindergarten-to-grade-12/performance-standards/social-responsibility/s4to5.pdf on June 11, 2018.

Government of British Columbia. (n.d.b). *BC performance standards: Social responsibility—Grades 8 to 10.* Accessed at www2.gov.bc.ca/assets/gov/education/administration/kindergarten-to-grade-12/performance-standards/social-responsibility/s8to10.pdf on June 11, 2018.

Government of British Columbia. (2016). *Building student success: BC's new curriculum.* Accessed at https://curriculum.gov.bc.ca/ on September 23, 2018.

Grant, M. C., Fisher, D., & Lapp, D. (2014). *Teaching students to think like scientists: Strategies aligned with Common Core and Next Generation Science Standards.* Bloomington, IN: Solution Tree Press.

Gregory, K., Cameron, C., & Davies, A. (2011). *Self-assessment and goal setting* (2nd ed.). Bloomington IN: Solution Tree Press.

Gross-Loh, C. (2016, December 16). How praise became a consolation prize. *The Atlantic.* Accessed at www.theatlantic.com/education/archive/2016/12/how-praise-became-a-consolation-prize/510845 on September 1, 2017.

Guskey, T. R. (2015). *On your mark: Challenging the conventions of grading and reporting.* Bloomington, IN: Solution Tree Press.

Halliday, J. (2000). Critical thinking and the academic vocational divide. *The Curriculum Journal, 11*(2), 159–175.

Harlen, W., & Crick, R. D. (2003). Testing and motivation for learning. *Assessment in Education: Principles, Policy & Practice, 10*(2), 169–207.

Hattie, J. A. C. (2009). *Visible learning: A synthesis of over 800 meta-analyses relating to achievement.* London: Routledge.

Hattie, J. A. C., & Timperley, H. (2007). The power of feedback. *Review of Educational Research, 77*(1), 81–112.

Hawken, L. S., Vincent, C. G., & Schumann, J. (2008). Response to intervention for social behavior: Challenges and opportunities. *Journal of Emotional and Behavioral Disorders, 16*(4), 213–225.

Heritage, M. (2007). Formative assessment: What do teachers need to know and do? *Phi Delta Kappan, 89*(2), 140–145.

Heritage, M. (2013). Gathering evidence of student understanding. In J. H. McMillan (Ed.), *SAGE handbook of research on classroom assessment* (pp. 179–196). Thousand Oaks, CA: SAGE.

Hobbs, R. (2017). Teaching and learning in a post-truth world. *Educational Leadership, 75*(3), 26–31.

Ibarra, H., & Hansen, M. T. (2013). Are you a collaborative leader? In *HBR's 10 must reads on collaboration* (pp. 1–14). Boston: Harvard Business Review Press.

International Baccalaureate Organization. (n.d.). *Middle Years Programme.* Accessed at www .ibo.org/programmes/middle-years-programme/ on June 11, 2018.

International Baccalaureate Organization. (2013). *IB learner profile.* Accessed at www.ibo .org/contentassets/fd82f70643ef4086b7d3f292cc214962/learner-profile-en.pdf on June 11, 2018.

International Society for Technology in Education. (n.d.). *ISTE standards for students.* Accessed at www.iste.org/standards/for-students on January 30, 2018.

Jackson, R. R. (2009). *Never work harder than your students & other principles of great teaching.* Alexandria, VA: Association for Supervision and Curriculum Development.

Jacobs, H. H. (2014). Curricular intersections of the new literacies. In H. H. Jacobs (Ed.), *Leading the new literacies* (pp. 5–22). Bloomington, IN: Solution Tree Press.

Jiménez-Aleixandre, M. P., Rodríguez, A. B., and Duschl, R. A. (2000). "Doing the lesson" or "doing science": Argument in high school genetics. *Science Education, 84*(6), 757–792.

Kallick, B., & Zmuda, A. (2017). *Students at the center: Personalized learning with habits of mind.* Alexandria, VA: Association for Supervision and Curriculum Development.

Kaufman, S. B. (2013). *Ungifted: Intelligence redefined.* New York: Basic Books.

Kaufman, S. B., & Gregoire, C. (2015). *Wired to create: Unraveling the mysteries of the creative mind.* New York: Perigee Books.

Krutka, D. G., & Carpenter, J. P. (2017). Digital citizenship in the curriculum. *Educational Leadership, 75*(3), 50–55.

Kurzweil, R., & Meyer, C. (2003). *Understanding the accelerating rate of change.* Accessed at www.kurzweilai.net/understanding-the-accelerating-rate-of-change on June 11, 2018.

Lake Washington Institute of Technology. (n.d.). *Communication rubric.* Accessed at www .lwtech.edu/about/instruction/outcomes-assessment/docs/lwtech-global-outcomes -communications-rubric.pdf on May 29, 2018.

Lane, S. (2010). *Performance assessment: The state of the art.* Stanford, CA: Stanford Center for Opportunity Policy in Education.

Lane, S. (2013). Performance assessment. In J. H. McMillan (Ed.), *SAGE handbook of research on classroom assessment* (pp. 313–329). Thousand Oaks, CA: SAGE.

Lopez, S. J. (2013). How can schools foster hope? Making hope happen in the classroom. *Phi Delta Kappan, 95*(2), 19–22.

Lunsford, A. A., & Ruszkiewicz, J. J. (2012). *Everything's an argument* (6th ed.). New York: Bedford/St. Martins.

Maag, J. W. (2005). Social skills training for youth with emotional and behavioral disorders and learning disabilities: Problems, conclusions, and suggestions. *Exceptionality, 13*(3), 155–172.

Maag, J. W. (2006). Social skills training for students with emotional and behavioral disorders: A review of reviews. *Behavioral Disorders, 32*(1), 4–17.

Mansilla, V. B., & Jackson, A. (2011). *Educating for global competence: Preparing our youth to engage in the world.* New York: Asia Society.

McKenney, Y. (2018). Making student writing matter. *Educational Leadership, 75*(7), 33–37.

McLeod, S., & Shareski, D. (2018). *Different schools for a different world.* Bloomington, IN: Solution Tree Press.

McTighe, J., & Seif, E. (2010). An implementation framework to support 21st century skills. In J. Bellanca & R. Brandt (Eds.), *21st century skills: Rethinking how students learn* (pp. 149–172). Bloomington, IN: Solution Tree Press.

McTighe, J., & Wiggins, G. (2013). *Essential questions: Opening doors to student understanding.* Alexandria, VA: Association for Supervision and Curriculum Development.

Messick, S. (1994). The interplay of evidence and consequences in the validation of performance assessments. *Educational Researcher, 23*(2), 13–23.

Miller, S., & Miller, P. A. (1994). *Collaborative team skills.* Evergreen, CO: Interpersonal Communication Programs.

Moon, T. R., Callahan, C. M., Brighton, C. M., & Tomlinson, C. A. (2002). *Development of differentiated performance assessment tasks for middle school classroom*s (RM02160). Storrs: University of Connecticut, National Research Center on the Gifted and Talented.

Moon, Y. (2015, April 24). An anti-creativity checklist for 2015. *Harvard Business Review.* Accessed at https://hbr.org/2015/04/an-anti-creativity-checklist-for-2015 on September 30, 2017.

Murawski, L. M. (2014). Critical thinking in the classroom . . . and beyond. *Journal of Learning in Higher Education, 10*(1), 25–30.

National Council for the Social Studies. (n.d.). *College, Career, and Civic Life (C3) Framework for Social Studies State Standards.* Silver Spring, MD: Author. Accessed at www.social studies.org/c3 on June 11, 2018.

National Education Association. (n.d.). *Preparing 21st century students for a global society: An educator's guide to the "four Cs."* Washington, DC: Author. Accessed at www.nea.org /assets/docs/A-Guide-to-Four-Cs.pdf on May 13, 2016.

National Governors Association Center for Best Practices & Council of Chief State School Officers. (n.d.). *Common Core State Standards for English language arts and literacy in history/social studies, science, and technical subjects: Appendix A—Research supporting key elements of the standards.* Washington, DC: Authors. Accessed at www.corestandards.org /assets/Appendix_A.pdf on August 16, 2018.

Next Generation Science Standards. (n.d.). *Read the standards.* Accessed at www.nextgen science.org/search-standards on August 30, 2018.

Next Generation Science Standards. (2012). *Science education in the 21st century: Why K–12 science standards matter—and why the time is right to develop Next Generation Science Standards.* Accessed at www.nextgenscience.org/sites/default/files/resource/files/Why% 20K12%20Standards%20Matter.pdf on June 11, 2018.

Next Generation Science Standards. (2016). *Fact sheet.* Accessed at https://nextgenscience .org/sites/default/files/resource/files/NGSSFactSheet2016revised.pdf on August 2, 2018.

Newmann, F. M., Carmichael, D. L., & King, M. B. (2016). *Authentic intellectual work: Improving teaching for rigorous learning.* Thousand Oaks, CA: Corwin Press.

NGSS Lead States. (2013). *Next Generation Science Standards: For states, by states*. Washington, DC: National Academies Press.

No Child Left Behind Act of 2001, Pub. L. No. 107-110, 20 U.S.C. § 6319 (2002).

Ohland, M. W., Loughry, M. L., Woehr, D. J., Bullard, L. G., Felder, R. M., Finelli, C. J., et al. (2012). The comprehensive assessment of team member effectiveness: Development of a behaviorally anchored rating scale for self- and peer evaluation. *Academy of Management Learning & Education, 11*(4), 609–630.

Ontario Ministry of Education. (2016). *21st century competencies phase 1: Towards defining 21st century competencies for Ontario*. Accessed at www.edugains.ca/resources21CL/About21stCentury/21CL_21stCenturyCompetencies.pdf on September 23, 2018.

Organisation for Economic Co-Operation and Development. (2010). *PISA 2009 results: Learning to learn—Student engagement, strategies and practices, volume III*. Accessed at http://dx.doi.org/10.1787/9789264083943-en on July 31, 2018.

Organisation for Economic Co-Operation and Development. (2017a). *Education at a glance 2017: OECD indicators*. Accessed at https://oecd-ilibrary.org/education/education-at-a-glance-2017_eag-2017-en on July 31, 2018.

Organisation for Economic Co-Operation and Development. (2017b). *PISA 2015 collaborative problem-solving framework*. Accessed at www.oecd.org/pisa/pisaproducts/Draft%20PISA%202015%20Collaborative%20Problem%20Solving%20Framework%20.pdf on June 11, 2018.

Organisation for Economic Co-Operation and Development. (2017c). *PISA 2015 results: Collaborative problem solving, volume V*. Accessed at https://doi.org/10.1787/9789264285521-en on July 31, 2018.

Owens, D. C., Sadler, T. D., & Zeidler, D. L. (2017). Controversial issues in the science classroom. *Phi Delta Kappan, 99*(4), 45–49.

Pandey, A., Nanda, G. K., & Ranjan, V. (2011). Effectiveness of inquiry training model over conventional teaching method on academic achievement of science students in India. *Journal of Innovative Research in Education, 1*(1), 7–20.

Partnership for 21st Century Learning. (n.d.). *Framework for 21st century learning*. Accessed at www.p21.org/our-work/p21-framework on June 11, 2018.

Patterson, K., Grenny, J., McMillan, R., & Switzler, A. (2005). *Crucial confrontations: Tools for resolving broken promises, violated expectations, and bad behavior*. New York: McGraw-Hill.

Paul, E. S., & Kaufman, S. B. (Eds.). (2014). *The philosophy of creativity: New essays*. Oxford, England: Oxford University Press.

Perkins, D. N. (2014). *Future wise: Educating our children for a changing world*. San Francisco: Jossey-Bass.

Piaget, J. (1970). Piaget's theory. In P. Mussen (Ed.), *Carmichael's manual of child psychology* (Vol. 1, pp. 703–772). New York: John Wiley & Sons.

Pink, D. H. (2005). *A whole new mind: Moving from the information age to the conceptual age*. New York: Riverhead Books.

Pintrich, P. R. (2002). The role of metacognitive knowledge in learning, teaching, and assessing. *Theory Into Practice, 41*(4), 219–225.

Piper, W. (1990). *The little engine that could* (60th anniversary ed.). New York: Platt & Munk.

Purcell, K., Rainie, L., Heaps, A., Buchanan, J., Friedrich, L., Jacklin, A., et al. (2012). *How teens do research in the digital world.* Accessed at www.pewinternet.org/2012/11/01/how -teens-do-research-in-the-digital-world on June 11, 2018.

Rainey, E. C., Maher, B. L., Coupland, D., Franchi, R., & Moje, E. B. (2018). But what does it look like? Illustrations of disciplinary literacy teaching in two content areas. *Journal of Adolescent & Adult Literacy, 61*(4), 371–379.

Ramdass, D., & Zimmerman, B. J. (2008). Effects of self-correction strategy training on middle school students' self-efficacy, self-evaluation, and mathematics division learning. *Journal of Advanced Academics, 20*(1), 18–41.

Reeves, D. (2010). A framework for assessing 21st century skills. In J. Bellanca & R. Brandt (Eds.), *21st century skills: Rethinking how students learn* (pp. 305–325). Bloomington, IN: Solution Tree Press.

Reeves, D., & Reeves, B. (2017). *The myth of the muse: Supporting virtues that inspire creativity.* Bloomington, IN: Solution Tree Press.

Resnick, L. B., & Resnick, D. P. (1992). Assessing the thinking curriculum: New tools for educational reform. In B. R. Gifford & M. C. O'Conner (Eds.), *Changing assessments: Alternative views of aptitude, achievement and instruction* (pp. 37–75). Boston: Kluwer Academic.

Reznitskaya, A., & Wilkinson, I. A. G. (2017). Truth matters: Teaching young students to search for the most reasonable answer. *Phi Delta Kappan, 99*(4), 33–38.

Richardson, J. (2017). Using controversy as a teaching tool: An interview with Diana Hess. *Phi Delta Kappan, 99*(4), 15–20.

Ritchhart, R. (2015). *Creating cultures of thinking: The 8 forces we must master to truly transform our schools.* San Francisco: Jossey-Bass.

Robinson, K. (2006, February). *Ken Robinson: Do schools kill creativity?* [Video file]. Accessed at https://ted.com/talks/ken_robinson_says_schools_kill_creativity on June 11, 2018.

Robinson, K. (2009). *The element: How finding your passion changes everything.* New York: Viking.

Robinson, K. (2011). *Out of our minds: Learning to be creative* (Rev. ed.). Westford, MA: Courier Westford.

Robinson, K. (2013). *Finding your element: How to discover your talents and passions and transform your life.* New York: Viking.

Robinson, K., & Aronica, L. (2015). *Creative schools: The grassroots revolution that's transforming education.* New York: Penguin Books.

Royalty, J. (1995). The generalizability of critical thinking: Paranormal beliefs versus statistical reasoning. *The Journal of Genetic Psychology, 156*(4), 477–488.

Runco, M. A. (2007). *Creativity: Theories and themes—Research, development, and practice* (1st ed.). Amsterdam, the Netherlands: Elsevier Academic Press.

Runco, M. A. (2014). *Creativity: Theories and themes—Research, development, and practice* (2nd ed.). Amsterdam, the Netherlands: Elsevier Academic Press.

Sá, W. C., West, R. F., & Stanovich, K. E. (1999). The domain specificity and generality of belief bias: Searching for a generalizable critical thinking skill. *Journal of Educational Psychology, 91*(3), 497–510.

Sampson, V., & Schleigh, S. (2013). *Scientific argumentation in biology: 30 classroom activities.* Arlington, VA: National Science Teachers Association Press.

Santelises, S. B., & Dabrowski, J. (2015). *Checking in: Do classroom assignments reflect today's higher standards?* Washington, DC: The Education Trust.

Sawyer, R. K. (2006). *Explaining creativity: The science of human innovation.* Oxford, England: Oxford University Press.

Schimmer, T. (2016). *Grading from the inside out: Bringing accuracy to student assessment through a standards-based mindset.* Bloomington, IN: Solution Tree Press.

Schmoker, M. (2018). Demystifying writing, transforming education. *Educational Leadership, 75*(7), 22–27.

Seyhan, H. G., & Morgil, I. (2007). The effect of 5E learning model on teaching of acid-base topic in chemistry education. *Journal of Science Education, 8*(2), 120–123.

Sheehan, T. (2017, April 19). Columnist Thomas Friedman says big forces are changing things in Fresno and the world. *The Fresno Bee.* Accessed at www.fresnobee.com/news /local/article145643094.html on July 31, 2018.

Slavin, R. E., Hurley, E. A., & Chamberlain, A. (2003). Cooperative learning and achievement: Theory and research. In W. M. Reynolds & G. E. Miller (Eds.), *Handbook of psychology* (Vol. 7, pp. 177–198). Hoboken, NJ: Wiley.

Smith, G. (2002). Are there domain-specific thinking skills? *Journal of Philosophy of Education, 36*(2), 207–227.

Snelling, J. (2018, February 1). *Top 10 sites to help students check their facts* [Blog post]. Accessed at www.iste.org/explore/articleDetail?articleid=916&category=Digital-and-media -literacy&article=Top+10+sites+to+help+students+check+their+facts on June 11, 2018.

Solari, H. (2018). *A mother has had enough with Snapchat until something amazing happens.* Accessed at www.momsrow.com/mom-life/2307161/a-mother-has-had-enough-with -snapchat-until-something-amazing-happens on June 11, 2018.

State of Washington Office of Superintendent of Public Instruction. (2017, September 29). *Career and technical education.* Accessed at www.k12.wa.us/CareerTechEd/Twenty FirstCenturySkills.aspx on September 23, 2018.

Sternberg, R. J., Jarvin, L., & Grigorenko, E. L. (2009). *Teaching for wisdom, intelligence, creativity, and success.* Thousand Oaks, CA: Corwin Press.

Sternberg, R. J., & Spear-Swerling, L. (1996). *Teaching for thinking.* Washington, DC: American Psychological Association.

Stiggins, R. (2007). Assessment through the student's eyes. *Educational Leadership, 64*(8), 22–26.

Stiggins, R. (2008). Correcting "errors of measurement" that sabotage student learning. In C. A. Dwyer (Ed.), *The future of assessment: Shaping teaching and learning* (pp. 229–244). Mahwah, NJ: Erlbaum.

Stoll, L., Bolam, R., McMahon, A., Thomas, S., Wallace, M., Greenwood, A., et al. (2006). *Setting professional learning communities in an international context.* Nottingham, England: National College for School Leadership.

Stringher, C. (2014). What is learning to learn? A learning to learn process and output model. In. R. D. Crick, C. Stringher, & K. Ren (Eds.), *Learning to learn: International perspectives from theory and practice* (pp. 9–33). London: Routledge.

Sugai, G., & Lewis, T. J. (1996). Preferred and promising practices for social skills instruction. *Focus on Exceptional Children, 29*(4), 1–16.

Sullo, B. (2007). *Activating the desire to learn.* Alexandria, VA: Association for Supervision and Curriculum Development.

Sussman, D. (2017). From partisanship to pluralism: Teaching students how to listen to each other. *Phi Delta Kappan, 99*(4), 50–53.

Terrell, S. S. (2017). *Hacking digital learning strategies: 10 ways to launch EdTech missions in your classroom.* Cleveland, OH: Times 10.

Thomas, J. W. (2000). *A review of research on project-based learning.* Accessed at www.bie.org /object/document/a_review_of_research_on_project_based_learning on June 11, 2018.

Topping, K. J. (2013). Peers as a source of formative and summative assessment. In J. McMillan (Ed.), *SAGE handbook of research on classroom assessment* (pp. 395–412). Thousand Oaks, CA: SAGE.

Tribuzzi, J., & Fisher, M. L. (2014). Bridging traditional and modern literacy. In H. H. Jacobs (Ed.), *Leading the new literacies* (pp. 25–53). Bloomington, IN: Solution Tree Press.

Vagle, N. D. (2015). *Design in five: Essential phases to create engaging assessment practice.* Bloomington, IN: Solution Tree Press.

Wagner, T. (2012). *Creating innovators: The making of young people who will change the world.* New York: Scribner.

Wallas, G. (2014). *The art of thought* (Rev. ed.). Kent, England: Solis Press.

Walsh, J. A., & Sattes, B. D. (2015). *Questioning for classroom discussion: Purposeful speaking, engaged listening, deep thinking.* Alexandria, VA: Association for Supervision and Curriculum Development.

Weber, C. (2018). *Behavior: The forgotten curriculum—An RTI approach for nurturing essential life skills.* Bloomington, IN: Solution Tree Press.

Weiss, J., & Hughes, J. (2013). Want collaboration? Accept—and actively manage—conflict. In *HBR's top 10 must reads on collaboration* (pp. 91–112). Boston: Harvard Business Review Press.

Welch, C. (2006). Item and prompt development in performance testing. In S. M. Downing & T. M. Haladyna (Eds.), *Handbook of test development* (pp. 303–328). Mahwah, NJ: Erlbaum.

Westheimer, J. (2017). What kind of citizens do we need? *Educational Leadership, 75*(3), 12–18.

White, K. (2017). *Softening the edges: Assessment practices that honor K–12 teachers and learners.* Bloomington, IN: Solution Tree Press.

Wiggins, A. (2017). *The best class you never taught: How spider web discussion can turn students into learning leaders.* Alexandria, VA: Association for Supervision and Curriculum Development.

Wiggins, G. (2012, February 3). *On assessing for creativity: Yes you can, and yes you should* [Blog post]. Accessed at https://grantwiggins.wordpress.com/2012/02/03/on-assessing-for-creativity-yes-you-can-and-yes-you-should/ on November 9, 2018.

Wiggins, G., & McTighe, J. (2005). *Understanding by design* (2nd ed.). Alexandria, VA: Association for Supervision and Curriculum Development.

Wildman, J. L., Thayer, A. L., Pavlas, D., Salas, E., Stewart, J. E., & Howse, W. R. (2012). Team knowledge research: Emerging trends and critical needs. *Human Factors, 54*(1), 84–111.

Wiley, B. L. (2014). Leading for global competence: A schoolwide approach. In H. H. Jacobs (Ed.), *Leading the new literacies* (pp. 123–160). Bloomington, IN: Solution Tree Press.

Wiliam, D. (2010). An integrative summary of the research literature and implications for a new theory of formative assessment. In H. L. Andrade & G. J. Cizek (Eds.), *Handbook of formative assessment* (pp. 18–40). New York: Routledge.

Wiliam, D. (2011). *Embedded formative assessment.* Bloomington, IN: Solution Tree Press.

Wiliam, D. (2013). Feedback and instructional correctives. In J. H. McMillan (Ed.), *SAGE handbook of research on classroom assessment* (pp. 197–214). Thousand Oaks, CA: SAGE.

Wiliam, D. (2018). *Embedded formative assessment* (2nd ed.). Bloomington, IN: Solution Tree Press.

Zhao, Y. (2016). Introduction: The danger of misguiding outcomes—Lessons from Easter Island. In Y. Zhao (Ed.), *Counting what counts: Reframing education outcomes* (pp. 1–10). Bloomington, IN: Solution Tree Press.

Zimmerman, B. J. (2002). Becoming a self-regulated learner: An overview. *Theory Into Practice, 41*(2), 64–70.

INDEX

Essential Assessment
Cassandra Erkens, Tom Schimmer, and Nicole Dimich Vagle
Discover how to use the power of assessment to instill hope, efficacy, and achievement in your students. Explore six essential tenets of assessment that will help deepen your understanding of assessment to not only meet standards but also enhance students' academic success.
BKF752

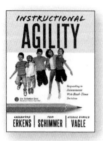

Instructional Agility
Cassandra Erkens, Tom Schimmer, and Nicole Dimich Vagle
This highly practical resource empowers readers to become instructionally agile—moving seamlessly among instruction, formative assessment, and feedback—to enhance student engagement, proficiency, and ownership of learning. Each chapter concludes with reflection questions that assist readers in determining next steps.
BKF764

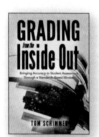

Grading From the Inside Out
Tom Schimmer
The time for grading reform is now. While the transition to standards-based practices may be challenging, it is essential for effective instruction and assessment. Discover the steps your team can take to transform grading and reporting schoolwide.
BKF646

Design in Five
Nicole Dimich Vagle
Discover how to work with your school team to create innovative, effective, engaging assessments using a five-phase design protocol. Explore various types of assessments, learn the traits of quality assessment, and evaluate whether your current assessments meet the design criteria.
BKF604

Collaborative Common Assessments
Cassandra Erkens
Foreword by Richard DuFour
Reignite the passion and energy assessment practices bring as tools to guide teaching and learning. Strengthen instruction with collaborative common assessments that collect vital information. Explore the practical steps teams must take to establish assessment systems, and discover how to continually improve results.
BKF605

Solution Tree | Press
a division of

Solution Tree

Visit SolutionTree.com or call 800.733.6786 to order.

"Excellent engagement
in what truly matters
in **assessment**.

Great examples!"

—Carol Johnson, superintendent,
Central Dauphin School District, Pennsylvania

PD Services

Our experts draw from decades of research and their own experiences to bring you
practical strategies for designing and implementing quality assessments. You can choose
from a range of customizable services, from a one-day overview to a multiyear process.

Book your assessment PD today!
888.763.9045

Solution Tree